Opening Doors
and Windows

'This memoir takes us from a savage and traumatic childhood to the world of faith and sacred art through the dynamic changes in British theatre in the mid-twentieth century, by way of some of the great artists who have worked with and benefited from James Roose-Evans. The story is told with enviable poise & fluency.'
Melvyn Bragg

'In these dangerous times, it is more important than ever that we try to understand the synthesis of chaos and order, freedom and discipline, intuition and ritual. And nobody has greater insight into these things than James Roose-Evans, who, alone amongst my teachers, opened the door to the nature of creativity for me at the beginning of my working life. ... What an illuminating, fascinating and inspiring read!'
Mike Leigh

'All who know him recognise in him a spirituality firmly rooted in his commitment to life and informed by his own hard-earned wisdom.'
Dr Anthony Stevens

'The entire life of the author ... has been a bravura performance from start to where it is at this moment ... The flow, however, is held in check by some remarkably good writing, and by the mining of a well-kept journal. Thus the rich detail of half a century ... Roose-Evans's description of his day-to-day work is structural, earthy and somehow inspiring.'
Ronald Blythe, *The Times Literary Supplement*

'A thoroughly good egg.'
Francis King, *The Oldie*

'His autobiography, *Opening Doors and Windows: a Memoir in Four Acts*, is a moving, vivid, often very funny account of a life devoted to uncovering the essence of things through the healing power of symbol, ritual and silence.'
Lucy Lethbridge, *The Tablet*

Opening Doors and Windows

A MEMOIR IN FOUR ACTS

JAMES ROOSE-EVANS

First published 2009
This edition published 2010

The History Press
The Mill, Brimscombe Port
Stroud, Gloucestershire, GL5 2QG
www.thehistorypress.co.uk

ROO

British Library Cataloguing in Publication Data.
A catalogue record for this book is available from the British Library.

ISBN 978 0 7524 5826 7

Typesetting and origination by The History Press
Printed in Great Britain
Manufacturing managed by Jellyfish Print Solutions Ltd

For Hywel,
always

and for
John Gordon, Margaret Lowy, Jane Rayne,
John and Lisa Rush, David Swift, Gillian and Paul Treuthard,
Laura Walker and Richard Wilson,
with gratitude

The only answers that really matter, the only authentic truths, are those that we find deep within ourselves.
Gerda Geddes

The quest is for authenticity, to discover and pay heed to the imperatives of one's own being, not to be satisfied with living by the often dubious standards supplied by the establishment. What is most called for is the exercise of powerful and intuitive minds without party allegiance that can reach behind the concepts of current theological controversies and illuminate what the religious quest is really about.
Dom Aelred Graham, OSB

Contents

ACT ONE

THE THEATRE BUG

In the Sixth Form at the Crypt Grammar School in Gloucester I decided to stage *Hamlet* out of doors on a semi-circular verandah with the audience inside. That it rained and the actors got drenched ('Too much of water hast thou, Ophelia!' murmured one of the actors to Michael Hurd who played Ophelia to my Hamlet) simply struck the staff as 'typically Roose-Evans!' Already that morning they had had to put up with my running in and out of classrooms, in my capacity as a prefect, wearing my Hamlet costume of sagging tights, baggy bloomers and flying black cloak, declaiming, 'The Headmaster wishes to see everyone in the hall at twelve o'clock!'

It was in the Sixth Form that I discovered a small record of Shakespeare speeches spoken by John Gielgud, then the most outstanding classical actor. I became, like many other budding actors of my generation, so intoxicated with his voice that I learned to speak Shakespeare in the same manner – only to have to unlearn it many years later! I also discovered in the school library a book by Rosamund Gilder which described Gielgud's performance as Hamlet scene by scene. On the strength of this and the small recording, and without ever having seen him act, I presumed to give a lecture on 'The Art of John Gielgud, the Actor' for which I was awarded that year's cup for Histrionics!

Flushed with my success, on a trip to London – my first – to stay with an aunt in Dolphin Square who was married to my father's only brother who worked in the Foreign Office, I went to a matinée of Rodney Ackland's adaptation of Dostoyevsky's *Crime and Punishment* which starred John Gielgud and Edith Evans. After the performance I went round to the stage door, asking if I might see Mr Gielgud as, I explained, I was writing a book about him. (I wasn't, but this was typical of the kind of behaviour that so often irritated my elders.) Back came the message that Mr Gielgud was resting, but that he would be very pleased to read the book when I had finished it. It was to be another ten years before I eventually met him, when I was taken to his house in Cowley Street for lunch by the actor Esmé Percy. After that we continued to meet over the years but it was to be forty years before we finally worked together when I directed him at the age of eighty-three in his triumphal return to the West End in Hugh Whitemore's *The Best of Friends*.

In between leaving school and going into the Army for my eighteen months' conscription service (the Second World War being ended) I went up on several more occasions to stay with my aunt. On one such visit I had observed a short, sturdy bearded man called Max, reciting Shakespeare to the gallery queue outside the New Theatre. I asked him if I might have a go as this seemed one way in which I could earn some money that would enable me to see more plays. (Until then, the only plays I had seen were *Humpty Dumpty* and *Peter Pan*, both at the Golders Green Hippodrome, and on two school outings, Donald Wolfit's company in *As You Like It* at Cheltenham, and *Macbeth* at Stratford-on-Avon with Valerie Taylor and Robert Harris as the Macbeths and an incandescent performance of Malcolm by a young Paul Scofield. In spite of this I knew that I wanted to be an actor more than anything else.)

'What can you do, my son?' was Max's unhesitating reply.

'Shakespeare, Keats, and some Oscar Wilde,' I answered.

'Right! We'll do a turn together!' he said, whereupon he tipped another busker half a crown for his space on the bill, for the buskers all worked in sequence as in a variety bill.

'My young friend and I,' proclaimed Max in his booming Wolfit-like baritone, 'will now entertain you with excerpts from the classics!' And so, turn and turn about, we recited. During Max's final oration I had to pass along the queue holding out a collecting bag made from a folded newspaper, which he afterwards taught me how to make. From the New Theatre we made our way to the Wyndham's, the Duke of York's and then on to the Coliseum, the bag getting heavier with coins. Afterwards we adjourned to the Salisbury in St Martin's Lane, which in those days and for many years was known as the actors' pub, where actors from weekly repertory companies from all over the country would meet on a Thursday, their one free day, to exchange news and gossip. Here Max bought me a soft drink, counted the takings and scrupulously gave me half. Finally he said (and oh, rare accolade for an aspiring actor) 'My boy, with your voice you should go to the Albert Hall!' and with that he instructed me to contact a man at the foot of the statue of Prince Albert and 'Tell him, Max sent you.' And so it was that my acting career began as a busker, a strolling player, in the heart of the West End!

The next day, without saying anything to my aunt, I arrived at the Albert Hall to find it encircled by a large queue of hundreds of people. After introducing myself to the head of the buskers I was placed second on the bill and began with Prince Hal's address to Falstaff from *King Henry IV*, Part 2, 'I know thee not, old man, fall to thy prayers! How well white hairs become a fool and jester!' I followed this with a speech from Leslie and Sewell Stokes' play *The Trial of Oscar Wilde* which I had heard on the radio. It was Wilde's reply to the question, 'What is the Love that dare not speak its name?'

Suddenly people stopped talking and some stood on their stools for a better view. I was making an impression – not because of my acting, as I thought at the time – but clearly people were curious that an obviously well-bred, well-spoken youth should be reciting such a speech. As I moved along the queue my collecting bag became heavier and heavier with florins, half crowns and shillings, to me untold wealth! Flushed with my success and the obvious sensation I was causing – I didn't know what the speech meant, I was a sexual innocent, but I was entranced by the words – I went from one part to another of that serpentine queue until I became aware of being followed by a tiny man who had strips of metal sewn onto his waistcoat on which he tapped out tunes with a spoon. Catching up with me he whispered, 'I've been waiting for you to finish!' Only then did I realise that I had gone over my allotted time and that he was next on the bill. At the same moment the leader of the buskers called out, 'Come 'ere, son!' In a panic, fearing he might be some Fagin among buskers, I ran and hailed a taxi (I had never been in one until then) and told the driver, 'Dolphin Square!' As we sped back to my aunt's I counted my takings for that afternoon: enough to pay for the taxi and to get me into the gallery at the New Theatre to see several performances, including seeing Laurence Olivier in *Oedipus Rex* and in Sheridan's *The Critic*.

MAUD ROOSE AND JOEY EVANS

It was my father who hyphenated the names 'Roose' and 'Evans', his parents' surnames. The only one of my grandparents I knew was his father, Joseph Penn Evans, always known as Joey. We often stayed at his house, The Laurels. 'Your grandfather was so careless,' my mother would say, 'he used to own nearly all of Ruardean and now there is nothing left.' Gradually, over the years, he sold off land to pay his debts so that all that my father inherited was the house.

Joey bred racehorses and was a familiar sight in the Forest of Dean in his grey overcoat with a velvet collar, his grey bowler hat and doeskin gloves, bowling along in his pony and trap, flicking a long whip. He married Maud Roose of Rhyll and he drove her out of her mind.

As a boy I heard stories of my grandfather horse-whipping my grandmother on the front lawn and how, on one occasion, he kicked over a bucket of dirty water when she was swabbing down the tiles, so that she had to start all over again. Once, when we were out walking in the woods, my mother told me what she believed had sent my grandmother mad. 'She was so troubled by the way your grandfather carried on with Mrs Warren, the chapel minister's wife, by whom he had two children.'

I remember Mrs Warren well. Once, when I was a boy, I saw her through a window coming up the drive of The Laurels. A strikingly handsome woman, she was dressed entirely in black with a veil over her face and was accompanied by a sickly looking girl and boy who must, I later realised, have been my grandfather's illegitimate children. They rang the bell and my mother answered the door. I did not hear what was said but Mrs Warren left a box of Turkish Delights for me, which my mother made me put on the fire, believing it was tainted with evil.

My grandmother ended her days in an asylum. As my mother explained, 'One day she ran away and walked as far as Ross-on-Wye where the police picked her up. She was trying to get home to North Wales but she had no money. If she ever had any she would always give it away to the Salvation Army or anyone who called. When they asked her who her husband was she kept replying, "King George". Eventually they found out and someone came and told Joey. He wanted me to go and get her. I said, "No, you've got to face this on your own." But he said, "She will only make a worse scene if I go." In the end I went with him and, of course, she agreed to come back home. But she got stranger and stranger. In the end it wasn't safe and so she had to go into a mental hospital. She died two years later. I visited her regularly. She would ask after everyone by name and sit there singing hymns.' My mother also told me how she had once given my grandmother two happy days from the asylum: 'I made her put on her best clothes, cleaned her nails, and took her out in the pony and trap. But your grandfather never forgave me for that.'

MY PARENTS

I was born just after midnight on 11 November 1927 and, according to my mother, my father and the family doctor toasted my arrival on Armistice Day with champagne.

My mother was like a gypsy and thrived on moving house. She would find a flat or a cottage to rent, do it up with great relish and a lick of paint, get to know everyone, enthusing about her new friends and then, after a year or two, would become bored and start looking for somewhere else. Everything would be packed into tea chests lined with silver tinfoil smelling of tea leaves (these we took everywhere with us) and loaded onto a removal van with our furniture and chattels. Curiously my father always seemed unfazed by this.

This pattern of moving meant that I attended some seventeen schools in all and lived in many more homes. It was probably because of the dislocation caused by this – never having long enough to put down roots or make lasting friendships, combined with the unpredictability of my mother's emotional weather and my father's tempers – that from early on I felt a strong sense of exile, of not belonging. It is, therefore, perhaps not surprising that the names of the two central characters that I was to create in a sequence of seven children's books were Odd, a small bear, and Elsewhere, a clown. As Elsewhere says,

> I've had all sorts of exciting adventures. I've been in many places, met many people, yet I could never feel that any of it was permanent. I always had the feeling that it could not last. Not in any sad way but just that things have a way of changing. And so I got to feel that wherever I was I could just as easily be elsewhere. That's how I got my name, of course. I've always had this feeling that somewhere, elsewhere, something was waiting for me and that when I found it I wouldn't feel lost any more. I'd be *here*, and not *elsewhere!* Odd has always felt the odd man out, too. I suppose that's why we understand each other so well.

As a young man my father had been a 'gentleman jockey' and my mother met him at the Cheltenham Races. He became a commercial traveller selling ladies' dresses and made frequent trips away, especially to Blackpool where he always stayed at the Palatine Hotel. It was in this way that we acquired a certain amount of cutlery, towels and linen napkins, all inscribed with the name of the Palatine Hotel. As I grew up my father remained mostly at a distance, erupting into the foreground at weekends. He always returned home on Fridays, having drunk heavily till the pubs closed. For years my mother lived in fear of Fridays and I, in my turn, was infected by her terror. Their fierce blazing rows became a weekly ritual. My mother and I would keep a look out for him from the window of the front room until we saw him staggering down the road, his arms laden with offerings of bananas, apples, oranges and nuts in brown paper bags, as well as a bundle of steaks wrapped in white paper oozing with blood.

On one of these occasions when I was about eight, my mother and I hid inside a large cupboard in the hall where, huddled in Oedipal darkness, we could hear him calling out her name. Not finding her he stumbled into the kitchen and proceeded to fry up a gargantuan meal of steak and onions after which he subsided into a stertorous heap. Creeping out to observe the lie of the land, I saw him going upstairs to sleep off his stupor, followed by our collie Raq, and vomiting as he went. Swaying and holding onto the banister he called out softly, even shame-facedly, 'Good dog! Go on, eat it all up!' and step by step our dog ate up my father's vomit.

On other occasions when my mother had cooked him a meal, he hurled the plate at the wall in anger and I would watch with fascination as pieces of plate hung precariously for a few seconds, before sliding down with the vegetables and meat to be wolfed by our dog.

Apart from Fridays, my mother also dreaded the new moon for then my father would be at his most dangerous. When I was five or six, I was woken one night by terrible screams. Creeping downstairs I saw my mother in the front room, sobbing and holding her prayer book, gabbling Hail Marys: 'Pray for us now and at the hour of our death!' as my father hurled china and glass at her. Woken by cries another time I peered through the partially open door of their bedroom and watched my father rip my mother's beautiful green velvet and lace evening dress off her back. Throwing up the sash window and holding a carving knife to her throat, she was screaming, 'I'll cut my throat! I'll cut my throat!' Once, decades later, when I was cross with her she said to me, 'You won't hit me, will you? I used to get so frightened when your father hit me.'

From my father I rarely received any display of affection: no hugs or embraces, not even the sharing of those activities which most sons enjoy with their fathers, while much of my boyhood seems to have been spent waiting outside pubs till closing time with my mother trying frantically to keep him under control.

I had one brother, Monty, who was four years older but of whom I have no memory of shared games or adventures. Indeed, looking back, both my father and my brother remain shadowy figures. My brother went off to boarding school and then, as soon as he was able, joined the Merchant Navy and travelled the world. Tall and blonde, he was an exotic figure in his braided uniform, while the mantelpiece would be stacked with postcards sent from different parts of the world. He eventually settled in America, married and became an American citizen. We have not met for more than fifty years although we write to each other at Christmas. He was very much our father's son and I was our mother's and for many years there was, I know from his letters to our mother, an underlying jealousy, he feeling that I had been given all the opportunities, where in fact I have had to fight every inch of the way. After our father died he wrote, saying, 'Jim, we had the best of parents.' I wanted to write back saying, 'No, it was not as simple as that. You escaped all the rows and the traumas', but I did not.

It is, however, not surprising that when, in my late teens, I had a breakdown and went into analysis, one of the areas I had to explore was that of my search for an elder brother figure, nor that when, at the age of twenty-two, I fell in love for the first time it was with someone who, like my brother, was four years older and who was to play the crucial role in my life as such a figure.

My poor mother; I was all she had and yet, in my teens, I so often rejected her. Returning home late from the village youth club, she would call from upstairs, 'Is that you, Jimmie?' and I, in my adolescent rebelliousness, would mutter, 'Who the hell do you think it is?' She would answer, undeterred, 'There's some stew on the stove.' My father, turning over in bed, would grunt, 'Can't you go to sleep! What the devil does he want stew for at this time of the night?'

'Well, the boy must have something to eat. He's been out all evening.'

'He'll find something. For Christ's sake shut up and go to sleep!'

In the kitchen I would pick up the paper and look to see how far Jane, in the cartoon series, had undressed that week. But I knew that my mother would be lying there in the dark listening.

Sure enough, perhaps an hour later, I would be tip-toeing up to bed, trying not to step on the squeaky boards, when she would whisper,

'Jimmie! Jimmie! Is that you? You just going to bed? It's late. Where have you been all this time?'

'Downstairs.'

'What doing?'

'Reading.'

How I hated this ritual interrogation, having to account for each moment. By now I would be standing by the side of her bed, a candlestick in one hand, my shoes in the other.

'Well, you are not going to read now, are you?'

'No, mother.'

'That's right. Goodnight. God bless you.'

There would be a pause and then she would add, pleadingly, 'Give me a kiss.' My father, grunting, would turn over, taking most of the bed-clothes with him.

'Go-ble-you!' I would mumble, hurrying to close the door behind me to escape, to shut her out.

'Leave the door! I don't like to feel shut in!'

Upstairs in my bedroom the paraffin stove cast a shadow on the ceiling like a paper cake-mat, while in my bed, placed there earlier by my mother, would be a now tepid hot water bottle. At one end of the room, propped against the wall, was a long mirror which had once been part of a wardrobe. At times of greatest frustration I would lay this on the floor, undress and lie naked on it, leaning on my arms, gazing at the pale face and dark eyes reflected in its depths. Slowly, like a swan dipping to the water, I would put my lips to those that came to meet mine, shivering in my loneliness, wanting to be one with that other whom I had yet to meet, in a perfect fusion of brothers.

My sense of drama I owe entirely to my mother whose humours, angers, impulses, laughter and tears were always heightened by histrionics. She put down in me ineradicable roots while, conversely, my roots remain deep in hers. Even after our parents are deceased we cannot escape them: they live on in us in the traits and characteristics which we have inherited, while what was unresolved in them falls to us to complete within ourselves. There is a deep psychological truth in the Old Testament saying: 'The sins of the fathers [but why not also of the mothers?] are visited upon the children of the third and fourth generations.' In so far as the next generation does not resolve these matters they will continue to be passed on from one to the next. It is all too easy to blame our parents for what and who we are and to remain fixated in anger and bitterness. Each of us, however, is responsible for our own actions and we cannot – must not – fall back upon our parentage or upbringing by way of an excuse. Perhaps also, as Jung once observed in a letter to Freud, 'It is not what our fathers did but what they didn't do that drives us on.'

If my father's mother was a gentle soul, brutalised by her marriage, my mother at least was made of sturdier stock and thus escaped a similar fate. On days when my father was particularly brutal she would take some bread and butter and go down to the woods below the village. 'I used to spend hours there. I would sit and have my tea. There was such peace there – and all the birds were singing!'

It was during one of my father's trips away that my mother made her first attempt to leave him. I was about fourteen. In the hamlet where we lived there was a local farmer who was keen on my mother, whom she easily persuaded to help by moving all our furniture into one of his barns. He arrived at midnight with his tractor when everyone was fast asleep and we loaded everything onto a trailer. The cottage, which was rented, was then locked, and my mother pinned a note to the door for my father, telling him that she had left him.

We sat up all night in the farmer's kitchen while he ground coffee beans, making pot after pot of strong coffee, and a three-legged white cat walked lopsidedly up and down the long table. The farmer's mother had died two years before and all the other rooms were shrouded in white dustsheets and kept locked. Early in the morning my mother and I ran across the fields, which were wet with a heavy dew, and caught the first bus into Gloucester where my mother gave me breakfast at Lyons Corner House before seeing me off to school and then catching her train to London, it having been arranged that I was to stay with the Pollards, a family I had got to know.

That first escapade of my mother's was to prove to be a dress rehearsal for the finished production for, some years later my parents, having come together again, were living in a house in Golders Green which my father had purchased in my mother's name so that she was, therefore, its legal owner. It was during my second year at Oxford, in 1950, that my mother decided to sell the house without telling my father and to leave him for good. For over a year she had had a couple renting the upstairs floor but, unknown to my father, when they left she would go upstairs each evening to pack the familiar tea chests with our belongings, talking aloud as though making conversation with the tenants. On coming down my father would ask her where she had been and she would reply, 'Upstairs, chatting with the Watsons.'

Then one weekend when, as before, my father was away on business, my mother invited me down from Oxford to help her with the removal. Through a dense fog a van arrived to take everything away into store, the agent locked the house, taking the keys, and my mother said goodbye, telling me I should hear from her in due course but that if my father were to get in touch I could truthfully say I did not know where she was. From time to time I would receive postcards from different parts of Norfolk where eventually she bought a small cottage which, after years of fear and brutal attacks, as well as lack of money, became for her – at least for a time, for she was never ultimately settled – Elysium.

PUTTING DOWN ROOTS

I had met Mary Pollard on my bus journeys to school. Four years older than I, she had one leg which was shorter than the other, strapped into a clumsy surgical boot with iron rods. As a small girl she had been violently kicked in the leg by a boy at school and the subsequent operation had gone wrong. Her mother, an experienced district nurse, always blamed the surgeon but in those days there was no established procedure or even precedent for suing an incompetent doctor.

Mary travelled each day to work in the Chapter House at Gloucester Cathedral, repairing a large medieval tapestry there. Later she went on to study in London at the Royal College of Needlework, returning to teach in Gloucester. Whenever there wasn't an empty seat I would give Mary mine and she would hold my satchel. These casual meetings soon grew into a friendship and I was invited to meet her parents in their small cottage at Pleasant Stile, high up above the village of Littledean. Her mother was retired from nursing, while her father had been invalided out of the Army after the First World War because of frostbite in his toes. Gradually I became one of the family and so, when my mother decided to go off and work in a munitions factory in Woolwich, this being wartime, it was agreed that I should go and live with the Pollards at Pleasant Stile. I was then fifteen.

My bedroom was above the tiny shop which Mrs Pollard ran as a source of extra income and in which we took turns to serve, selling cigarettes, tobacco, sweets, Beechams Powders, shoe polish and laces, as well as lemonade for those who made the steep climb from Newnham-on-Severn below, before descending to Littledean. Sometimes we were just asked for a glass of water by regulars such as the herbalist who used to push his bike uphill, laden with his wares, wearing a large dock leaf under his trilby hat to keep his brow cool.

Mrs Pollard had once been a member of the Plymouth Brethren and she remained very much an evangelical Christian. Each day we would sit in the kitchen for morning and evening prayers, Mary and I on a prickly horsehair sofa covered with black oil cloth, Mrs Pollard in a wooden carver and Mr Pollard opposite in an upright chair. Mrs Pollard would read first from the large Bible on her lap, and then follow this with a long improvised prayer which knitted together all the needs of the world, or so it seemed, with those of our neighbours, families and friends, 'remembering Mrs Roose-Evans and her husband', and concluding with the Lord's Prayer which we said together.

Often, coming in late of an evening I would find her asleep, her household tasks completed, seated by the last embers of the fire, the Bible tilted on her lap, her spectacles slipped forward on her nose, and her arthritic feet soaking in a bowl of now tepid water. Waking, she would smile gently and kiss me goodnight.

Convinced that I was destined to be a missionary in deepest Africa she set about teaching me to be self-sufficient. As a result I learned to chop wood, saw logs and split kindling wood (which had to be put in the oven overnight to dry), how to grow vegetables, cook, sew and darn my own socks (weaving the wool over and under in a neat patchwork). Regularly I would bring in buckets of coal as well as slack for damping down the fire. I peeled the carrots (which were also used for making imitation marmalade, for this was wartime and rationing) and potatoes (keeping the peelings for the chickens).I emptied the slops, fed the hens and collected their eggs. I also regularly cut out small squares from the daily newspaper, threading these on a string as toilet paper for use in the privy at the top of the garden, the contents of which I had to dig out and bury once a year.

Although there were times I felt rebellious, especially at having to polish the linoleum and black-lead the grate first thing on Sunday before going to church, nonetheless there was a part of me that responded to all this discipline. I relished being one of a family, with each day structured; no longer at the mercy of emotional whirlwinds. I began to feel I had a place and a function. It also enabled me as a Rover Scout to win armfuls of proficiency badges! Above all, I was encouraged to work hard at my studies. Before I went to live with the Pollards I used to sink regularly like a heavy weight to the bottom of the class at school but with their support I rose to the top of the class, passing both my School and Higher School Certificates, and winning a place to New College, Oxford to read English. All this I owed to Mrs Pollard, while between Mary and myself a deepening affection made us each other's confidante.

The senior English master in the Sixth Form at the Crypt Grammar School was W.N. Hook, known as Wilf. A tall man, with black hair and piercing eyes, he would lean back in his chair, wrapping his academic gown around him like two black wings, clasping his hands around his knees which he propped up on the desk in front of him. An inspirational teacher, he believed that the advancement of knowledge was no good without the development of the whole person. He made enormous demands upon our time and creativity, expecting us not only to study our set texts but to read books on psychology and history, write poems, paint, and make puppets. He loved introducing us to poets not on our syllabus, such as Edward Thomas and C. Day Lewis. Observing that I was prone to taking myself a little too seriously (I was in any case born with a vertical frown, which I inherited from my mother, which added to this impression) he liked to tease me, as when on one occasion he reshaped a line from Milton, 'Pure as the naked Heavens' to read 'Pure as the naked Evans', watching me blush as the rest of the class laughed. He was quick to deflate any form of pretentiousness, and never hesitated to point out inanities in our texts such as the unfortunate line in one Hardy novel, 'Her breath came in short pants'.

He ceaselessly encouraged us to probe and question. Once, in a mood of rebellion against his incessant demands, I painted a picture of myself strapped to an operating table and, towering over me, a tall surgeon-like figure. At the bottom I wrote 'Portrait of W.N.N' and handed it to him. Wisely, he made no comment. With his understanding of psychology (he often expounded to us some of the theories of Freud) he must have realised that by giving expression to my feelings I had dealt creatively with my rebelliousness and so was able to move on.

From childhood onwards this ability to act, or visualise through movement, sound, writing or drawing, has enabled me to shed skins and go on growing. It is by gaining conscious control of our unconscious imagery that we bring into order our chaotic psyches. Mrs Pollard, however, was suspicious of all art, of artists and of the imagination. I was once listening to a Beethoven concerto on the radio and Mrs Pollard, on entering, switched it off telling me to stop mooning around and get on with my homework. To her, the creation of stories was a form of lying. When she discovered that I was reading Thomas Hardy's *Jude the Obscure*, one of our set books, she wrote to Wilf to protest. Similarly she did not approve of my becoming friendly with the poet Donald Cowie and his wife Ruth who lived with their lively young son Peter in a nearby cottage.

I loved being invited to supper by the Cowies and being treated as an equal. It was they who encouraged my early attempts at writing. Through their sense of fun and love of words they opened doors and windows through which I began to glimpse another world, one that was far more mine than that of the mission fields of Africa. Although they were atheists they never sought to undermine my beliefs, but their questions, like those of Wilf, encouraged me to develop my thinking, rather than my feeling, responses. All too often, however, when I returned from these stimulating evenings, there would be scenes with Mrs Pollard who was convinced that the Cowies were trying to corrupt me.

I joined the local youth club and a group of us would descend the hills on our bikes, swooping like hawks on the village below. As we sped down the lanes on frosty nights we would let out yells of 'Whoopee!' accompanied by a jangling of bells.

A travelling cinema used to come to the village hall every Monday. That the film often broke down, with a kiss or a murder suspended, or that the reels got mixed up, only added to the fun and the excitement. There were always two showings, the first being for the younger ones, so that those waiting for the next performance would hear from inside the stamping, cheering, and banging of chairs – as well as of each other – as Roy Rogers rode the inevitable ride, or police cars screamed round inevitable corners. As the younger children streamed out, their faces flushed, – 'Cor, that was bloody marvellous!' – so the next audience moved in. Money was passed through a hole in the wall where a man's fingers could be glimpsed tearing tickets off a roll. Inside the hall photographs of chapel elders, texts painted for Sunday school prizes, and faded Christmas decorations, hung from the wooden walls.

Once the shutter of the improvised box office was slammed down, the lights were switched off, and the film would hover drunkenly onto the makeshift screen, half on, half off, freckling the portraits behind like mildew, before finally righting itself. The older boys always sat at the back. Whenever a pretty girl, any girl, appeared there would be whistles from the back where rows of glowing cigarettes moved jerkily up and down amid clouds of smoke. Every now and then a face would be illuminated by the sudden flash of a match, or the red glow of a cigarette being inhaled.

Returning home from these evenings, pushing our bikes up the hill, we could occasionally see a light crawling up behind us, climbing over the hedges on either side, reaching up into the tops of trees. Then we would pull in our bikes to one side as the car drove past, its lights swinging and swaying on into the night, leaving only the faltering light of our dynamos to blink on the road's surface. Passing a cottage we might see an oil lamp being carried upstairs, or someone putting out the cat before locking up for the night. 'There, go along puss!' The cat, its eyes gleaming in the reflection from our lamps, would cross the road and clamber up into a hedge on the other side of which we could hear sheep coughing, or a horse blowing through its lips.

THAT FIRST IMAGE

From the window of my bedroom I could see the valley below with the River Severn lying like a glittering scythe and Gloucester Cathedral in the distance. Often, kneeling at night to say my prayers, I would gaze up at the moon reflected in the river, and be discovered asleep on my knees. In the morning I would wake to see the sun heaving and shouldering its way through the clouds, as a flock of birds darted like arrows shot by the retreating night. Almost the first sound I would hear would be the clatter of milk cans as Rob Morgan from the farm below drove up to deposit them at the Stile for the milkman to collect. Somewhere in the valley a train rattled like a box of small bones, roaring into tunnels, then rushing noisily out again, belching smoke and snorting.

In the holidays I worked on the Morgans' farm, helping out with the hay-making when we would often have to race against the dark storm clouds in order to get the stack built and covered over with a black tarpaulin before the rains pelted down. In the summer I took part in the harvest, beginning early while the day was still fresh and cool and working until late in the evening. At midday we would sit in the shade of a hedge eating thick chunks of bread and cheese, while the cider bottle, which had been left standing in the ditch covered with large rhubarb leaves to keep it cool, was passed round. As the fields of corn grew ripe for gathering so they were cut to the last island when terrified rabbits, having retreated to the centre, would make a last forlorn run for cover, only to be brained with a stone or have their necks wrenched until their eyes bulged out. Swathe by swathe the corn subsided to the ground to be stooked and left to stand like sentinels of the harvest. When the moonlight shone on the bare fields of stubble, night's gleaners, the surviving rabbits, would emerge to nibble at the shortened stems, their ears cocking at the slightest sound of footsteps in the lane, where stitchwort gleamed palely in the hedgerows, and overhead the sky was strewn with stars like daisies in a field.

Although Robbie, as his family called him, was two or three years older than I, we soon became good friends, so that whenever I had finished my homework, or during the holidays, I would drop in to help out with whatever jobs needed doing. In winter, observing how his hands grew cold and chapped as he clenched and released the teats of the cows when milking, I quickly learned how to milk, our heads leaning against the warm flanks of the animals as they munched the hay. Sometimes if Robbie was out ploughing up on the ridge he would shout out for me to join him, keeping the tractor running until I was perched beside him. The soil up there was fine and fell softly as the tractor moved steadily with the plough.

Once, however, the sky misted over and the rain fell steadily, drenching the fields which began to steam. Quickly Robbie covered up the plough and draping old sacks over our shoulders we climbed back onto the tractor, leaving the plough behind and made for the farm where Mrs Morgan, looking out through the dairy window, saw us coming down the hill and hurried to put on the kettle. At the farm I leapt down to open the huge barn doors. The chickens that had been sheltering from the storm clucked and scattered as the tractor drove in. Placing an old khaki coat over the engine, we washed our hands under the gulping pump in the scullery, before going in to have our tea. Through the windows we could see the rain slashing down across the valley, veiling it like twilight, while rainwater gurgled along the gutters of the house and plopped into wooden water butts. 'Some storm!' commented Robbie. Then, almost as suddenly, the sky cleared and over against the river clouds hung, torn and empty, like burst paper bags. While the trees dripped, thrushes, wagtails and blackbirds gathered on the front lawn for slugs and worms.

I envied Robbie his physical strength, his indifference to church or religion. I was always riddled with anxieties, scruples and an all-pervading sense of guilt. One summer he and I went off for the whole day, climbing and swimming. On our way home it began to pelt with rain and we ran swiftly down a steep slope, making for a barn by a group of hazel trees. We arrived breathless, soaked to the skin. Robbie's shirt was open at the front, clinging to his body, the rain trickling down his long neck and through the hairs on his chest. Inside the barn there was the scent of wet earth and dusty hay. Chickens fluffed their feathers, murmuring contentedly, as the rain deluged down outside. I was content just to be there with Robbie but then I became aware of him looking intently at me. He was so close that the warm odour of his body became mingled with that of the rain-soaked earth, and I could feel his breath on my face. I felt his arm encircle my shoulders and then the rain-wet imprint of his warm lips outlining mine. Our teeth chinked and for one teasing moment our tongues met. It was all over before I realised what had happened. One moment we were close, warm body against body, and the next he had released me. That was all. But then he began to speak in a low voice almost as though to himself. I let him talk, for rarely did he talk so much, or so vulnerably. I knew that I wanted to hold that moment for always. It was a profession of friendship coming from one who I had not dared to hope could ever feel towards me as I did towards him. It was as though we had been bonded as brothers by that one kiss.

By the time we had returned to the farm it was late and Mrs Morgan insisted I stay the night, having already sent a message to the Pollards. 'You can just about share Robbie's bed,' said Mrs Morgan, 'and I've put out an old pair of his pyjamas for you.'

In the night I woke to find Robbie fast asleep, lying half across me with one arm over my chest. Listening to his breathing I began to breathe in as he breathed out, making an inter-twining pattern of sound, weaving the two of us together. Slowly my breath moved in unison with his until we lay like one person. I felt encased in him like Ariel in the cloven pine and yet, unlike Ariel, not imprisoned, but enveloped in a warm comforting darkness, wrapped in safety, while through the window of the attic bedroom I could see the moon, high up and full, with dark clouds racing past it. It seemed that we had melted into one another.

But we had not had sex, and what happened in the barn was never referred to again. In due course Robbie married, had children, and put on weight. Yet that memory stays with me from more than sixty years ago. Camus says somewhere that we devote our lives to rediscovering the two or three essential images on which we first opened our eyes. That time with Robbie was a promise of what lay ahead, although I was not then to know this. Decades later I came across a definition by Charlotte Woolf of homosexuality as 'ideal twin-ship', and I think often of Plato's description of love as a restoration: not just a longing to be reunited with our missing half, but the longing for the restoration of a grander self. Love is a quest for perfection and through our identification with 'the other' we regain our lost perfection and the two halves become one. All our loves tend towards union; they are the central forces in our lives. This longing for union finds its most complete expression in Plato's *Symposium* where we find the ancient myth that once upon a time man had four hands and feet, but a single head with two faces. Like Lucifer, however, he was so filled with pride that Zeus punished man by cutting him in two. Until that moment each individual had been complete and love was unknown. But now each half yearned for the other, 'and when one of them finds his other half, the pair are lost in amazement of love and friendship and intimacy.'

As Cathy says of Heathcliffe in *Wuthering Heights*, 'He's more myself than I am. Whatever our souls are made of, his and mine are the same.' Such love I was in time to find.

JIMMY PROSSER

Each evening from my bedroom window at Pleasant Stile I would hear the church clock at Newnham-on-Severn in the valley below playing the hymn tune *We love the place O God wherein Thine honour dwells*. Opposite the church was a tiny row of cottages, in one of which lived Jimmy Prosser who was to have a profound spiritual influence upon me. Severely injured in the First World War he had always, as a result, to wear a steel corset which caused him to walk with a lurch and a tilt. Thrown up in the air by an exploding shell, his neck was broken and he was paralysed. He lay for some hours in the squelching mud, the rain pouring down, until the Catholic chaplain arrived and began to say the prayers for the dying. 'No! No!' he cried, 'I'm not to die!'

Evacuated back to England to die, his mother was informed and given precise instructions about his coffin and she was asked to be sure to 'return the enclosed Union Jack for which a label is enclosed' after the funeral. By now his paralysed flesh had fallen off his back, and his wound was discharging spinal fluid so that every morning he was stuck to his sheets.

'I was utterly helpless, little more than a parcel of bones: Three times I was given the Last Sacrament as I was not expected to live. And then one day I was told that a young woman from Avila, who was preparing to become a Carmelite nun, was praying for me, and would be coming to see me. She came and she talked to me of the love of God, saying that she knew God was going to spare me because He had work for me to do. I only saw her face as I was immobile under a hospital cradle. I only saw her that once in 1917 until last year, 1945, when I went to the Carmelite Monastery at Reading where she is now Prioress.'

Gradually, over many months, he was able to stand up although his legs were very weak, but eventually he was able to walk with the aid of crutches.

'I used to play the piano but because I had no power in my legs a fellow named Green, who had no legs at all, would work the pedals with his hands at my instruction. For hours I would play Protestant hymns such as *Rock of Ages*.'

He was then suspended from a wall while bandages soaked in plaster were wound round him from the waist to the chin. He had to hang there until the plaster hardened so that a mould could be made from which a leather cage was made which he had to wear for seven to ten minutes each day and then gradually for longer periods. The other men painted a collar and tie on it! Slowly, over the years, he began to recover but for the rest of his life he had to wear this steel corset.

Fiercely independent and never complaining, he cared for his blind mother with whom he lived. I used to cycle down the hill from Pleasant Stile and sit for hours in his cottage, drinking blackcurrant cordial from large cut-glass goblets, listening to him talk of Lourdes and of Our Lady to whom he had a great devotion. It was in gratitude for his life being spared that each year he would make a pilgrimage to Lourdes, helping to look after the stretcher cases, and always, as an act of extraordinary faith, he would drink a glassful of the water from the Grotto which was swimming with pus from the wounds of the sick.

Jimmy was an impressive sight in his Breton beret and black cloak. I remember standing outside Gloucester Cathedral for the enthronement of a new bishop, unable to get in because it was packed. Jimmy appeared with a staff in one hand and the other uplifted as though in blessing, whereupon everyone made way for him as easily as the Red Sea responding to Moses. The officials in the main entrance, assuming he was some dignitary who had been overlooked, at once found him a seat. His flamboyant style was also reflected in his handwriting – he always used purple ink – with its many ornate flourishes, like missives from some Firbankian cardinal.

His was a story of remarkable courage and determination but most of all it was his devotion to Our Lady, the Eternal Mother, that moved me. As I sat listening to his stories, I knew that one day I would become a Catholic. But I knew also that I did not have to do anything about it, that I would know when the moment had arrived.

EXILED FROM EDEN

I was deeply happy at Pleasant Stile, and began to call Mrs Pollard 'Mother', which she, though I was always conscious of the inverted commas, strictly discouraged. Gradually, inevitably, my own mother became aware that I never stopped talking about the Pollards, about how happy I was there and she became jealous. By now, having returned from London, she insisted that I leave the Pollards and go back to live with her. I was almost seventeen. Snatched abruptly from my Eden, from the one place where, for the first time in my life, I had felt secure, nurtured and fulfilled, this was an intensely wounding period and one from which it took me many years to heal.

The cottage which my mother had found to rent was in the middle of an isolated common, a breeding ground for snipe and curlew. By the side of the cottage was a small orchard where I used to sit for hours in one apple tree from which I could see, up in the hills, Pleasant Stile and the Pollards' cottage. In the mornings before school and again in the evenings I would sit in the branches of this tree, weeping bitterly. The experience led to terrible struggles with my mother. She and I appeared to be alone in that isolated cottage, for I have no memory of my father at this time. One night, having packed a bag, I ran out of the house saying I was leaving home. My mother chased after me, wheeling her bicycle, stumbling and falling across the muddy fields, the two of us shouting wildly at each other terrible, tearing words, blind words, wounding indelibly. Suddenly there was an almighty reverberation of thunder as though the sky was about to be torn apart, and my mother, screaming against the thunder, ran dementedly along the lane, away from me, as though fleeing from the monster I had become. By now I was frightened that she had gone out of her mind. She kept crying out, 'Don't touch me! Leave me alone! Go away!' Her stockings were torn, her face spattered with mud, bruised and tear-stained. Dear God, how we torture one another. Was it this way, I wonder, that my grandfather drove my grandmother mad, through verbal and physical torture?

It was during this period that I took to beating myself with a leather strap, flagellating myself in an attempt to atone for the stain and smear of my faults, and for the wildness in me of my father and grandfather which I seemed to have inherited. I even took to hurling myself against a brick wall until exhausted, or walking barefoot among nettles. Once I even tried to hammer nails through my hands but lacked the courage for that extra thrust that would have driven them through the flesh. I used to pray for long hours, pleading with God to forgive me, until I fell asleep, exhausted, on my knees. Such histrionics surely marked me out as my mother's son.

Yet she loved me deeply. I was all she had and we were locked into each other. For years I was haunted by her frequent quoting of a neighbour in Ruardean who seeing me in my pram had remarked, 'He's evil, that one! He'll come to no good!' If one moment my mother overwhelmed me with kisses, the next she would castrate me with such negative remarks. She both set me on a pedestal as her idolised son and, at the same time, kept dragging me down from it. It seemed as though I were both her saviour and her devil. Even in my more mature years she always knew how to reach my weakest spot, to nag and needle me in the same way that she did with my father.

Once, when I was forty-six, and visiting her in Wales, she came into my study carrying a sepia photograph of me at the age of six with full Shirley Temple curls. She had wept when they had to be cut off for me to go to school, and kept them for decades, wrapped in newspaper. Referring to this photograph a few days before she died, she remarked, 'If only you could have stayed like that!' Now, holding me from behind, she began to sob, running her hand through my hair and saying, 'Your hair's still silky!' and then, torn out of her, came the cry, 'I wish I could do something!' I knew then that what she lamented was that lost paradise when I was small and she and I were close, a world within a world, of mother and child.

So often her own suffering and loneliness would invade me as though with each visit I was a sponge to absorb it all. Such visits would drain and exhaust me, especially as this was during years when I was earning very little. I could never discuss financial matters with her for then she would talk about ending her life. She also became jealous of any women friends I might have, such as the post mistress in our little village. One morning she observed me going down to the post office, which was also a small shop, to buy some butter. On my return to prepare lunch I found she had gone to her room, drawn her curtains – even though it was a beautiful summer's day – and was lying on her bed in the dark, listening to the radio. Although she said she did not want any lunch I left a tray outside her door. Later I heard her come downstairs and found her in the kitchen, a cloth around her neck, hacking at her hair with a pair of scissors, causing blood to flow.

'Cut it all off!' she shouted. I was so shocked at this disfigurement that I cried out, 'Oh, God! God!' over and over, going from room to room, not knowing what to do with myself. Finally, going into my study, I closed the shutters and lay on the floor roaring with pain. I could not take any more. I had done all that I could for her: bought her a home, paid for her operations. All I knew was that I must go back to London. I could not stay any longer in that house even though I had only arrived the day before. I went in to tell her gently that I must go back to London, knowing, however, that she had heard my cries and was clearly shaken. When the local taxi arrived to take me to the station I turned to wave and she smiled. Then suddenly her mouth opened in a silent cry and her tears cascaded. She turned and shut the front door, going alone into that empty house. Oh, how terrible were her griefs, and yet there could have been such happiness in that house which she had found and I had bought for us.

The basic problem was one of loneliness. She once told me that whenever I returned to London she would open all the doors, 'and then it doesn't seem so lonely. Then, later, I shut them all up.' On another occasion, when I was working in my study, I smelled bacon frying. 'I felt so hungry,' she said, 'so I cooked myself some bacon and fried bread. It's because I've got company.'

Do all women, I wonder, from their collective experience know how to penetrate their children's armour and render them impotent? It is not only sons, but daughters too, who testify to such love/hate relationships with their parents. We speak of a mother's love as though it were automatically something noble (as indeed it can be, especially at the heroic moment of giving birth) but we ignore at our peril the *shadow* side of the mother. It has taken me many years to understand the nature of Kali who, as the Divine Mother, is both destructive as well as creative, a primal force. Yet my mother really did love and care for me, watching anxiously over me, always wanting the best for me, and it was her sadness that as I grew up and away from her there was so little she could do for me.

To let go of one's child, even more so when there is no love in the marriage, is a pain that perhaps only a woman can understand. Sadly, like many of her generation, my mother never found her own role in life, outside that of being a mother. With so much energy and drive, which I have inherited from her, she could have achieved a great deal more. But I am always indebted to her gaiety and laughter, and her ability to make any place feel like home, as well as her sense of drama! In later years, when there was so little she could do for me, whenever I stayed with her, she would place on my desk an egg cup filled with tiny flowers which she had picked from the garden or hedgerow. Through this recurring ritual she was still able to express her love and watchfulness over me.

POSTSCRIPT

Around the time of my twenty-first birthday Mrs Pollard and Mary came to London to visit us. We were standing on a street corner when suddenly my mother verbally attacked Mrs Pollard who was stunned by her wholly unfair accusations. There was a terrible scene and my mother said I was never to see Mrs Pollard again. She, being a scrupulously honest woman, replied, 'If your mother doesn't want you to see me you must honour that.' Although I wrote regularly to her over the years she never did see me and it was only after her death that Mary and I met again.

That was in May 1963 when I returned after so many years to find myself in an alien landscape. The view from Pleasant Stile was as fine as ever but it no longer spoke to me with the intensity it once had. Mary, who had remained unmarried, seemed to have changed little: a greyness in the hair but the same, clear skin and serene countenance. After a fragile meal we sat before the fire where, holding her cup and saucer as a point of concentration, she spoke of her mother's last illness and of her final, painful and distressing delirium before passing into a coma. Seated in the dusk Mary talked on in a clear but shadowed voice, 'I cannot weep. I prayed that mother would die and so I must thank God for this answer to prayer. But I would not look at her once she was dead. I had done everything for her when she was alive but I could not bring myself to wash and prepare her body. Her funeral was an occasion of such joy and happiness, all the blackbirds were singing. I know that I shall meet her and my father and other friends in Heaven.'

The cottage seemed more crowded than I remembered, with pots and jugs, trinkets, photographs, and gifts from abroad, her mother's old crutches and other invalid accessories – and chairs, chairs. 'Mother would never get rid of anything'. In pots and saucers there were more than fifty cactus plants while in the outside toilet was a pile of newspapers ten feet high. As she talked I observed the shadows under her eyes, and I sensed tiredness – a vulnerability in her. I wondered why I had not been invited to stay overnight (my old room was still there, unused). I invited her to dine with me at the Speech House in Littledean but she said no, she would not enjoy it, nor could I afford it. She was, I realised, afraid, and was now alone.

Standing outside in the moonlight, looking at the cluster of lights below in Newnham-on-Severn, and hearing the church clock there peal out the tune *We love the place, O God, wherein Thine honour dwells*, I was aware of how we had once loved each other, even if only in a platonic, adolescent way. Had I stayed that night perhaps she might have wept for what might have been. We were both too naked, without defences, and I think also we both knew we could no longer return to the closeness we had once known: and so, because of this, there was that night between us a restraint.

A SOLDIER'S LIFE

On 7 November 1946, four days before my nineteenth birthday I joined the Army. During my Infantry training I refused to take seriously those manoeuvres which involved charging with bayonets at stuffed sacks, pretending they were Japanese soldiers whilst screaming at the top of our voices. As a result I was the only one in our platoon not sent to the obligatory battle camp: doubtless those in command suspected it might be unwise to allow me to handle live grenades! Instead I was put backstage for the pantomime at the Garrison Theatre in Oswestry where among my tasks was that of sitting up in the flies and dropping leaves on the Babes in the Wood.

During one weekend leave from Oswestry early in 1947, I arranged to meet my mother in Gloucester, when it began to snow. Because a heavy fall had been forecast we ran to catch the bus, fearing it might be the last. (My parents by then had got together again and moved back to Ruardean.) My mother slipped on the wet pavement, breaking her ankle, though she did not know this at the time. We arrived at the bus stop to learn that all buses had been cancelled. We managed, however, to find a taxi but a mile outside Littledean the drifts were so bad the driver was forced to abandon us and turn back. We were still miles from home and so we struggled up the hill to Mrs Pollard's, where my mother was put to bed immediately. Having been a district nurse Mrs Pollard had at once diagnosed the broken ankle and knew that my mother should not be moved until a doctor could be sent for.

That night the snow baled out faster and faster like pillow cases being emptied of feathers: sifting into hedges, slipping under gates and forming thick mats on doorsteps. All night it fell quietly and steadily until the woods were veiled by a curtain of falling snow. Cattle huddled together and rooks flew into the hollow spire of the village church. Doors were barricaded with banks of snow and in the morning the road down to the village was blocked with drifts five feet deep. And still the snow tumbled down. No traffic was able to get through. Listening to the radio we learned that it was not just Littledean that was in a state of siege but much of the country. Clearly there was no way I could get back to camp. Then the wind blew the snow into deeper drifts so that houses were half buried. The next night it froze. It was as though nature, like a sculptor, had put a varnish over everything to preserve its delicate folds and wrinkles. Sledges appeared and snowballs whizzed through the air as armies of small boys took up strategic positions and every garden took in a snowman.

On the third day men from the village turned out with spades to cut a way through the drifts as far as the Pollards' house, flinging the snow from left to right, until a narrow tunnel was made, in some places six feet high. The first person to appear was the doctor who examined my mother and ordered an ambulance which could only come as far as the village. The ambulance men brought a sitting stretcher to the house and when my mother saw it she broke down, crying, 'I don't want to go to hospital! Please, please, don't let them take me. I hate hospitals!' At the hospital in Gloucester she broke down again. I was shaken by this. Suddenly she, who had always appeared so strong, seemed as helpless and as vulnerable as a child, her face appearing to break into fragments. It was then that I understood Picasso's painting of *A Woman in Grief* which Wilf had shown us one day in class, with the face broken into many pieces like shards of glass.

From Oswestry I was drafted to Alton Towers in Shropshire to be trained for the Royal Army Education Corps. In the hot June and July of 1947, along avenues of flamboyant rhododendrons, between neglected lawns and lakes full of weed, we marched to classes in the stables and outhouses of that many-roofed and turreted pseudo-Gothic castle where in its Puginesque chapel I organised play readings by candlelight. It was on those battlements that I was once spotted by the Sergeant Major in the middle of a thunder and lightning storm reciting King Lear's 'Blow, winds, and crack your cheeks! Rumble thy bellyful! Spit, fire! Spout, rain!' On another occasion he caught me walking through the grounds wearing on my head a fez which I had found in a basket of theatre properties. 'For Christ's sake, Evans!' he shouted, 'Take that bloody thing off your head!'

After our training several of us were posted to our first billet, the Education Centre on Salisbury Plain. Having until then shared a barrack room with some twenty other men it was a relief to be told that at Salisbury we could expect, as qualified sergeants, to have individual quarters. However, on arrival we found that we were to be crowded into a small barrack room as there was no other accommodation. On one side of my bed there was a curtain which, clearly, had once been used to divide the room. This I pulled to the length of my bed to form a partition on one side while on the other I placed an old bookcase I had found, thereby creating a degree of privacy for myself. But this did not go down at all well with my fellow sergeants. One night, on returning to the barrack room and going to switch on the lights, I discovered that all the bulbs had been removed and that the others were inside, waiting in the darkness. 'Come on in!' one of them called out. Sensing trouble I replied that if they wanted me they could come outside. There were about seven of them, all journalists or teachers in Civvy Street, and they proceeded to beat me up. Lying on the ground, looking up at the stars, I could not understand their antagonism as they rammed their fists into me. 'He doesn't even bloody fight back!' shouted the ringleader, spitting in my face. 'The yellow spunk!' Eventually they replaced the electric bulbs and I returned with them to the barrack room where they proceeded to put me on trial. Who did I think I was? Why did I think I was different from anyone else?

I answered all their questions truthfully but because their interrogation was one-sided I began to emerge as a monster of egotism until suddenly one of them said, 'This is wrong. We are trying to make out that black is black and white is white but the truth is more complex!'

In retrospect it is easy to see that while I showed initiative and got things moving – on arrival at the Centre I had launched a newspaper for the camp, as well as a regular radio programme – I nonetheless lacked tact, and all too often charged ahead without stopping to find out what anyone else thought. I was too much a loner and had not then learned how to be part of a team, something I really only learned when I started working in the theatre.

I was so unhappy that the next day I volunteered to go on a draft to Palestine, then one of the most dangerous fighting areas left. I was prepared to do anything to escape this atmosphere of hostility. And so, en route for Palestine, I was posted first to Buchanan Castle at Drymen, outside Glasgow, where I found my former Commanding Officer from Alton Towers who said, 'Why on earth do you want to go to Palestine? Why not stay here on the permanent staff and then towards the end of your eighteen months, I'll get you on a posting to Trieste. You will enjoy that!'

I was placed in charge of the small theatre and given a room to myself backstage. Apart from acting in and directing various productions in the theatre, my main task was to teach elocution. Although I had had no formal training I had a lot of confidence! I would take a group of men up onto the battlements and get them to sing out in long drawn-out syllables the Welsh girl's name, Angharad. I had got this idea from seeing the film *How Green Was My Valley* which opens with the young Huw calling across the valley to his sister.

One day when my group were performing this exercise, the Sergeant Major was trying to drill a platoon of men down below.

'Ang-har-ad! Ang-har-ad!' my men sang out, over and over. Finally the Sergeant Major brought his men to a halt and bellowed up to me (he, at least, had excellent projection!) 'Sergeant, for Christ's sake, take those bleeding men somewhere else!' I looked round the battlements and, observing a line of chimney pots, I instructed each man to take a chimney pot and resonate down it a rhyme my mother had taught me as a child: 'A big bow-wow prowling round about the house.'

One after another, and then in unison, they chanted. After several minutes a trapdoor in the roof was pushed up and an officer appeared, saying wearily, 'Sergeant, really! I am trying to teach a class down below and all this canine gibberish is coming down the chimney! Please take your men somewhere else.'

One day, when it was raining heavily, I used the banqueting hall for a class with two of my men. At one end was a massive oak staircase leading up to a balcony where I positioned one man as Juliet and, at the bottom some thirty feet below, I stationed the other as Romeo. As Juliet began to cry out, 'Romeo! Romeo! Wherefore art thou?' the double doors at the far end of the hall opened and there appeared a phalanx of senior officers from Whitehall led by Colonel Salisbury, the head of the Royal Army Education

Corps. I saluted smartly and he asked me what I was doing. Surprisingly he complimented me on my ingenuity, adding that he hoped I would be organising some form of entertainment for the banquet to be held there that evening in his honour. I can't now remember what we did, but I do recall that at the climax I swung in on a rope, attached to the balcony thirty feet above, and landing on the long refectory table, recited *Richard III*'s 'Now is the winter of our discontent'!

AN AIR I BREATHED DEEPLY

For the final months of my National Service I was posted to Trieste. It was my first time abroad and on arriving in Italy I immediately felt at home. Opposite the Education Centre was the parish church of St Vincent de Paul where I began to attend Mass regularly. I loved the natural way Italians had of wandering in and out of church at all times, pausing with bags of shopping, or accompanied by small children, to light a candle and say a prayer, then out again into the noisy streets. This to me was an air I breathed deeply where religion was seen, not as a Sunday activity, but impregnating the whole of life. Lighting a candle is a small piece of theatre, an outward expression of an inner activity, the physical action springing from something deep within. When we leave a church having lit a candle we experience a simple comfort in the knowledge that the candle burns on in our absence; knowing that as it diminishes and finally sputters out, it will be succeeded by other candles and other prayers. In the long hours of the night and throughout the day, in thousands of churches and temples all over the world, candles and votive lamps are burning as a symbol of our need to invoke a power beyond that of our limited selves. To light a candle in this way is an act of poetry as well as an act of piety, reminding us that we each carry a single lamp for humanity.

The Italians have a natural sense of theatre, and seemed at home with images and symbols. I shall always remember the Feast of Corpus Christi in Trieste when the Blessed Sacrament was carried through the city in a golden monstrance under a large ornate canopy, the streets lined with people, while from every window and balcony brightly coloured bedspreads were displayed, and flowers thrown down as the procession passed beneath them. Only when it came to the Communist part of the city did those standing on the pavement express a cold hostility. When finally the procession reached the Altar of Repose, showers of roses were thrown up into the air as everyone burst out singing.

Such spontaneity was again evident when Renzo Ricci, then Italy's most famous actor, comparable to Laurence Olivier, returned to Trieste for the first time since the war to play *Hamlet*. At the end of the second act the audience showered bouquets of flowers onto the stage, waving flags of Italy and repeatedly calling 'Ricci! Ricci! Ricci!' On his ninth appearance he addressed the vast auditorium, saying how good it was to be back and to see once more the flag of Italy in Trieste. After this he returned to his dressing room to prepare for the rest of the play. But still the audience would not let him go and continued to chant, 'Ricci! Ricci! Ricci!' waving their flags and banners as though at a football match. When, after a long wait, he reappeared, an enormous shout went up from everyone present. Finally, in a silence deep with emotion, during which many were weeping, he recited by heart Carducci's long patriotic poem, *The Song of Italy*.

Listening to his performance as Hamlet I fell in love with the Italian language and set about learning it. Its melodic phrasing even improved on some of Shakespeare's lines, as in Horatio's last words to Hamlet: 'Buona notte, dolce principe, e voli d'angeli ti conducano al tuo riposo' ('Good night, sweet prince, and flights of angels sing thee to thy rest.') It is the long vowel sounds of Italian that make it so mellifluous.

At the church of St Vincent de Paul I found myself sitting next to two brothers, Carlo and Mario Luigi. Although they spoke no English they always turned warmly to greet me and as my Italian improved we got to know each other. It was then that I knew the moment had arrived that I had long sensed: that one day I would become a Catholic, and so finally in Trieste I began to receive instruction to be received into the Catholic Church. I asked Mario and Carlo if they would be my godparents, for although I had been baptised and confirmed in the Anglican Church it was considered best that I should also have what was termed a conditional baptism, followed by confirmation.

On Sunday 6 June 1948, I made my First Communion as a Catholic at the church of St Vincent de Paul. Returning from the Communion rail, the first person to greet me was Maria who did the laundry for the Education Centre, who had walked several miles with her mother in order to be present at my First Communion and give me a bouquet of white carnations. Afterwards, standing outside on the steps of the church under its high portico, the parish priest said to me, '*E contento, adesso?*' meaning 'You are content now, fulfilled, at peace?' I knew only that I had 'come home'. And although now I am no longer a Catholic, but have reverted to my original Anglicanism, my years within the structure and tradition of Rome have remained a lasting influence on me.

Carlo, Mario and their father were very poor but they had prepared a special meal for me that day, as well as an iced cake inscribed with the words 'Viva James!' Their mother had died some years previously, but the two boys continued to live with their father who was a carpenter. Each evening he brought home a bag of sawdust with which he filled the stove. Into the centre of this he would insert a taper and the heat from the glowing sawdust would be enough to heat their evening meal of pasta. I spent as much of my spare time with them as I could. I loved the freedom of being able to walk arm in arm with them through the streets. After a midday meal we would take a siesta and I would lie between the two brothers on the family's large double bed. Carlo, the older brother, who was engaged to be married, would always kiss me on the cheek when he woke up.

The decision to become a Catholic was one I took entirely on my own. Being in the Army, away from the umbilical attachment to my mother, having to learn to be one of a group, I was taking my first step towards independence and in that sense it was a true rite of passage. As the theatre director Peter Brook has observed, 'A great ritual, a fundamental myth, is a door and he who can experience the door within himself passes through it most intensely.' All rites of passage involve three stages. First there is the ritual of separation, achieved in my case by being in the Army, and then this is followed by the initiate being stripped of all familiar associations before finally being inducted into the spiritual context of his tribe. This stage is aptly described as a *liminal* state, from the Latin word meaning 'threshold.' The initiate crosses from one stage of life to another and once he has crossed that threshold he cannot return. As Anthony Stevens writes: 'Now I am a boy belonging to my mother. And I die as a boy and am ritually dismembered. Now I am born as a man among men.'

And so it was that taking that independent step in Trieste marked my entry into independence but also a deepening of the inner journey of the spirit.

FIRST STEPS AS AN ACTOR

'It's Titian, isn't it, darling?' Seated behind her desk, like a large toad with glittering eyes, Miriam Warner, the theatrical agent renowned for her toughness, glared at me in silence. It was some moments before I realised she was referring to the colour of my hair. She got me my first jobs after coming out of the Army, playing one-night stands of light comedies in the East End of London, where the audiences sat at rough trestle tables with enamel jugs of beer, drinking and smoking and talking throughout the performance. After one such evening, as we made our way between the tables, I was accosted with cries of 'We could hear you, luv!'

Although the Army paid for me to travel from Italy to audition for the Old Vic School, as well as for the Royal Academy of Dramatic Art, I failed both auditions. Over ambitiously and, I suspect unwisely, I had chosen to do Sir Epicure Mammon from *The Alchemist*, an exercise on my part of pure overacting!

Determined to be an actor I had already given up my place at New College, Oxford and so, on being demobbed, I made one more attempt to enter RADA. Again I failed. Hearing of a small dramatic academy, the New Era, run by an elderly actor named Horace Sequeira and his wife, I enrolled, but left after one week as I was in search of the holy grail, the Stanislavsky Method. At the suggestion of a drama teacher, Oliver Reynolds, who had worked with Michel St Denis, I entered the Hovel Theatre Studio, which was supposedly run on Stanislavsky principles by its owner, Lady Neysa Graham. I was immediately cast as Leontes in *A Winter's Tale*. One day in class Neysa Graham, floundering in an attempt to expound Stanislavsky's theories, turned to me, saying, 'Oh, James, you explain, you understand it so much better!' It was then that I realised I was not going to learn very much at the Hovel and so I left at the end of the first term.

Unable to find the training I wanted I began to go the round of theatre agents until Miriam Warner took me under her wing. She got me a job playing Lieutenant Colbert in Terence Rattigan's *While The Sun Shines* for one week at the Palace Theatre, Walthamstow. Applying my Stanislavsky – I had devoured both his *An Actor Prepares* and *My Life in Art* – I practised short steps in order to suggest those of a little man, worked on my French accent, and grew a moustache. (I suspect that it was these attempts at over characterisation that caused me to fail my auditions for RADA.) During rehearsals, Freddie Tripp, our producer (as directors were then called) said, 'You're not going to play it like that, are you? Didn't they teach you how to walk at the Academy? Legs out from the hips and swing both arms! And you're not going to use that accent, are you? They won't understand what you're saying.' Then he added, 'By the way, that moustache, not a good idea, old chap!' And so overboard went all my attempts a characterisation and I played Lieutenant Colbert as straight as any juvenile.

My lonely attempts to apply Stanislavsky's Method (the very words were suspect in those days) were the means of teaching me a basic lesson on one occasion. I was in a production of *Othello* at the Marlowe Theatre, Canterbury, doubling Desdemona's father, Brabantio with Ludovico, the Prince, who appears at the end. For half an hour before the performance I would sit in the wings in my costume and make-up, pretending to be

Brabantio. At the dress rehearsal, as Iago called for Brabantio in the opening scene, I hurried on, as though woken from sleep, dragging on my dressing gown, only to find the actor, Kenneth Mason, who was playing Iago, dragging me upstage. 'My dear boy!' he said as I protested, 'it doesn't matter how well you are acting, if the audience can't see you. I am only trying to get you into your light!'

Some years later, when I was in Esmé Percy's production of Shaw's *St Joan* at the Q Theatre in Richmond, with Rachel Kempson as St Joan and Robert Shaw as Dunois, I had to double the role of Brother Martin with that of the Steward in the opening scene. The latter has to come on crying excitedly, 'Sir, sir! The hens are laying like mad!' Before each performance I used to hide the prop eggs backstage and while the first scene was progressing, I would be hunting around in the wings muttering under my breath as I found each clutch of eggs, 'Glory be to God, a miracle!' in order that I might have the right degree of fervour when I rushed on to say my line. Esmé Percy always used to say that the audience missed the best part of my performance as the Steward!

My first proper audition as a young actor was for Harry Hanson who ran a series of weekly repertory companies all over the country, providing a lot of actors with regular employment in mainly commercial plays. It provided an excellent opportunity for young actors to learn their craft working alongside more experienced actors; an opportunity and an experience sadly lacking today. If I succeeded I knew I could be in regular work.

I was met by his general manager Douglas Neil who, in a black and white suit, bow tie, and curling moustache, looked more like a bookie.

'You do know I'm not Mr Hanson, don't you? I've been with Mr Hanson for twenty years and I know exactly what kind of actor he likes. I can see you have great power and I'm impressed. He can't stand people who come on stage and you don't know they are there at all. After all, the stage is larger than life, isn't it?' He beamed at me and put me down as a Leading Man, inviting me to return at the end of the week to repeat my audition pieces for the great man himself. 'You mustn't be nervous of him. He'll sit back in his chair, looking like the Emperor of China, but he has a heart of gold.' The following Friday I met the legendary Mr Hanson: plump, with rouged cheeks, and on his head a blonde wig.

There was a story (I learned later) that he once had a business manager who was his lover and who also was bald and wore a wig. One Thursday when there was no rehearsal there was an urgent call at the theatre for Mr Hanson and so a young stage manager was sent to find him in his digs. The landlady directed him upstairs where he knocked on a door, and hearing Mr Hanson say, 'Come in!' entered, to find two bald men tucked up in bed, with their wigs on stands on either side of the bed. Harry Hanson was so furious that the poor stage manager was sacked.

Once again I performed my audition pieces: Ernest Piaste, the Polish student from Bridie's *Daphne Laureola* and Owen Morgan from Emlyn Williams' *The Corn is Green*. I then asked if I might do Monsieur Henri from Anouilh's *Point of Departure*, apologising for it being a bit highbrow, to which Mr Hanson replied in his thin lisping voice, 'Oh, you never know, I might stoop to it one day! It's not commercial but I love it!' He asked if I had done any weekly repertory before and then trotted out what was clearly one of his set speeches:

> It's hard work, you know. But it brings out the best in people. There are many who have been with me for years and who will go no further, but there are those few who I know will get there in the end because they have the essential spark: actors like Emrys James, Pauline Jameson, and others. Emrys was with me for years at Peterborough and then Edith Evans saw him when she was on tour and offered him a part. When he asked me what he should do, I said, 'Take it, my boy, take it!' And another thing: I like all my companies to work hard together. I'm a self-made man and it irritates me to see these young people just out of drama school, impatient to be in the West End. I say to them, 'If you've got anything you'll get there in the end.' Now rest assured, dear boy, that I shall use you. But I've yet to sort everyone out.

And so it was that I arrived in Hereford to play the juvenile lead in R.F. Delderfield's *Worm's Eye View*, to be greeted by Douglas Neil, fluttering with smiles.

'I hope you won't think I've been neglecting you? Do you need any money? Everything all right at your digs? This week's rather busy as I have to keep going up to town but I hope soon to let you know where you'll be going next. I shall see the play on Monday night so as to see it fresh. Now! I have a sort of message for you from Mr Hanson. We both feel, and I discussed it with him after your audition, that you are very intense. You may not know it but the sooner you do the better. Not that it's altogether a fault. But Mr Hanson feels that for a year or two it won't hurt you to play all sorts of parts until you gradually find your forte. So you mustn't be disappointed if the plays we do are all commercial. But that doesn't mean we don't do a straight play every now and then. For instance, Mr Hanson is very fond of

Rebecca. But you need to get away from that intensity and get the feel of an audience. It's an old story but I can best illustrate what I'm trying to tell you by using it. It's about two young men in the bar of the Arts Theatre Club in London – now remember this is not meant to be a dig at you! – who were discussing rather intensely how to get a laugh. Standing next to them was Bud Flanagan who interrupted them, saying, 'Much of what you've been saying is very true, but you know the great thing in the end is to know how to fall on your arse. That's the secret, because even in Shakespeare you have to fall on your arse!'

In the end I found it very difficult to believe in the one dimensional character I was called upon to play, that of an earnest young schoolteacher who had lines like, 'This is a grand country! The kids are grand too! A great country that produces Browning and Shakespeare and Shelley!' In addition I had difficulty with the young actress playing opposite me who kept telling me I didn't kiss her properly: 'You should push your tongue into my mouth! Didn't they teach you that at Drama School?!'

The truth was that I didn't fit in. I lacked the social ability for small talk, the sitting around in the pub after the show. I was indeed altogether too tense and intense. Harry Hanson was right. And I was also ill at ease in that kind of play. And so, at the end of the week, I returned to London knowing I would not be further employed by Mr Hanson.

BREAKDOWN

Having had no proper theatrical training, lacking professional contacts, seemingly unable to earn a living, coupled with a traumatic home life, and cut off from contact with Mrs Pollard and the one place that had been truly home, I suffered a nervous breakdown. It took the form of breaking out in sweats whenever I went off to be interviewed for an audition. Halfway there I would turn back and retreat to my bed for twelve hours or more. My parents by then were once again living together in a house in Golders Green.

Quite clearly I was regressing from the challenge of adult life but undoubtedly there was more to it than that. It was my good fortune that the priest in Ogle Street to whom I went for Confession recommended me to a Jungian analyst, Dr Franz Elkisch, a German Jew who had been trained by Jung in Zurich, and who at the outbreak of war had managed to escape to England.

I went to Franz Elkisch over a period of some twenty-three years, though there were occasional gaps in that time when I was away working. For several years, when I could not afford it, he urged me not to worry about payment, saying that it was much more important that I continue the analysis. Franz used to tell one of Jung's favourite stories of how once upon a time there was a drought and at last, in despair, the people of that country sent for a holy man to see if he could bring rain. For three days he just sat and did nothing, and on the third day the rains came. 'But what did you do?' asked the people, to which he replied, 'First I put myself in order and then all nature was in order around me.'

The discovery of realms within each one of us is a rich and at times a perilous process, one that calls for a skilled guide. I was indeed fortunate in not only being sent to a Jungian, which was what I needed at the time in order to explore the world of images and symbols, but also someone onto whom I could safely project 'the father' I had always sought. Decades later, shortly before he died, and long after my analysis had ended, Franz acknowledged our special relationship in a letter:

> My dear Jimmie, *son*, let me use this way of addressing you as it is, I feel, the proper way of giving our contact its proper expression. You care for me and I'm very grateful to you. My love and gratitude that you exist and are there,
>
> Franz.

On another card he wrote simply, 'The lost son is found again'. It was he who helped me, not only to find my own centre, but also to reassemble the pieces of my jigsaw, until the picture of who I was meant to be began to emerge more clearly. The day was to come, some twenty or more years later when, after recounting one particular dream I had had, he declared, 'Your analysis is ended', and from that moment we became Franz and Jimmie, and on meeting he would often share with me his own dreams.

VOCATION

It was in the spring of 1949 that, floundering in the attempt to carve a career in the theatre, I made a trip to Ampleforth Abbey in Yorkshire where I found myself drawn to the monastic way of life and to St Benedict's mixture of prayer, study and manual labour. As a result I went to the Abbot to ask if I might join the community. He wisely suggested that I should go to St Benet's Hall in Oxford, the House of Studies for the Benedictine Congregation, take a degree and 'find out more about what kind of person you are and what kind of people monks are.' Fortunately, although I had turned down my place at New College, I was still eligible for a grant to study at Oxford.

Before going up to Oxford in the autumn of 1949 I took a job for the summer term teaching English and Religious Knowledge at All Hallows, a Catholic Preparatory School at Shepton Mallet in Somerset. An old country house with a courtyard and stable block, it was set in parkland with a fine avenue of lime trees under which, on Sports Day, I observed Evelyn Waugh in a grey check suit, bow tie, and grey bowler, walking deep in conversation with Monsignor Ronald Knox in his old-fashioned black frock coat and round-brimmed black hat.

I often used to take my youngest class out to a nearby wood where they would sit in a row on a fallen beech tree like fledglings, while I read to them from *Wind in the Willows*. One afternoon I suggested that each boy should build a hut in the woods from branches and bracken. One seven year old, Simon, who had a pronounced stammer, asked if he might go to the lavatory in his 'house'. Such was the urgency of his request – for I could as easily have told him to walk back to school – that I agreed but stressed he must dig a proper hole, filling it in afterwards. A little later he reappeared, running up excitedly and saying, with hardly a stammer, 'P-Please, Sir, I've *done* it!'

Each afternoon the staff used to sit down to tea at one end of the panelled hall, with the French windows open to the lawn. On a round table covered with a starched white cloth were plates of thin bread and butter (white and brown), scones, cakes, honey and jam. I was so full of what had happened that I could scarcely wait to get back to tell everyone about Simon. Suddenly there was an embarrassed silence, broken by the clunk of the Matron putting down her cup and saucer, exclaiming, 'How disgusting!' I was so upset by the Matron's reaction that I discussed the incident with one of the monks, Dom Oswold Sumner, who came over daily from Downside Abbey to celebrate Mass in the school chapel, and was an authority on psychological matters. He at once assured me that

I had done the right thing but, he added, perhaps it was not a good idea to recount the episode at the tea table!

I used to spend many hours listening to Simon stammering out long and convoluted stories. I even encouraged him to take a small part in a one-act play. When he came on and delivered his lines without a single stammer there was an audible sigh from the rest of the school, knowing how important it was for him. Afterwards he ran up to me, his face shining, as he cried, 'I did it, Sir! Sir, didn't I?'

Discovering a swarm of bees I bought a hive and encouraged the boys to look after them. Then I found a jackdaw which we tamed. All went well until the day it flew through the open window of a classroom and perched on a boy's desk.

'What's that?' demanded an irascible Irish master.

'Please, Sir, it's Mr Roose-Evans' jackdaw!' came the excited reply from the whole class. When the master moved forward to catch the bird it hopped onto the next desk until, as he pursued it from desk to desk, the whole classroom was in an uproar.

A little later the jackdaw took to flying in at the windows of the top dormitory in the early mornings, when the boys would lean out to try and catch it. The Matron was understandably irate, and that was another black mark against me. One day Jaarko, as the bird was onomatopoeically named, vanished. Had the Matron poisoned him? No one knew but the whole school was in a kind of mourning. Then on the third day, in Biblical fashion, just as the boys were seated on the lawn in a large circle for their post-prandial rest, Jaarko appeared out of the sky like a black Holy Ghost, spiralling downwards and landing exactly in the centre of the circle to great cheers from the boys. In the end he became so tame that he was caught by one of the cats and found floating in a dam which, incidentally, I had also got the boys to build. Eventually I was summoned to the Headmaster's study where Mr Gregory Dix, the owner and principal of the school, boomed disapprovingly at me, 'You are taking the boys away from their nets and their Latin!'

There was a small group of boys who used to meet regularly with me in an attic room of the stables under its blue and gilt clock. Probably because I was much closer to them in age, and also because they knew I was only there for one term, they confided in me all manner of things which they would not normally have discussed with a member of staff. As one nine year old observed, 'If our parents knew half the things that went on here they'd have a fit!'

In teaching Religious Knowledge I devised my own system. For the first half of the lesson I would explain the meaning of a section of the Catechism in a way they could understand, using drawings and practical illustrations;

while for the second half of the lesson I would get them to recite the passage aloud, over and over, until they had it by heart. It was by this method that a bright, red-haired boy, with pale blue eyes and a cheeky grin, rose to be top of that class. He was Auberon Waugh, son of Evelyn. However, the sound of chanting voices drifting out through the open classroom windows did not endear me to other members of staff.

I was much attracted to one of the boys. He and I would exchange notes, hold hands briefly on stairwells, and go for walks. It was all very intense and platonic. The Judas figure in this sad tale was a permanent member of staff who also acted as sacristan at Mass: a tall, fleshy man with large white hands, who loved to ingratiate himself with the visiting clergy. He used to watch me closely, wet lipped and bulging eyed, scenting scandal. It was he who reported the friendship to the Headmaster. What he should have done, of course, knowing I was young and inexperienced, was to have taken me aside and gently suggested I see less of the boy. As a result the boy and I were summoned, each individually, to the Headmaster's study. We were allowed one last conversation, for which I remain grateful, for I have never forgotten the remarks made to me then by this ten-year-old boy: 'Sir, you cannot go around as you do wearing your heart upon your sleeve! You must hurry up and become a monk.' He also remarked, 'Sir, I feel tied to you!' And yet without question the relationship had to come to an end. I grieved for several years over this loss and owed much to the sympathetic understanding of the writer, Eleanor Farjeon, who by then had become a close friend.

ELEANOR FARJEON AND WRITING

Dere mister roost-in-heaven
Yu are the nicest fan male
I ever had.

Yours devotedly, Nell F. x

It was when the actor Denys Blakelock was invited to play King Nollekins at the Arts Theatre, in Eleanor's musical play for children, *The Silver Curlew*, with music by Clifton Parker, that I first met Eleanor. She was then in her seventies. An inveterate theatregoer – her father had been a friend of Sir Henry Irving who always gave the Farjeon family his box when they went to see him act – I became her frequent escort to first nights where her large, comfortable figure was a familiar sight. Because she was shortsighted – she had to wear very powerful magnifying glasses – she liked to sit in the front row of the stalls, and actors soon became used to the sound of her opera glasses being lifted to her spectacles with a large clunk, while her sighs and gasps of appreciation seemed to underscore every detail of the acting and the production. Then, after she became a Catholic, another sound was added to her repertoire: the rattle of her rosary beads which she kept wrapped round her right hand and from which she would not be parted. One night, at her home in Perrins Walk in Hampstead, her chair collapsed beneath her weight and, unable to get up, she lay on her back all night until her 'daily' came in the morning. When I saw her later that day she lay back on her sofa, laughing, 'You see, Jimmie, I had my rosary, didn't I? So I was able to say my beads. And also the radio was switched to World Service, so I could always listen to that. And I knew Joan would be coming in the morning, and would rescue me. But don't tell Denys! He will only be upset.'

Eleanor had a special love of cats. The most wary and battle-scarred of tom-cats would come daily to her window to be fed, while always she had her own marmalade cat, the most famous of which she wrote about in a book called *Golden Coney*. Her current marmalade cat when I knew her was named Benignus, after Father Benignus who had received her into the Catholic Church. It is when I read her poem, *Mrs Malone*, that I catch something of what she meant to so many of us:

It's our mother,
It's Mrs Malone
whose havings were few
and whose holding was small,
and whose heart was so big
it had room for us all.

Eleanor had two brothers. Herbert, who had been a journalist but resigned when, after a gruesome tragedy, he was told by his boss, Lord Beaverbrook, to 'go and get that woman's grief!' became a successful writer of revues for the West End, in one of which Joyce Grenfell was to make her professional debut. Her other brother, Harry, was a musician and a wonderful teacher. 'Harry claimed that no sound ever ceased to exist, but that all silence was made up of every note of music, fragment of speech, sigh, laughter and crying, that there had ever been: a tingling, vibrant silence like the singing inside a seashell.'

Eleanor had never married but for many years her companion was George Earle, called Pod, who was a superb teacher of English. He had never forgotten his father saying to him, 'Consider the nature of the metaphor, dear boy. There is nothing else.'

'Wood and words were his two passions,' said Eleanor. 'He learned the former from the village carpenter who would say, "Now, Master Jarge, measure twice and cut once!" To Pod a word was a kingdom, a mine of mythology and meaning.'

There was a period of about two years when Eleanor suspected he was having an affair with a nurse, but she said nothing, 'I was never very good at sex, Jimmie, and I knew that this was what Pod was getting from this woman, and that it would eventually die out, for we had so much more in common. He was with me to the end. I shall never forget the day he died. Golden Coney, my beloved marmalade cat, sat on that chest of drawers, keeping watch over the bed on which Pod's body lay, and stayed there for three days without moving, not even to eat, until the body was taken away.' I also learned from Eleanor about the poet Edward Thomas, who was killed in the First World War, 'He counted on me for my friendship, Jimmie, and although I loved him with my whole heart, he relied on me never to tell him of my feelings for, if I had, our friendship would have come to an end.'

Eleanor gave me the original manuscript of one of Edward's poems, one that celebrates the walks that he and Robert Frost used to take: 'I loved him beyond any man in my young thirties, so much that I really would have died for him, if it could have served him, only that's not what can serve the strange complicated Hamlet-like nature that was his. So I just had to be his friend to death, and only by one word in a letter from France, just before his death, did he let me know that he was aware of what I felt for him as a woman.'

It was Eleanor who, more than anyone, first encouraged my writing, and who also became the first patron of the Hampstead Theatre which I was later to found. I was seventeen when my first short story was published in the *Strand Magazine* with a glowing introduction by the Editor which rather went to my head. I at once sent in a second story only to have it soundly and rightly rejected by the Deputy Editor. This dose of cold criticism was sorely needed and I wrote nothing more until, in my early twenties, I completed a novel which I asked Eleanor to read. She was so impressed that she sent it off to the head of Methuen, strongly recommending it for publication. As a result she and I were summoned to Methuen where I was told that at 30,000 words it was too short but that if I would be prepared to rewrite it to a more conventional length, they would seriously consider publication. Some four or five years later, having rewritten it, I once again asked Eleanor to read it.

'I have to tell you,' she said, 'that in the re-writing you have lost the quality the book once had and that made it special.' This was indeed a blow but as I listened to her detailed criticisms I knew she was right. It took a while to absorb but eventually I realised that while I could write I lacked the talent to be either a novelist or a playwright. Long afterwards Eleanor spoke about this occasion. 'You were to me the son I might have had and I thought: I have to be honest with him, but he may not be able to take it, and this could mean the end of our relationship.'

However, I have always been deeply grateful to those who have not hesitated to challenge or criticize my behaviour, or my work, for without such feedback how else is one to grow? This is why the role of an editor in publishing is so important, for the relationship of an editor to an author is similar to that of a director and a playwright.

Although later I began to keep a journal I thought no more about writing books until, in the 1960s, David Herbert of the Studio Vista Press commissioned my first book, *Directing A Play*, with a long introduction by Vanessa Redgrave whom I had directed when she was a student at the Central School of Speech and Drama. It was David Herbert who also commissioned my next book, *Experimental Theatre*, which in more than forty years has never been out of print. Then, quite unexpectedly, I began to write a sequence of seven children's books, *The Adventures of Odd and Elsewhere*, set in Fenton House in Hampstead which belongs to the National Trust.

C.S. Lewis says somewhere that in writing for children you write for the child in yourself. The first of my sequence of the Odd and Elsewhere books, which was dedicated to Eleanor Farjeon, was published in 1971 and was written when I was running the Hampstead Theatre. How did this wholly unexpected thing happen? It was only after a time that I realised what had triggered it all. The first book opens with these words:

> Sprawled in a corner, the small bear could see the removal
> van move away. Everybody had gone and he was left alone
> in the empty house. 'The odds are,' Odd murmured to
> himself, 'that I am the only person left in this house, and
> what could be odder than that?'

Suddenly I remembered how when I was six we moved house. I was seated with my mother, alongside the driver, in the removal van, about to drive away when, looking down into the empty front room, I saw my teddy bear lying there and burst into tears, begging to be allowed to go and get him. My mother said there was no time to go back, but she would get me another. Clearly the memory had lain buried for years but somewhere in my subconscious I must have wondered what ever happened to my first, much loved teddy bear.

It was Pam Royds, the children's editor at André Deutsch, who suggested that the first book I had written was really two books and that if I would rewrite it as such they would publish. It was while writing the second volume *The Secret of the Seven Bright Shiners* that I realised I wanted to write a sequence and that the underlying theme was, as Mary James wrote in *The Times Educational Supplement*, that of capturing 'the strange excitement and loneliness of growing up.' Although the books are now out of print, the National Trust has a special Odd and Elsewhere room at Fenton House in Hampstead, with photographs of the originals of Odd and Elsewhere on sale.

THE ELDER BROTHER

Oxford, like Cambridge, is an enchanted place, and perhaps even more so because of its enclosed college gardens, each awaiting discovery, unlike Cambridge with its famous 'Backs' open for all to see. But it is an enchanted world only while one is part of it. Once one has gone down one can never get back inside that charmed circle of youth and privilege – indeed it is a privilege to be given three years in which to grow up and find one's way – for, after leaving, the next generation of undergraduates claims it for its own. One is pushed out of Eden, never to return.

In the Michaelmas Term of 1949 I arrived in Oxford. I saw Kenneth Tynan in baggy tights playing Pelleas in *Pelleas and Melisande*, while everyone was still talking about Neville Coghill's magical production of *The Tempest*, in Worcester College gardens, in which Ariel ran across the lake at the end (on concealed planking) to bid farewell to Prospero. As his barge sailed into the darkness, Ariel ran back across the lake and up a ramp, disappearing in a burst of fireworks.

St Benet's Hall is two houses knocked into one at the far end of St Giles along from Blackfriars and Pusey House. The long front room on the ground floor served as the refectory, where we ate our meals, while at the back was the chapel. On the first floor was the caleo-factory where we assembled for coffee, read the papers and chatted. Next to it was the Master's study and bedroom, occupied at that time by the shy and scholarly Dom Gerard Sitwell. On the floors above were rooms occupied by monks from Ampleforth, Belmont and Fort Augustus. I was the only layman.

One of the youngest monks was Dom Jerome Hodkinson, later to become Abbot of Belmont in Herefordshire. He and I sat opposite each other at the bottom end of the table in the refectory, and because we were both reading English, we shared the same tutor, Dr Catherine Ing. Although the front door was locked every night at nine o'clock, which in all Benedictine communities is the beginning of the Great Silence, many of the younger monks used to leave open the catch of a window in the basement in order to climb in that way.

On going up to Oxford I had been given an introduction to David March, an actor at the Oxford Playhouse. He was a deeply committed Catholic, a member of the Third Order of St Dominic, widely read in literature, art and Jungian psychology. We began to meet regularly and to attend Mass together at Blackfriars. In that first autumn of 1949 we took long walks, trudging through the fallen leaves in Addison's Walk, feeding the deer in Magdalen Park, after which we would cross the road to the tropical swelter of the Botanical Gardens, often finishing up for tea at the Cadena or returning to his flat to listen to music about which he was very knowledgeable. Aware that I was testing a religious vocation he exercised great restraint in his growing affection for me. Just once he laid his hand gently on my head, until one day as we were lying chastely on his bed, listening to music by the light of the gas fire, he said, 'I love you.'

It was only gradually that I realised what was happening; that after so long waiting I had found the elder brother I had always been seeking and that I, too, was in love. And so, within three months, I moved out of St Benet's and went to live with David, while everyone we knew, including the monks at St Benet's, accepted that we were a couple.

Those were days of such discovery and sharing, long imagined but never before realised. And so it was that slowly, gently, we moved towards the consummation of our love. 'But we must be fraternal in our loving,' said David. 'Our love must not be enclosed but flow out to others.' And when, during the vacations, we separated, letters flew backwards and forwards. 'Do you think people know we love each other?' he asked.

And then in no time at all it seemed spring had come and then summer. One evening in the Jesuit church at Oxford, while I was kneeling in contemplation of the Blessed Sacrament, David went to confession. At the edge of my consciousness I was aware that the queue for the confessional was getting longer and more restive. Finally David appeared, in a state of distress, having been refused absolution unless he agreed never to see me again. This he could not for he was convinced that our relationship was 'meant'. He went straight round to Blackfriars and asked to see Father Conrad Pepler (later to become Prior of Spode House) who at once gave him absolution. He told him that the Catechism is but a rough guide for the faithful who need some rules by which to lead their lives and that St Thomas Aquinas, in the last year of his life, had asked that his great work, the *Summa Theologica*, be destroyed because, in the light of a vision he had had, he realised how inadequate it was. 'A good Catholic,' said Father Conrad, 'should have an informed conscience. He must know what the Church teaches but, in the final analysis, he must follow his own conscience, working out his own salvation "in fear and trembling."' In blessing our relationship he said that we must not seek orgasm but that if it happened we should not let it burden our conscience: what mattered was that we should love one another. His blessing meant that we were able to bring our love to the altar, there to be nurtured by the Sacraments. Sadly, and in many cases tragically, few of my Catholic contemporaries who were homosexual were so fortunate but instead had the bitter experience of being rejected by the Church.

While at Oxford I travelled up to London once a week to have a private lesson with David's former teacher Litz Pisk. Born in Vienna she came to England in 1937 where shortly after she was invited to join Michel St Denis, George Devine and Glen Byam Shaw at the newly formed Old Vic Theatre School. Later she became Head of Movement at the Central School of Speech and Drama. I used to love performing for her the very formal pavane dances but I had great difficulty in doing the more physical and erotic Elizabethan gavottes, for though I longed to be physically and emotionally free, I was still deeply inhibited.

Each week a young actress used to have the session before mine. On one particular Saturday I was seated outside waiting for her session to end. The studio doors were locked and all I could hear was the rhythmic beat of Litz's drum. Suddenly the young actress began to laugh, a sound that cataracted into laugh after laugh, like a dam being released. When she emerged with shining face she said, 'At last I've broken through! It's been difficult but I've found the release.' I felt very envious, longing to experience a similar liberation, but I had to wait a few more years before I was able to achieve that freedom.

In teaching Litz always referred to a centre of stillness as she worked to eliminate an actor's psychological or emotional problems. 'It's important that you break these limitations,' she once said to me, 'and empty yourself out, which means giving yourself up to what you are doing at any moment, and when you give like that, you are emptied: you don't have any more problems.' Litz's brilliance as a teacher was that she sought to release movement from within the performer rather than choreograph it from the outside, recognising that every individual is different. 'One must collect inwardly in order to reach out' she would say, and I have often thought how seminaries and theological colleges would benefit if such teachers were included on their faculties.

But for David March's love and guidance I might have drowned in a sea of feelings. He constantly challenged me intellectually. 'Think, think!' he would say. Like the Pollards he taught me discipline, encouraging me to persevere in my studies especially when, realising I was not called to the religious life, I wanted to go down from Oxford and start acting straight away. He taught me that it was important to complete what I had begun even though as an actor a University Degree would not be a necessary qualification. Also through him, both in conversation and observing him at work, for he was a protean actor, I learned more about the craft of acting which increasingly I saw to be my task.

A VERY SPECIAL FRIENDSHIP

Why, above all, you can find happiness in this funny, out-of-date, benighted undeveloped little corner of the earth, passes my comprehension. But then I am out of date. You ought to hear Denys's complaints! They continue. You see, if people really and truly do like it, and come to pass the time of day with me, it expresses itself in them and so reflects on me and makes me happy, and I do love them to come. Pick.

I had been introduced to Mrs Ethel Spencer-Pickering who lived at the Granary, outside Harpenden, near St Albans, by the actor Denys Blakelock who had known her for many years. One of four daughters, Pick had been brought up in that house: three Elizabethan cottages converted into one dwelling, set in its own grounds.

Because her widowed father had little money, he used to rent the gardener's cottage at one end to various Pre-Raphaelite artists, including Holman Hunt, Evelyn de Morgan, and William de Morgan who wrote his first novels at the Granary. Pick's father also rented it to a young man of private means, Spencer Umfreville Pickering, who used to dabble in scientific experiments at the Harpenden Laboratories to which he left the bulk of his estate for further research. Eventually he bought the Granary and married Pick.

Born in the 1870s Pick was some fifty years older than I and yet age made no difference to our friendship, which grew into a very special and close relationship. Every home I have had since has been a reflection of the Granary which in my twenties and thirties became for me a way of life, the place where I felt most at home and where I did my early writing. The rambling house with its overgrown garden and orchard, through which Pick would mow paths that didn't lead anywhere, 'just for the fun of it!' reflected her personality. There was a stillness about the house and garden which seemed to invite one to sit in contemplation of the mystery of things, every object seeming to possess its own enigma and secret life. In the guest bedroom where I slept in a large mahogany double bed, a pile of leather-bound books was placed on top of the wardrobe to hold up the sagging plaster of the ceiling. There was no central heating and the rooms were lit by gas lamps which purred like contented cats. At night there would be flasks of tea and tins of biscuits – 'to ward off night starvation!' – while in winter there would be thrice-daily wine glasses of cinnamon – 'to ward off winter colds!'

Pick loved the theatre but rarely went to the cinema. However, having once met Vivien Leigh with Denys Blakelock (he and Laurence Olivier had known each since boys) she went to the local cinema to see *Gone With the Wind* and, when asked how she had enjoyed it, replied 'The afternoon I went Miss Leigh had a cold.'

She had enormous energy and zest for life. On one occasion when her equally elderly neighbour Sir William Beach-Thomas, who wrote a weekly gardening column for *The Observer*, came to tea in his wheelchair, she insisted on sitting in it and racing around the garden, laughing with delight. Often, distracted by some new pleasure, she would forget the task in hand, so that milk being heated for coffee would boil over or, rushing to the kitchen we would find a saucepan of bones, intended for stock, ablaze and the kitchen filled with acrid smoke. She was not fazed by such events nor when the best china or glass got broken. 'Things should be used!' she would insist and then collapse into a chair with laughter. Only when her sister Ivy, who was an evangelical Christian, came to stay, was she constrained, knowing she was expected to be on her best behaviour. 'It is sometimes irksome,' she once sighed to me, 'to be regarded as a lost soul. I try to bear it, but I am never allowed to forget it, and I know I am, but some day I hope to see the light.' Often, on retiring to bed I would find that Ivy had placed a small religious tract under my pillow. Ivy liked everything to be neat, orderly and predictable, whereas Pick was impulsive, with a child's sense of wonder. When given a present she would lift the parcel, turning it this way and that, trying to guess what was inside. This would then be followed by a slow unwrapping, lingering as long as possible the final moment of discovery. Her face was an intricate network of spider-web lines, her hair still yellow from being regularly dipped in a mixture of flowers of sulphur and water.

In 1955 I went to work in America, to teach at the Julliard School of Music and on my return the following year I went down to see Pick for my twenty-eighth birthday in November. After dinner we sat in front of the fire quietly talking, and then I went to the grand piano (its top covered with books and William de Morgan pottery) to play for her. Although I can't read music and have no ear, I love to sit at a piano and make up my own melodies. Suddenly I saw Pick shaken with tremors, her eyes dilated. 'It's been too much!' she said, reaching for my arm, as she struggled to move to another chair, and I knelt at her side. 'I shall be all right,' she said and then began to speak with an urgency as though wanting to communicate to me all the things that were deep inside her. 'You are precious. Oh, my darling! You will be happy. We shall all be happy!' As she kissed me closely and tenderly, her weight hung heavy about me. Then she lay back, saying, 'Play to me!' but abruptly began to struggle up, saying, 'I don't know whether I can get upstairs but we will try it quietly. Don't say anything to Ivy.'

Halfway up the wooden staircase (that staircase where, in Spencer's lifetime, the servants were expected to turn their backs to him if he were passing) she paused to look out of the landing window at the night sky, and murmured, 'It has been a happy day, hasn't it? Happy!' Then seeing her sister hovering at the top of the stairs, with a final spurt of determination she ran up the remaining stairs and flung herself onto her four poster bed.

Downstairs I sat at the piano and played, letting the music sustain her in the room above for I sensed a finality about everything. Ivy then joined me downstairs as Pick, having rejected her help, had asked for Helen, the elderly German refugee who lived in, to help her undress. I could see that Ivy was very tense, unable to relax, asking unnecessary questions whilst stooping to pick up fallen petals from a bowl of orange blossom.

Suddenly Helen called out sharply, 'Mrs Beere!' and then I knew. I heard the telephone being used and a little later the doctor arrived to give Pick an injection and a sleeping draught.

'You pray,' said Helen to me. 'We need prayers.'

After a while Pick sent for me, her face swollen, the eyes frightened, her speech indistinct, and it was clear she had had a stroke down one side. Waving her sister out of the room she clasped me with one arm, saying, 'We're going to be happy, happy, aren't we, darling? I'm going to be all right, and even if not, even if I never see you again, you know I love you, don't you? That's all that matters, isn't it? Goodbye, my darling, goodbye!' During the months that followed she was so ill that I was not allowed to visit but I wrote a weekly letter with drawings which her sister read aloud to her. If I helped to sustain Pick with amusement and interest through those letters and cartoons, there was no doubt that it was her sister's devoted nursing and constant care that did as much as anything to restore her. And so it was that on 3 June 1957, after seven months in her room, Pick walked downstairs for the first time, leaning heavily on my arm, and we took a short walk around the garden. From then on I visited regularly, getting in buckets of coal, chopping firewood, clearing the undergrowth, weeding, and mowing the lawn.

Pick's speech had always been idiosyncratic, so that she would say things like, 'Mrs Jones has died-dead, don't you know?' She loved Lewis Carroll and would use words such as 'galumphing' and 'uffish'. After her stroke, however, her speech became even more like eccentric. On one occasion I asked her what she had been doing that morning and she replied, 'This morning the Church of Chingleman brought me Holy Calypsion.' Then, hearing what she had come out with, she fell back laughing.

In 1960 Pick had to leave the Granary, which was sold and razed to the ground to be replaced by a housing estate. She went to live with her niece Phyllis before being moved to a nursing home in Barnstaple. In a bare attic room with only linoleum on the floor, her bed not even facing the window, she lay there, unravelling a fantasy that the Duke of Bedford (who, in reality, had been a childhood sweetheart) was in a room down the corridor: 'He was six and I was five. We were husband and wife. Then I married Spencer and his wife was killed in an air-crash, and he said to me, 'I always wanted to marry you.' I've not seen him for years but he's here now. He's bought this place, don't you know, and he's dying.' She was convinced I was dead, telling me she had seen me through the window trying to get in and that I had put a gun to my head and shot myself. A few weeks later her niece Phyllis sent me a card saying Pick was dying and so once again I travelled down to Barnstaple. Pick was lying back on her pillow and her teeth had been removed so that her mouth was fallen sideways. As she saw the blue irises which I had brought, her eyes widened and her unparalysed hand drew them towards her as she smothered her face with the blooms, breathing in their scent.

'Look, who's come!' said the Matron. 'Here's your boyfriend!' Pick's eyes widened as she took me in and her hand pulled mine to her face so that she could feel it against her cheek; but she could no longer speak, only make noises. The Matron left us and Pick lifted one of the irises, holding it upright. She shook it, listening to the squeaky rattle of its stiff sheathed leaves, and then plunged it through the air like a blue and yellow bird. Gathering the flowers with one hand she held them upright in a bunch, gazing at them as though she would paint them, as once she would have done. We kissed and held hands. Suddenly she lifted a single flower and hit me with it. I took another and we began to fence and foil until she fell back laughing. She began to make noises and I pressed a button.

'Is it a vase you be wanting for the flowers?' asked the nurse, but what she wanted was the bedpan. When I returned I placed the irises in a tall glass vase which the nurse had brought, and placed it on the floor so that Pick, lying in bed, could see the flowers more easily. For a long time she engaged in an elaborate, detailed speech of croaks and whispers at the end of which I said, 'I don't understand what you are saying', whereupon her face creased and wobbled with laughter.

The Matron came in and gave us each a glass of champagne. Slowly Pick subsided into sleep and I sat on, holding her hand, as the daylight faded. Suddenly she groaned, putting her hand to her head which, she had once described as 'itching like an ant's nest'; a result of the stroke. She now took my hand and got me to scratch her head. Her mouth, fallen sideways, was like a black and purple wound. Occasionally her legs kicked spasmodically and she emitted short high cries and her shrunken body trembled. At intervals, her eyes wide open, she would gaze wonderingly round the room as though newly come to it. Then her eyes would alight on me with a smile of recognition. At these moments we were as we had always been, not needing words, and I marvelled at how close we were in spite of the years between us.

Outside in the churchyard on the edge of the cliff, the coffin was lowered into a grave that had been hewn out of rock where Spencer had also been buried. The final words of the Committal were blown on the wind and at the same moment the sun appeared so that the sands of Woolacombe, where Pick had spent every summer of her life, glowed golden as the waves raced in to the shore. Two days later Phyllis wrote to me:

> After the funeral Rupert and I collected Aunt Pick's clothes. I tied them all in her grey coat, bound the neck, arms and ends, and at sunset put it in the full moon flood tide and it went silently out into the sunset, uncannily like a turtle. She would have laughed: it even had a 'head' which moved as it swam, the arms moving like a turtle. I suppose it was a good thing you saw her as you clearly got through to her but I hope the toothless image faded. I wish you could have seen her dead, with the good looks and dignity of her father, and a faint enigmatic Mona Lisa smile.

Long afterwards Phyllis sent me the following transcript she made of a conversation she had with her aunt before the stroke. It serves to conclude this quiet memorial of a very special friendship:

Once, when the trees were full of apples and the squirrels busy in the branches of the beech tree Jimmie came to see me with Denys Blakelock. We talked a lot of nonsense, I daresay; at least I did – about ghosts and ogres and witches, don't you know. Poor Denys was bewildered for Jimmie and I seemed to be talking in a secret code. He was still up at Oxford then. But we had fun, that I remember. And then after lunch on that first day of our meeting he disappeared when we were sitting on the verandah having coffee. Suddenly I saw him, bare-armed and bare-footed, come running through the trees, turning a somersault on the lawn, and throwing a cascade of small green apples into the air. How can I find words to describe it? It was Puck, it was Pan. It was the garden come alive! I loved him from that very moment. Oh, he was difficult, I know – strange, elusive, moody, but after all I was an old woman and he was a young man with all his life before him. But he always came to see me and always, to my amazement, he returned like a homing pigeon.

Once, I remember, he filled the trees with night-lights, and acted for me all of Puck's speeches, crouching among the branches of the apple trees, leaping down, dancing in and out like a shadow in the lamplight from the house. I shall never forget the way in which he spoke the words, 'Night….and SILENCE!' with such a sense of the mystery of night. I sat in a corner of the garden, wrapped in a blue blanket. He never knew how I shivered with cold and was subsequently ill with this wretched chest of mine. But that's why I would never have the apple trees felled.

Then one day he went to work in America and I thought that I should never see him again. It was autumn. I remember going to the door and giving him a last embrace, then dropping my arms, letting him go – as one does a wild bird – for I never hoped to possess him. How can the old contain the young? Besides, I wanted him to be free. I stood there, watching him go down the long drive between the chestnuts and the lime trees. It was dusk, the sky touched with pink, and a mist rising. Just before the bend in the drive, where that one tree was struck with lightning – you know the one I mean? – he turned and held up his hand in salutation. I wanted to cry out, but I didn't. I thought: this is the last I shall see of him.

I remember going out into the garden to do some pruning. I couldn't bear to go back into the house and when I did it was to wander restlessly from room to room. Everything was so full of his touch: the desk where he wrote, the flowers he had picked that morning, the rumpled cushions where he had sat on the sofa after lunch trying to do a Chinese puzzle, and his sherry glass on the mantelpiece. At least I was alone. I could not have borne it had anyone been there.

He used to write to me from America: lovely letters, full of descriptions of places and people, but sad, too. I felt he was lonely there, yet I could do nothing. Then he wrote to say he had decided to stay in America. I suppose it didn't really come as a surprise to me. I think I had always known it, as one knows the most important things in life, deep down inside one. I still have that letter. In it he revealed all that I and this place meant to him. I knew then that he loved me. It was like a beautiful dream ending in a golden sunset full of colour and hope – which was magic indeed, because of the disturbing news it contained. And yet, of course, he did come back after all.

He used to dance to music. He would make up dances like poems. Often I wished that he would show my friends but always he refused, would grow reticent and withdrawn. In a way I suppose I wanted to show him off. But I'm glad he always refused. It seemed as though it was something that just existed between the two of us.

One particular afternoon we had been watching the snow drift down, reflected in that big mirror, and then when it was dusk we made tea and sat by the fire. He switched on the wireless to find the right time – you know what the clocks are like in this house! – and there was this music. He got up and began to dance, at first slowly and pensively. And though this was some time before he went to America I sensed that deep down he was already saying goodbye. It's like the birds, they know when it is time to go: you see them circling, restless, fore-gathering, and then one day they are gone. Well, that night he filled this house with benediction. He seemed to be the earth bearing crops, the trees growing high, the stars entangled in their branches. It was as though he was lifting and blessing this house, as though he were singing a child to sleep, the world cradled in his arms. It was all those things. He seemed to be pouring out everything for which no words could be found. I have never forgotten that evening and often, when I lie awake at night, unable to sleep, I seem to hear the music and see him dance again, and then I know that all is well between us. It was the most precious thing he gave me.

A REAL EDUCATION

I once asked Vanessa Redgrave when, as a finalist student at the Central School of Speech and Drama, she was acting in a production of Shaw's *In Good King Charles' Golden Days*, how she found working with the actor Esmé Percy who was directing. 'We don't get much rehearsing done, but it's worth everything to hear his stories. That is a real education.'

'I think I am the only successful actor who may be said to have begun his stage career with a fall!' remarked Esmé Percy, lolling on a leather banquette at the Savile Club where we were lunching shortly after his return from a triumphant tour of America in Christopher Fry's *The Lady's Not For Burning*. As a boy he had run away from school in Brussels and gone to Paris where his idol Sarah Bernhardt was performing. He sent round a note saying that he was waiting at the stage door and that if she did not see him he would throw himself into the Seine. She at once sent for him, saying it would be a great shame for such 'un brave garcon' to throw himself in the river. She asked him what he wanted and he replied, 'To be an actor, *et seulement près de vous, Madame.*'

Wrapped in chinchilla, holding a large bunch of Parma violets, she gave him a signed photograph of herself, making him promise to go back to school for just one more term and then, if his parents agreed, she would supervise his tuition as an actor. 'And so in the summer of 1900 I said goodbye to school and the first chapter of my actor's life began.'

The Divine Sarah, as he always called her, found an old actor of the Comédie Française to teach him during the week. Then at weekends she would get him to repeat for her all the pieces he had learned when 'not a false tone, not a careless rhythm, a superfluous gesture, would escape her eagle eye.' Eventually she allowed him to appear with her at special matinées. He returned to England armed with introductions from Sarah to Frank Benson, Beerbohm Tree and Forbes Robertson, then the three leading actor-producers. Although Benson had no vacancy he said, 'With such an introduction I must make one!' Tree snatched him from Benson, eager to have Sarah's protégé, and he was cast as Britannicus in Stephen Philips' *Nero* in which he had a sensational fall backwards down a staircase. That fall was the talk of London in 1906!

From Sarah Esmé inherited a remarkable vocal range from high falsetto to basso profundo, a range that few actors today can command. This vocal range made him an ideal Shavian actor and for a number of years he toured with the McDona Players, performing in all Shaw's plays. In the long speeches from *Don Juan in Hell* he taught me how to build a speech to a climax and then to pause on a preposition or a conjunctive, such as 'and' or 'but', making the audience wait in expectation, like a pause in music, before starting to build to a fresh climax.

His flat in Warwick Avenue was like a womb of memories. The front rooms where his mother had lived and died were untouched, full of fin de siècle furniture, the walls crowded with portraits of Esmé: as an altar boy, as a young cadet, as Hamlet, Lord Byron, Hassan and many other leading roles. The landing was piled to the ceiling with books, while he lived in one small room at the back, crammed with more books, holy pictures, brass candelabras, a mother-of-pearl rosary dangling from a broken ivory crucifix, and a picture cut out of a magazine of a small boy curled up in bed with a book, a box of chocolates and his dog. 'That's my mental age!' he would say, 'and there's always doggy!'

Because so many asked to hear his stories about Sarah Bernhardt he put together a recital, *The Legend of Sarah Bernhardt* which he first performed for the Shaw Society and then with great success at the Edinburgh Festival. He also produced a long playing record of it – thereby providing for future generations an evocation, as much through his own personality as through his anecdotes, of a style of acting and a vocal command that is rare today. Thus, in speaking of Sarah's performance in *La Dame aux Camélias* he observed how she would read Armand's last letter in a whisper 'and yet,' added Esmé, 'in the vastest theatres of France not a syllable was lost!' – and of course in those days there were no microphones.

Seated in front of his puttering gas fire, a box of coins to one side for feeding the meter, a bowl of water in front of it to prevent dehydration, Esmé and I would go over and over the lines of what was to become a bravura performance, while his shaggy, uncombed spaniel Skippo lay as close to the warmth as he could. It was a previous dog that, quite accidentally, had clawed out one of Esmé's eyes. The glass replacement had a tendency to slip out whenever he got emotional. Once at the Oxford Playhouse, in a play in which he portrayed Hitler, the eye fell out during an impassioned speech and rolled onto the floor. Without pausing, Esmé stooped to pick it up, turned and, while continuing to speak, popped it back in – ending with a round of applause!

For me, as for Albert Finney and many of my generation, one of the greatest actors of the twentieth century was Wilfred Lawson. He was also Laurence Olivier's favourite actor, the one he most admired. I was fortunate to see his performance twice as the Captain in Strindberg's *The Father* at the Arts Theatre in 1953. Here, indeed, was an actor who had an eye like Mars to threaten and command, born to play King Lear – which sadly he never did. Actors all too often today, as Peter Brook has observed, instead of raising themselves up to the challenge of these great roles, scale them down to their own selves. But Lawson was a giant among actors.

At the opening of the third act the stage was empty and then a growling was heard, as of a wounded animal breaking loose, and the sound of timbers being sawn through, followed by the approach of heavy boots. An axe smashed through a panel of the locked door, accompanied by a hand reaching through the gap to turn the key.

As Lawson erupted into the room, hurling over chairs that stood in his way, advancing inexorably, something happened on the last night which had not occurred when I had seen it before. Two people in the front stalls, clearly frightened by the ferocity of Lawson's performance, made ugly jeering sounds of rejection. At once Lawson turned on them with a thunderous growl, silencing them, before continuing with the scene. Suddenly he dried; there was a prompt but, ignoring it, he swept on, improvising, and only later weaving in the prompt.

The Captain attempts to shoot himself but the gun is empty. When his old Nanny enters he asks, 'Why did you take away the cartridges, Nanny?' Gently she moves him to a chair where he sits, his arms hanging slackly between his knees, his face puckered, smiling like a lost child, the tears streaming down his face, as she talks to him about the nursery days. He sighs with contentment, gurgling and cooing like a baby, while Nanny gently removes the gun and then slowly, as though dressing him for bed, puts him into a straitjacket. Laughing and crying he lifts his arm to wipe his nose on one of the long sleeves before she removes him to the sofa so that she can cross the two sleeves to tie behind his back, thereby pinioning his arms. 'Time for bye-byes!' she sings and he giggles in response, 'How can I go to bed when you have just dressed me!'

Strapped in the straitjacket, lying back on the sofa, he suddenly becomes aware of what has happened. He tries to get up but falls back until, with a deep rumbling sound that grows to a roar, he hurls himself up by brute force, only to fall off the sofa. Crying out in frustration he bumps himself forward along the ground, beating his head against the floor as he goes. 'Forgive me!' cries Nanny as she kneels, laying her head alongside his on the ground. Suddenly, in one concertina-like movement, he jerks himself up, crying out, 'Traitors! Take her away!'

As his wife enters he watches her cross the room, inveighing against all the women who have betrayed him, savagely carving in words an image of Woman until, gathering all his energy, he spits violently at her, the liquid curving through the air. Then exhausted, all passion spent, he leans his head on Nanny's breast, singing with mocking irony the words 'Gentle Jesus, meek and mild' until he chokes on the words 'Blessed art thou among women!' and falls back silent.

The ovation on the final night for this unforgettable and great performance resulted in the entire audience rising to its feet, stamping on the floor, and roaring with one voice, 'Bravo! Bravo! Bravo!' Repeatedly the curtains opened upon the shy figure of Wilfred Lawson standing, his head bowed, smiling and bashful, as the audience continued to roar its gratitude in great waves of sound until finally the curtains remained open. Then it was that, reluctantly, he stepped forward to say thank you. He shifted sideways and then, with an allusion to his alcoholic problems, added, 'I have been away a long time. You must know what such a reception means to an actor. Tonight has helped to wipe away a lot of the bitterness. Thank you!'

The totality of such a performance, the sense of the actor giving wholly of himself, not just resting on technique, is indeed rare in the theatre. The greatest performers in any art are those who give wholly of themselves.

It is only by listening to older actors that a youngster learns so much about the tradition and craft of acting. In his autobiography the actor Peter Barkworth described how he and a fellow student were seated in the front row of the gods, when they observed how the leading actress every now and then raised her eyes towards the gallery. Leaning towards his companion Barkworth whispered, 'You see? We must remember that when our time comes.' Today, when the majority of actors have only the experience of working in television or in small theatres, when they transfer to a larger theatre, many continue to play to the stalls, and do not know how to reach out to a larger house.

FROM LEADING MAN TO DIRECTOR

In the spring of 1954 I was engaged as leading man for a new weekly repertory company at Bridgewater in Somerset, where the juvenile character actor was Kenneth Williams, then an unknown actor who had come from working with the equally unknown Richard Burton in Swansea. It was a low point in Kenneth's career, during which he talked seriously about giving up the theatre and becoming secretary to a History don. Little did any of us then forsee that he would become a household name on screen and stage. Kenneth and I became chums and would talk for hours. As he wrote many years later, 'Yes, we have lasted a long time, and it's always the same. Once we start talking the clock's forgotten!' He was, behind his brilliant and outrageous façade, a deeply lonely person. He once sent me the following quotation from George Eliot's *Adam Bede*, which expressed his longing for a true friend:

> Oh, the comfort, the inexpressible comfort, of feeling safe with a person; having neither to weigh thoughts, nor measure words, but pour them all out, just as they are, chaff and grain together, knowing that a faithful hand will take and sift them, keep what is worth keeping, and then, with a breath of kindness, blow the rest away.

It was while acting opposite Kenneth that I learned how not to 'corpse' on stage; that is, collapse into giggles. He would often stand downstage, his back to the audience, and even while acting, make faces at the rest of us, muttering under his breath, determined to make us laugh. In one play, *Give Me Yesterday*, I played a famous old Viennese maestro and Kenneth my brilliant protégé, a concert pianist, returned after many years to thank me. In the middle of a very moving scene, Kenneth so reduced me to helpless laughter at one performance that I had to leave the stage even though we were in the middle of a scene, leaving him alone on stage. Of course when I returned, having pulled myself together, it was even worse as he raised his eyebrows at me, signalling, 'Well, look at *her!*' From then on I learned that the only way to act with him was to avoid eye contact and always act to one side or other of his face.

Kenneth admired me as an actor but he kept saying, 'You should direct, Roosey!' and so when our producer (director) fell ill he said, 'Now's your chance!' As a result, I directed St John Ervine's *The First Mrs Frazer*. It was then that I realised how my love of dance, of literature, painting and theatre, all came together in the art of directing.

On my return to London I bumped into the actor Alec McCowen who said 'If you want to go on directing why don't you apply for the job of Director of the Maddermarket Theatre in Norwich? They are looking for someone and if you like I'll drop a line to Nugent Monck for you.'

MY FIRST THEATRE

The Maddermarket Theatre in Norwich, modelled on an Elizabethan playhouse, had been founded in 1921 by Nugent Monck, a protégé of William Poel who had done so much to revolutionise the acting and staging of Shakespeare and in the process influenced a whole new generation including Harley Granville Barker and John Gielgud. Nugent Monck had retired and been succeeded by Lionel Dunn whose job was then being advertised. The artistic director, designer, and stage manager were professional appointments but all the actors and the other members of staff were local amateurs. Many of the actors, however, had a long experience of acting and a wholly professional approach to their work. Each production was rehearsed for six evenings a week over four weeks, often also at weekends, followed by a run of the play. In the season of 1954-5 I directed eight productions, opening with Chekhov's *The Seagull* for which John Gielgud tried in vain to find for me Komisarjevsky's prompt copy for the famous production in which he and Peggy Ashcroft had played.

'Aren't you nervous?' he said to me and I, with all the confidence and ignorance of being, at twenty-seven, a late starter, replied, 'Oh, no!' The other plays of that season included Shakespeare's *Much Ado About Nothing*, *Macbeth* (in which I also played the lead), John Whiting's *A Penny For A Song*, Bernard Shaw's *Pygmalion*, Shakespeare's *Henry IV, Part I*, and Henri Ghéon's *The Marriage of Saint Francis* (in which David March came to play St Francis) and to mark the centenary of the birth of Oscar Wilde, *An Ideal Husband*. We were the only theatre in the country to mark the occasion, and in the foyer I assembled an exhibition of Wildeana, loaned by Montgomery Hyde MP, Louis Wilkinson and others. There was also a large photograph of Wilde, with a vase of green carnations in front of it, while every male member of the cast wore a green carnation in his buttonhole. Ten years later I was to direct an all-star production of the play, with Margaret Lockwood as Mrs Cheveley, which ran in the West End for over a year.

LORCA AND THE LANGUAGE OF FLOWERS

The other major production of the season was the English première of Garcia Lorca's *Dona Rosita*, or *The Language of Flowers* in a translation by C.A. Rossner adapted by the actress Selma vaz Dias. For this production I persuaded the Governors of the Maddermarket to let me fly to Spain in order to do research on the background of the play which Lorca had subtitled: A Poem of Granada. In it are assembled many of the different people he knew while growing up in Granada. He himself described the town as 'a Paradise closed to many with gardens open only to a few.' Thanks to introductions from Señor Rossner it was my good fortune to be one of the few to enter houses and gardens frequented by Lorca, to talk with his friends, and listen to recordings of him playing the piano. In Madrid, en route for Granada, I visited his sisters and studied photographs of him, one of which they gave me. In nearly all of them he appears sad, even dissipated. As a youth he was slim, elegant, almost a dandy in pose and dress but as he grew older he became puffier, rounder in the face with shadows under the eyes. Only in those pictures taken with children, whose company he loved, and one rare picture of him alone, seated cross-legged in one of the courtyards of the Alhambra, is he seen laughing. Yet the sadness in his face and the preoccupation with death in his poems and drawings were but the other side of his essentially optimistic and happy nature: the two extremes are typically Spanish.

Lorca's sisters gave me introductions to other members of the family in Granada as well as to various close friends of their brother; in particular Don Alfonso Gamir de Sandoval who lived in a handsome villa in the Generaliffe and who taught English at the University of Granada. Don Alfonso, who spoke a precise and elegant English, prided himself on his English teas. Seated in a high-ceilinged drawing room at a large round table with a starched linen table cloth, there was a choice of India or China tea, plates of scones, rich fruit cake, and thinly cut bread and butter, with an assortment of jams. One might have been having tea in Cambridge with E.M. Forster.

One afternoon he took me to visit a family with whom Lorca had been friendly and who possessed some records of Lorca which he wanted me to hear. On our way he mentioned that he had to be at the University at half past five for a tutorial with his students. On arrival I had first to be introduced to each generation of the family as well as watch a demonstration of flamenco dancing by a group of small girls. Finally, after two hours of courtesies, glasses of liqueur and small cakes, and after a long search for the records – no-one could remember where they had been put – in a room crowded with children, parents, grandparents, servants and the parish priest, we sat or stood, listening to these crackling recordings of La Argentina singing, accompanied on the piano by Lorca. A clock in the house chimed six and turning to my companion I remarked, 'But Don Alfonso, what about your students?' 'Do not worry,' he replied. 'They will go to a café and wait. In Spain we do not worry about such things. There is always time.'

Another afternoon a large taxi drew up outside the Thomas Cook Travel Agency where I had been told to wait. The de Lopez family, accompanied by the President of the Carmens, were taking me on a visit to the *carmens*, those houses in the Albaicin whose high walls protected their middle-class owners from the poverty in the cobbled streets outside. In such a house would Dona Rosita's uncle and aunt have lived and, as I was now told, I was being taken to the house in which lived the real Dona Rosita on whom Lorca had based his play and who indeed never married; I was warned not to ask any questions, but simply to observe.

The play is the story of a girl who, betrothed to be married, waits year after year for her fiancé to return from America, only to realise too late that he never will and as a result she never marries. It seemed to me that Lorca was both these characters. As a homosexual living within the social, religious and political restraints of that period, he was unable to declare himself and so, like Rosita, remained alone. At the same time, however, like Rosita's fiancé, he had been able to escape to America and breathe for a time a freer atmosphere. Back home in 1935 from touring with his own company La Barraca he was, as Ian Gibson records in his biography, referred to by the local bourgeoisie of Granada as 'The Queer with the Bow Tie.'

In the play the uncle cultivates a rare rose which lasts for only one day: 'It is white in the morning, at noon it turns red as blood, and then at night, on the edge of darkness, its petals fall'. This powerful erotic image dominates the whole play.

In the street outside, as we waited at a tall iron gate to be admitted, a child was squatting to urinate, the steaming yellow liquid trickling between the stones and soaking into a slice of bread which a dog came to sniff at. We entered a large garden full of flowers, vegetables, fig and olive trees, bordered by box hedges. Later, standing on the roof of the house, among stone pots of cacti and lilies, I could see across to the Alhambra and the Generaliffe, and I thought of Rosita's words:

Arum lilies whirling glad
Will send my roof-top mad.

Suddenly a picture of the young girl deep in love, almost swooning in the afternoon heat and the perfume of the lilies, fell into place. We were ushered into a large salon, newly decorated, littered with objets d'art, as though an auction were about to take place. Our hostess entered, a fur coat incongruously draped around her shoulders, her dimpled hands flying to the back of her untidy hair. As she darted about the room showing us various things I thought of the words of the servant in the play who says of Rosita: 'She is all over the place from one minute to the next. She's always in a hurry for everything!'

As we departed the lamps were being lit indoors and someone – perhaps our hostess? – was playing a Chopin Nocturne while outside in the street the gypsies, gathering for the dancing in the caves, circled our car with curiosity and then spread out as it moved slowly down the hill.

Don Alfonso had spoken to me several times of one of Lorca's closest friends, Don José Navarro, a barrister. That evening, my last, it was arranged that I should meet him at midnight at the Capri, a new American-style bar that had just opened. For two hours Don José talked to me about Lorca, recalling how Lorca told him when he was in Buenos Aires, touring with his theatre company, La Barraca, his success shamed him. 'Once upon a time', he said, 'I had no money but my pockets were stuffed with poems. Now my pockets are stuffed with dollars but I have no poems any more.'

In 1931, when Lorca returned from America, Spain was in a political upheaval. Don José himself was on the Right and whenever Lorca came to visit him his friends used to say, 'Don't talk to that man. He is on the other side. He will convert you!' The Left wanted Federico to come over to their side, they wanted to use him as a flag, but he was uninfluenced by the ideas of either party, stressed Don José.

'He was too vital a person, cared too deeply for everything and everybody. He did not care sufficiently for politics. He was not dogmatic but to the official mind he remained an enigma and, as such, was considered dangerous. Moreover he wrote verses to traditional tunes which were widely sung, especially by the poor and, like many of his poems, they were often anti-Franco, attacking the brutalities of the Civil Guard. Many a man was shot for less in those days. And so one morning Federico was taken out onto the hills above Granada and shot. We are told that it was an accident. That is what we were supposed to believe.'

Afterwards we walked slowly, arm in arm, through the empty streets to see his house, one frequently visited by Lorca and which was, said Don José, typical of the play. Opening the front door we entered a courtyard with a stone carved lion spouting water into a pool and climbed to the first floor. Standing in the doorway of the drawing room I gasped. 'But this is it! This *is* the Language of Flowers!' Don José laughed with pleasure, nodding emphatically as he said, 'This, this is what Federico had in mind when he wrote the play. This is what Dona Rosita's uncle and aunt's home would have been like at the turn of the century.'

The panelled walls were painted with swags of flowers; on the carpet was a floral pattern, while flowers were painted on silk cushions and embroidered on the covers of chairs. Even the piano keys were covered with a strip of canvas embroidered with garlands of flowers. At once in my imagination I saw the room peopled with Rosita's girl friends, as they are in the second act of the play, gathered round the piano, singing their favourite song: *What The Flowers Say*. And all this detail I was later to weave into the production itself.

As we parted Don José embraced me, holding me closely to him and weeping. 'Federico! Federico! Federico!' he cried. It was as though on that spring night of 1955 I had been transmuted into Federico Garcia Lorca. And as I walked up the hill in the moonlight to my hotel in the Alhambra I murmured to myself, over and over, as though to the poet himself, the words of Rosita:

> *I long to see you coming*
> *Through Granada's twilight to me,*
> *And all the air salt-glittering*
> *With yearning for the sea.*

ACT TWO

MEETING WITH MARTHA GRAHAM

In Herman Hesse's novel *Steppenwolf* the owner of the Magic Theatre says to the hero, 'It is the world of your own soul that you seek. Only within yourself exists that other reality for which you long. I can give you nothing that has not already its own being within yourself.' That theatre I was to find in the work of the great American choreographer and dancer Martha Graham when for the first time she came to London with her company at the beginning of 1954. Having seen Agnes de Mille's invigorating choreography for *Oklahoma!*, and having read her autobiography *Dance to the Piper*, I already knew something about Graham's legendary qualities as a pioneer of the Modern Dance. As a result I was almost the first in the queue to book for the opening performance of the season.

Many in that first-night audience, accustomed to classical ballet, were bewildered, even angry. I listened in the intervals to all the voices. The following evening I returned to see the same programme and suddenly, *coup de foudre*, I understood what Martha Graham was about; as a result of which I went to every performance, seeing each work several times, and making detailed notes. Although I love all forms of theatre, from farce to drama, I was also in search of something beyond words and that in visual terms was more akin to poetry, a form of theatre which would be capable of profoundly changing people's perceptions. As Antonin Artaud had written in the 1930s,

> The theatre will never find itself again except by furnishing the spectator with the truthful precipitates of dreams. I say that there is a poetry of the senses as there is a poetry of language and that this concrete physical language is truly theatrical only to the degree that the thoughts it expresses are beyond the reach of spoken language.

Artaud's concept of a non-verbal theatre was to be developed first by such pioneers as Martha Graham who, single-handedly, created a whole new form of theatre. In turn she was to be followed by Peter Brook, Jerzy Grotowski, the Living Theatre, the Bread and Puppet Theatre, and many more. As Peter Brook was to write in his seminal book *The Empty Space*, 'The search is for a necessary theatre, one which is an urgent presence in our lives, speaking to a man in his wholeness.'

In addition, I recognised that Martha Graham was rediscovering the sacred and religious origins of theatre. Thus, when in *Errand into the Maze* Graham as Ariadne came face to face with the feared Minotaur, mounting and riding it out of the maze, she was also confronting the darkness or *shadow* side that is in each of us; coming to terms with it both in herself, as well as on our behalf.

Without ever being in any obvious way autobiographical all of Graham's work sprang out of her own life experience and her dancers were only too familiar with those occasions when they would find the doors into her main studio locked and a scarf looped through the handles to indicate that she was not to be disturbed. 'When I have a problem,' she once observed, 'I go into my studio and dance it out.' Whatever emerged would then become the raw material for a new work although, as her remarkable Journals reveal, months of research as well as experiment would go into the creation of each work.

'The basis of all dancing,' Martha Graham once said, 'is something deep inside you. There is a necessity for movement when words are inadequate.' If audiences were sometimes distraught at the imagery in many of her works, it was because they were ill-prepared to face the psychological reality which was the basis of her art. If certain of her works could disturb, such as *Dark Meadow* (which was booed so loudly in Italy, because of the phallic symbols used, that the dancers could not hear their music cues), or *Cave of the Heart*, then other works such as *Diversion of Angels*, *Canticle for Innocent Comedians*, and *Ardent Song* (which John Martin, the leading American dance critic, once described to me as 'perhaps the most haunting, and most beautiful, of all Martha's rituals'), were intensely lyrical.

As Craig Barton, Martha's manager, wrote to me:

Martha's dancing is about something. It does not entertain or provide distraction. One sees a visual masterpiece in which the dancers move in a masterly and special way, but the reaction of the spectator moves onto another plane of inner revelation, of excited unrest. Even a lyrical abstraction like *Diversion of Angels* has a radiation that shakes one's interior. One has had a serious experience.

In *Appalachian Spring*, to a commissioned score by Aaron Copland, Graham as the Bride had a moment when, lying on her back, she rocked to and fro on the threshold of her new home. Referring to this, Cyril Beaumont – then the elder statesman among English ballet critics – said to me, 'But why does she roll about on the floor like that? It breaks the line!' In that remark he revealed the essential difference between the classical ballet, especially at that period, and the modern dance. In looking for an external aesthetic he had failed to respond to the inner rhythm of the movement, expressive of the Bride's intimate identification as a virgin with the virgin prairie, soon to be sown, as well as with the Bride's crossing the threshold of her new life and her expectation of bearing children. Curiously Nijinsky, whose memory Cyril Beaumont hallowed, would have understood for he once wrote, 'Any imaginable movement is good in dancing if it suits the idea which is its subject' while he himself demonstrated in his choreography for Stravinsky's *Rite of Spring*, to the initial scandal of the world of classical ballet, that that which at first sight may be considered ugly can have its own intrinsic and sculptural, rather than linear, beauty.

During that first season I wrote at length about the works to Miss Graham and received a reply from Craig Barton informing me that Miss Graham would like to meet me. 'Your grasp of what the works are about,' he wrote, 'and which you have so beautifully expressed, is deeply gratifying to her and, I would like to add, to me also.'

And so it was that one evening after a performance I was ushered into Miss Graham's dressing room by Leroy Leatherman (who was later to write a book about her work). We sat side by side on a low divan while Leroy Leatherman, like a friendly chaperone, sat at a distance. As I spoke about the works she turned to him, laughing and saying, 'He understands it all. We don't have to explain to him!'

Learning that I was in the theatre she talked about the first time she saw the great Eleanora Duse act: 'I was playing in the *Greenwich Town Follies*, goodness, how long ago! I shall never forget where my seat was that afternoon. Duse was old, riddled with disease, at the end of her life, but she held us. I remember one moment when she slipped off her shawl and the way she did it. She became at that moment, in front of our eyes, a young woman! Then there was the way she clenched one hand and in that simple gesture there was everything of agony and of acceptance. One was moved because she had *vision*.

'One is a servant of the public. And every performance must be approached in a spirit of dedication. One has always a great responsibility, for one can never tell what effect one is going to have on an audience.'

She then told the story of how, after a performance of her solo work, *Lamentation*, a study of grief, a woman came backstage after the performance to thank her. It transpired that she had seen both her children killed in an automobile accident. She had been unable to grieve until that evening when, for the first time, she had been able to weep 'because you have shown me that there can be dignity in grief.'

Speaking about the work *Canticle for Innocent Comedians* I referred to it as a Franciscan celebration of the sun, moon, stars, fire, earth, and water: like being present at the creation of the world with each of the elements being given its task; while in *Diversion of Angels* she had movingly evoked Thomas Traherne's vision of 'Boys and girls tumbling in the streets and playing were moving jewels. I knew not that they were born or should die but all abided eternally as they were in their proper places.' 'In the end,' Martha Graham replied, 'we have to return to these simple, elemental things, for they are what endure while civilisation itself changes. In my work I have always sought to reveal an image of man in his struggle for wholeness, for what one might call God's idea of man rather than man's idea of himself.'

On my remarking that she must be tired – for each day she was rehearsing the new work *Ardent Song* which had its world première in London that season – and dancing at night, she answered, 'One is only tired when one has messed things up for oneself. Sometimes people give one peace and you have given me peace.' Smiling, she added, 'I should like you to write to me from time to time. I should like to hear from you and what you are doing. You have vision and passion and that is rare.'

On the last day of the season Craig Barton telephoned me to say how much Miss Graham had appreciated my visit and that my letters had been read by all the company. That evening after the final performance there were prolonged cheers led by Madame Rambert, founder of the Ballet Rambert, who came down to the front of the stalls, holding her hands high in applause, while Frederick Ashton, Margot Fonteyn, and many other members of the Royal Ballet were also present. Afterwards I was taken backstage, past a long queue of people waiting to see Martha Graham into Craig Barton's office where I was handed a copy of Barbara Morgan's book of photographs of Graham's work which had been inscribed for me on the title page: For James Roose-Evans – You have given me so much – Martha Graham.

Craig Barton said, 'You have come into our lives and you are going to stay.' On my way out Leroy Leatherman appeared and, taking me by the arm, said, 'Miss Graham would like to see you.' He led me past the waiting queue into the hushed atmosphere of the Number 1 Dressing Room.

'You'll write?'

'Yes!'

Suddenly Miss Graham laughed, relaxed and happy.

'You look like one of the Brontes tonight!' she said to me.

We met again in 1964 when she returned to London in triumph – heralded in advance by Kenneth Tynan as 'one of the great artists of the twentieth century' – at a special luncheon in her honour at the American Embassy, where she was the only woman present. The other guests included Sir Frederick Ashton, Sir David Webster, Sir John Gielgud, Robert Cohan and Bertram Ross, Martha's leading male dancers, and the critics Richard Buckle, Sir Arnold Haskell, Clive Barnes, Peter Williams and lastly that remarkable man Robin Howard who was to devote his personal wealth and the last years of his life to setting up a Graham-based school and company, The London Contemporary Dance Company with Robert Cohan as its first artistic director. After the luncheon we were all asked to pose for a group photograph. Then Francis Mason, the US Cultural attaché, came up to me and said, 'Miss Graham would like to be photographed with you.' Holding her hand, I gazed at her. 'You should look at the camera!' she laughed. It was then that I thanked her for all that she had given me.

THE VOYAGE OUT

Although the year at the Maddermarket Theatre had been an intensely rich and rewarding baptism for a young director I was restless to learn more about the American Modern Dance, and although the Governors of the Maddermarket were wanting to renew my contract, I began writing to various foundations and universities in America in search of a fellowship that would enable me to pursue my studies. By the early summer of 1955, when the Governors were pressing for an answer to their invitation I decided to leave, even though I had no job to go to, and I went to stay at the Granary, writing, gardening and waiting for the next move. This came in the form of a letter from Germany inviting me to fly to Amsterdam to be interviewed for a post on the faculty of the prestigious Julliard School of Music in New York. In Amsterdam I met Professor Harold Grey, Head of the Humanities Department of the Julliard, who told me that correspondence of mine to Stanford University in California had been forwarded to the Julliard, the American equivalent of the Paris Conservatoire, which was then looking for someone who would explore the possibilities of integrating music, dance and drama.

Where today the Julliard is based at Lincoln Centre, in the 1950s it was housed on Claremont Avenue near Columbia University. In 1945 the composer William Schuman had been appointed President and in 1951 he established the Julliard Dance Department with, among its faculty, such outstanding figures as Martha Graham, Doris Humphrey, Louis Horst, José Limon, and the English choreographer, Anthony Tudor.

Inside the Julliard the corridors were filled with students hurrying from one class to another. The whole place was like a beehive. From endless cell-like studios could be heard the rise and fall of many different sounds: a virtuoso cascade of notes from a piano, the spiralling of a violin, or an aria being interrupted and recommenced. Higher up the building were the various dance studios, the largest being on the top floor from the windows of which at night could be seen the lights of Harlem. In the far corner of this studio was the storeroom where all the percussion instruments were kept under the careful eye of Felix. Often, during a class or a rehearsal, Felix would make his portly way between ballet dancers at the barre, or weave in and out of a modern dance class where the dancers would be spread across the floor, contracting and stretching their limbs. Once, when Martha Graham was giving a class, Felix crossed and re-crossed so many times that Martha, unable to endure these interruptions any longer, went into a contraction and released a long scream. Felix never entered that studio again while Martha was teaching!

Before flying out to New York I had drawn up a detailed schedule of work for the whole year but at the last minute I threw this away, realising that if the work was to be truly experimental then there could be no map of territory that was as yet uncharted. I knew only that as a director I wanted to experiment with the juxtaposition of bodies, sounds, voices, movement, dance, shapes and colours, in search of new forms of expression. I called the course *Theatre of the Imagination*, and at my first meeting with my students – including professional dancers, singers, musicians and a composer, Anthony Strilko – I explained that the main purpose of the course was to give them a personal experience of theatre rather than an academic course. In this way I hoped to enable them to find within themselves the 'why' of theatre and out of this to create a work, or works, which would speak for them as individuals. How we would achieve this I did not know; all I knew was that we would have to proceed by trial and error, exercising considerable faith in the creative principle to declare itself and point the way. But first, out of a group of various backgrounds, ages and experience, we would need to forge a unity so that we could all arrive at a point where we could feel free to express ourselves without fear.

I also told them that they would be expected to work in bare feet in these classes, as a way of enabling them to be more at ease in their bodies and with their emotions. As one student subsequently recorded:

> When I entered Studio 201 for the first time I saw a red-headed young man wearing a blue T-shirt, blue jeans, and bare-footed. I was somewhat astonished to learn that he was the teacher, since he was the first teacher I had seen without shoes. In the following hour and twenty minutes he told us that we also would be expected to remove our footwear for the rest of the year in his class. The entire session was quite a shock.

For a long time rumours spread of the barefoot class that sat in the dark or performed strange exercises with rubber babies, birds in cages, and wooden hoops, laughing and screaming. My own appearance barefooted in the corridors of the august Julliard caused quite a stir and I was dubbed, after a recent movie, 'the Barefoot Contessa.' Sometimes I would take the group out along the Hudson River, past Grant's Tomb, encouraging them to jump, run and turn somersaults on the sidewalk with the spontaneity of small children, all in an attempt to release their creativity. Such freedom of expression, before the more liberated 1960s, was something of a shock to a more inhibited generation of students, especially in the highly competitive professional atmosphere of the Julliard.

There were times, however, when I despaired as much of myself as of them. If they were often in the dark as to what we were doing, so was I; while the process of getting to know one another was often painful. That they were American and I English seemed often to get in the way. I began to learn that although we spoke the same language, our cultural and social associations were very different. Then, too, I worked instinctively in terms of images and symbols – (Jung was then a dirty word in America at a time when Freud was the only acknowledged psychological authority) – while, in addition, several of the group argued in terms of 'what use will this be to me as a dancer, musician, singer?' I found that I could not even assume the normal – to me at least! – references to folklore, myth, fairytale, the Bible; even history. And so they remained stubbornly on the defensive, distrustful of spontaneity, afraid of opening themselves up to the experimental and the unknown. Finally, of course, the very nature of the work was bound to arouse deep resistance so that for a time there was near chaos: mutinies, calculated insolence, and fierce destructive arguments. Only the support of other members of the Faculty – in particular that of the English choreographer Anthony Tudor, and that of Doris Humphrey, one of the pioneers of Modern Dance, and of Pearl Lang, one of Martha Graham's principal dancers and a choreographer with her own company – enabled me to persevere. Martha Graham herself was away on a Far Eastern tour at this period. I was also encouraged by the response of a small core of students who were committed to the work. At the end of the first semester, therefore, I went to William Schuman and insisted that the disruptive and uncooperative students be removed since clearly they were deriving no benefit and merely preventing the others from achieving anything constructive.

So it was that in the New Year of 1956 there came the first signs of real growth and it was now that I set each student an individual assignment, to create an original work of theatre, however small, by drawing upon some life experience of their own, taking as their definition of theatre: the objectification, through the medium of performance, of an inner reality.

The histrionic is a natural tendency in all of us: when we are happy we sing and dance; when frustrated we stamp and swear; when in pain we rock and moan. It is the performance of these actions that, in dramatising the mood, affords relief. To that extent art is also therapeutic. The histrionic, however, is not necessarily art, but simply self-expression. Art implies a form, rhythm and shape in time and space, as well as the ability to communicate its content to others so that it can become a shared experience. What is subjective must be made objective through the use of craft and technique.

I now began to work with individual students separately outside of the regular class. Each would bring a theme or an image and try to find its inherent form. I insisted on only one thing: that however abstract the piece might become it had to have a firm basis in reality. The abstract must always grow from the concrete, the universal from the particular. So, if the theme were that of 'feeling lost' we would look at actual examples of getting lost: as a child, or being on the subway after midnight with the panic of not being able to find the right train. There was to be no attitudinising, no vague expression of emotion.

Seated in a corner with a drum I would try to follow and assist whatever was being improvised. The beat was there solely to act as an inner pulse, not to dictate or impose. For as long as was needed I would continue to beat the drum while the student sat or lay on the floor until eventually a spontaneous movement or sound would manifest itself which the student would then follow through. Once a key image was discovered this would be explored through many improvisations until, detail by detail, it was crystallised into a work that could be performed before an audience.

Such a way of working involved certain dangers as well as responsibilities on my part as I was not a therapist. In order to minimise the degree of emotional involvement on my side I always avoided personal comment on the content of the emerging work, discussing it solely in terms of its dramatic and kinetic shape. There is a character in Virginia Woolf's novel *The Voyage Out* who, when asked what kind of books he wants to write, replies, 'Books about silence, about the things which people do not say.'

Increasingly in the twentieth century psychologists, painters, sculptors, writers, poets, dancers, had been concerned with the attempt to build a bridge between the conscious world of the ego and the unconscious world that lies within. Yet the theatre, as I saw it, still lagged behind, was still trapped in naturalism. Franz Marc, the painter, spoke of breaking the mirror of life 'so that we may look being in the face', while in the thirties the lone voice of Antonin Artaud in France declared 'I say there is a poetry of the senses as there is a poetry of language.'

But even more than this, what I was beginning to learn was the importance of ritual in which theatre has its origins. Ritual is one of the keys which can open a door into the realm of the imagination, that realm which is, in fact, the world of what Jung termed 'the collective unconscious'. Jung considered it the task of each individual to rediscover and reawaken those images that lie within and which he termed 'archetypes', to awaken them and to meditate upon them as they manifest themselves through dreams and through works of art. In certain dreams, as also in the work that I was doing, key images will manifest themselves and serve often as sign-posts on life's journey.

One of the dance students, Carolyn Gracey, had been distressed by the death, some months earlier, of a much loved teacher. Her first attempts to find a form that would express her sense of loss proved either sentimental or melodramatic, more like psycho-drama. She was deeply disturbed also by the group's response to what she was attempting, as well as by their attack on her and her belief in a personal God. She subsequently wrote:

> I was so upset that I spent a tortured night, unable to sleep.
> The following day when I met with James in the studio, I
> was so uptight that when he asked me to relax and just let

something come, I became even more tense until suddenly the conflict in my mind spilled over into the improvisation out of which the final ritual evolved.

It was the discussion with the group which helped her to face the central issue: What is beyond death? Is there a God? Is there an ultimate meaning to life? As a result, her unconscious began to work, releasing in the improvisation the essential images she needed. Carolyn called this piece, *From Forth This Circle* and it remains for me one of the most vivid examples of a personal ritual that I have experienced, a true rite of passage in that it enabled her to move forward and beyond the initial sense of loss.

She began seated on the floor inside a child's wooden hoop, rocking backwards and forwards in an agitated manner, repeating over and over the words, 'No God! No God!' She began to wrestle with the hoop, an image of her dilemma, rising up with it as though trapped inside it, at the bottom of a deep well. Repeatedly she cried out the words of her private terror until, at the climax, she gave a cry of despair and collapsed to the floor, the wooden hoop rattling round her until it was silent. She remained quite still, waiting. In the silence a flute was heard playing the Shaker melody, *Simple Gifts*. Slowly opening her eyes she gazed at the wooden circle inside of which she was seated, as though now seeing it from a different perspective, as though inside that terror lay the answer she was seeking. Reaching out her hands she fingered the hoop gently and began to sing, like a child's nursery rhyme, the words, 'My circle is my God, my God is my circle!' Then, lifting the hoop, she stood up, holding it high above her head like a spinning halo of light, and sang out with joy the words of her inner revelation, 'My circle encompasses me!' The simplicity of this short work, the intensity of its emotion, the crystallisation of a real and recognisable human dilemma, recalled some of those delicate poems of Emily Dickinson, each one a minute but precise graph of a mood and of her own spiritual journey.

Long afterwards I came across these words by Joseph Campbell: 'The great realisation of mythology is the immanence of the divine – you don't have to go anywhere else for it.' It was to be many years, however, before I fully understood that the work I was doing was about helping people to create their own rituals that would enable them to integrate certain life experiences. As Sandra Goldberg, another dancer in the group, observed of the whole year, 'It was a journey, not through books to acquire factual material, but through ourselves. With the aim of finding within ourselves the heart of theatre.'

THE MAKER OF SOULS

With its insistent pressure on the individual to 'be someone', New York is a fiercely competitive city, and yet slowly I learned how not to compete. One evening, sitting cross-legged in my brown-stone apartment by Columbia University, rocking gently backwards and forwards, I found myself saying over and over like a mantra, the words 'I am alone! I am alone!' Once, opening a volume of Emily Dickinson's poem I came across the line: 'Loneliness is the maker of souls', and I thought, Wow! She knew. For ultimately each of us has to learn not only how to be alone but how to deal with existential loneliness.

When I set off for New York I had been armed with introductions from John Gielgud, Esmé Percy, and Ram Gopal (with whom I had studied Indian dancing). One of these introductions was to Mercedes d'Acosta, a colourful character who for years had been a scriptwriter in Hollywood, and a former lover of Greta Garbo. In her youth she had worshipped the actress Eleonora Duse and whenever Duse was on tour in America Mercedes would be present in the audience, wearing a large black cloak, a silver crucifix round her neck, and a black patch over one eye. As soon as Duse came on stage Mercedes would stand up in the stalls and make the sign of the Cross.

Mercedes introduced me to many people but most importantly to Dr Masha Rollins, a Jungian analyst who had trained with Jung, and who agreed to see me once a week without charge. When, much later, I expressed concern about this, she replied, 'I make my rich patients pay for you. Besides,' she laughed, 'you are much more interesting!'

Each week I would take her a tangled collection of dreams to be explored. On one visit, during a discussion about my mother, she cut very deeply and I was angry. It was only then I realised how much more work I had to do and that I had not yet forgiven my mother for taking me away from the Pollards.

It was Masha who encouraged me to keep a journal. 'It is like talking to an intimate friend,' she said, 'to someone who really understands.' One dream in which a boy whispered to me, 'I so want to trust someone' brought to the surface my existential loneliness. 'That is what we desire: to communicate,' said Masha 'and there are few with whom this is possible. If we have one such person in our lives we are blessed.' The keeping of a journal enabled me to come safely through a lonely but challenging year in which I did a lot of growing up.

There were other lessons I learned from Masha as when I was distracted by a bluebottle fly which was zooming clumsily about her consulting room and which I offered to kill with a rolled up newspaper. 'Let it be!' said Masha quietly. 'It has been here all winter.' And so I began to learn to be alone with my own bluebottle thoughts.

On another occasion when I commented on how during the winter months I always wanted to withdraw and sleep, she replied, 'That is only natural. Many animals hibernate in the winter, conserving their energies for the spring.' She told me how one winter in New York, when she was much younger, she moved from her apartment to a smaller one down town without telling anyone, and hibernated there for the whole winter.

'It was a wonderful experience, a luxury, something you can only afford to do once. But it taught me the importance of listening to one's body. As the days shrink and darkness comes even earlier, inevitably we feel, as did our ancestors, that life is ebbing away. Once one understands this one learns how to endure the winter darkness and to conserve essential energies.'

AMERICA'S MOST LOVED POET

'It doesn't matter how calm you keep,' said the cabbie, 'in this business you always end up with ulcers!' I was on my way to meet the poet Robert Frost and the cabbie, unable to take a short cut through Central Park because of a procession on Fifth Avenue, had to make a long detour.

'What is it?'

'Greeks! They are always having processions! And if it isn't the Greeks, it's the Italians or Spaniards. These people, they are all fanatics, waiting to get to Heaven, to a private Valhalla of their own. If we had a proper Mayor this wouldn't happen, but he is so anxious to get votes. They are all the same, politicians!'

Robert Frost, on the eve of his eighty-second birthday, was in New York to give a reading of his poems at the Young Men's Hebrew Association where Dylan Thomas first performed *Under Milk Wood*. I had sent a note to Robert Frost conveying greetings from Eleanor Farjeon who, forty years previously, had known Frost when he came with his wife and children to live for a time in England and when he became a close friend of the poet, Edward Thomas.

Opening the door of his suite at the Westbury Hotel he gestured, laughing, towards the television set in the room. 'I don't know how to work these darned things! Where I live in the country there is no radio, television or telephone, but I like this for the boxing.' A tall man, slightly stooping, his face and hands freckled from exposure to all weathers, lined and wrinkled like an old apple, the soft white hair falling in a boyish lock across his forehead, his eyes were a startling blue beneath the shaggy white eyebrows. The whole face was smiling, yet shy, evasive, self-mocking.

'Ha! They call me a poet! But I can never get used to it, you know, even after forty years. I always put "farmer" on my income tax returns. I've put "teacher" – but never educationalist! – even "retired", because of course I've been out of things so long. I've even thought of putting "resigned" and, in brackets after it, "to everything", but it doesn't do to joke with the authorities! The last time I saw Tom Eliot in London I asked him what he put and he replied, "publisher" but never "poet".

'I took on a farm in New England and didn't write a thing. Then I saved up enough money to go to England with my wife and four children just before the First World War. I guess I had three reasons for going to England that first time: one was a desire to live under thatch; one to experience being poor, living really cheaply as one could in England then; and one was my feeling for the country of lyric poetry. I used to live with Palgrave's Treasury. I never was carried away by any particular poet. There were just two things I cared for: short lyrics and eclogues, Theocritus, Vergil, and some of Wordsworth. T.E. Hulme, the philosopher, in his unwisdom, wanted me to name my second book (which I called *North of Boston*) *Yankee Eclogues*!

'Those two and a half years in England were the best in my life, and the best thing that happened there was knowing Edward Thomas. He read a poem of mine and wrote asking to meet me. How much he did for people, other poets, especially Walter de la Mare whose work he kept quoting in his reviews until people started saying, "Who is this Walter de la Mare?" A lot of people were unkind to Edward and he had to put up with a lot of hack work, journalistic stuff such as an article on the pubs of England which would entail his tramping around, getting people's reactions. He could do it but it wasn't any satisfaction. Sometimes I would go with his wife Helen to meet him off the train from London when he had got one of these reviewing jobs. "Oh, how marvellous!" Helen would enthuse, and he would be angry and go off, leaving us. Helen loved him too much and didn't really appreciate his work in the way that Eleanor did. Eleanor loved Edward but he never reciprocated it. She used to type out all his poems when he started writing.'

As I was leaving he said, 'Thank you for coming. It has made me very happy. I'm not a letter writer but I will try and write to Eleanor. Tell her that I still care, and maybe I will bring out a collection of Edward's poems over here with a preface by me, and Eleanor's article from the *London Magazine*. My publishers will do anything for me. I've stayed with the same publishers all through their vicissitudes and only the other day the managing director said to me that no other American writer had been so long with one publisher. I'm proud of that. I often think about loyalties; how you get from an attraction to an attachment. One of these days I want to write an essay about that.'

That evening the YMHA was packed with people of all ages, even standing down the side aisles, to hear 'America's most beloved poet' as John Malcolm Brinnin introduced him. Then Frost ambled on, clutching a sheaf of poems, and began to talk discursively. Suddenly I heard him saying

> There is someone in this audience tonight who has been reminding me of my very great friend, Edward Thomas, the English poet, who was killed in the First World War. He was very close to me, the closest friend I ever had, and this poem which I am going to read, *The Road Not Taken* is really his poem. It is more his character than mine, and indeed when I sent it to him out at the Front, he replied, 'What do you mean by sending me my poem!'

Frost next read the poem *The Soldier*, describing his reaction on hearing the news of Edward's death, and finally *Iris by Night*, the original manuscript of which Eleanor had given me, which describes a walk they once took together 'in a relation of elected friends.' Afterwards he came from backstage to sign copies of his books, moving slowly down an avenue of people, until he came to me.

> Oh, there you are! You know that was a wonderful thing you did to me tonight. You brought it all back. Thank you for that. And give my message to Eleanor when you write, and come and see me again before you go back to England. Come to Bread Loaf Writers' Conference this summer.

'IF WE ASK YOU TO STAY, WILL YOU?'

At the end of their year my students gave a performance of their works in the main dance studio at the top of the Julliard before an invited audience which included Pearl Lang. There was also a young dancer from her company, Bruce Marks, who was to become Principal Dancer of the American Ballet and then Artistic Director of the Boston Ballet. Years later he said to me, 'At that time there was no one talking like you, saying the things you were saying. They just didn't understand.'

Pearl Lang, who had sat absorbed and deeply moved, told me that I had given her fresh hope. 'We need you here and at Yale,' she said. 'We need you more for dancers than for actors. If we ask you to stay, will you?' It was to be a long time, however, before I was able to assess the exact value of what had been achieved but it laid the foundation for my later work in ritual.

As a result of that evening I was invited by Ted Shawn to teach a course at Denishawn, the home of Modern Dance, founded by Shawn and Ruth St Denis. In addition, Alwin Nikolais invited me to start a school of theatre at the Henry Street Playhouse where he was working experimentally with his own dance company and whose work, within a very few years, was to take London, Paris and other cities by storm. The Alwin Nikolais Dance Company was also to have the unique experience of performing in Persia before the Shah and his Queen, in the great amphitheatre under the stars on the same night that Man first landed on the Moon.

THE BREAD LOAF WRITERS' CONFERENCE

Suddenly there arrived an invitation to give a poetry reading at the Bread Loaf Writers' Conference in Vermont of which Robert Frost, who lived nearby, had been President since its inception. The conference, the first of its kind, had been launched in 1926 by John Farrar, editor of *The Bookman*. Its aim was to bring together the best available staff of writers and editors and to work it mercilessly for two intensive weeks of daily and evening lectures, workshops, manuscript reading, and private conferences with contributors.

On my arrival I found a letter from Eleanor Farjeon enclosing another for Frost. 'I must tell you,' she wrote, 'what living happiness your letter has given me with that account of Robert and his plain message after forty-one years: "Tell Eleanor I still care". And tell him, I still care also!'

The next day I went to call on Frost. Seeing him a field away, in white trousers, his shirt hanging outside, climbing the hill in the afternoon heat, having been to visit his grandchildren, I delayed my arrival in order to give him time to recover. Behind his simple log cabin rose the blue-shaded mountains. As I climbed the steps to his verandah I knocked over a rake and he emerged laughing to tell me the story of an English woman who was so anxious to be thought upper class that she assumed a refined accent. One day, going down the garden, she saw a rake lying in the grass. 'What's that?'

she asked the gardener in her lofty voice. At that moment she stepped on it accidentally. It sprang up and hit her in the face at which she lost her accent and cried, 'Damn the bloody rake!'

He sat before an empty grate, a little flushed after the exertion of walking, one eyebrow sagging, hiding the eye. Early photographs of Frost reveal him to have been as romantically handsome as Rupert Brooke but now in age his face was intricately lined and weathered like an old tree.

It was in this cabin he told me that he had written his most celebrated lyric *Stopping by Woods on a Snowy Evening*. 'One night after supper I sat down to work at a long piece of blank verse with which I wrestled all night, but which refused to resolve itself. Finally, putting down my pen I got up to watch the dawn from that window. And it was at that moment that *Stopping by Woods* came into my head in its entirety. All I had to do was to write it down. I call that the luck of the work, and probably if I hadn't been struggling over that bad poem, the better one might never have come to be written!'

Referring to Eleanor's letter prompted him to reminisce about Edward Thomas.

'He was a big strong man but he didn't want to fight. Yet the war represented a kind of challenge. It was a real struggle for him. He was quite prepared to fight but he couldn't stand patriotic talk or the kind of person who said it was going to be the war to end all wars. His father was a close friend of Lloyd George, you know, and twice they tried to get Edward off the active list but he insisted on being treated like everyone else.

'It was I who started him writing poetry. When I read his prose I said to him, 'This should be in verse!' Once he started he never stopped. Edward and I were more than fellow poets; we were more than friends – we were affectionate friends. And when I returned to England in 1928 his death had changed everything. It wasn't the same.'

His voice faltered, the eyes darkening, and we sat a while in silence. Then, placing his large square hands on his chest, he continued. 'Edward was like a man who takes the spear into his own hands. Where some would try to shield themselves from it Edward received it into himself.'

Taking my copy of the first edition of Edward's poems, which Eleanor had given me, which was dedicated to Frost but published after his death, he inscribed it: 'to James Roose-Evans from his friend Robert Frost, the wish that we might see something come from this little book out of our having met. Ripon, Vermont, USA, August 20th 1956.' He then said, 'When you give your reading, will you tell them about Edward? I can't.' As I rose to leave he told me that he had to give a lecture at a university at the end of the week. 'I do about twenty a year, few enough to give me time to think of something fresh to say! I go about barding! I'm a sort of travelling Homer, and I live on property that once belonged to someone called Homer Noble, so you see there is some sort of a connection!' I asked him what he did with all the academic hoods he received for his many honorary degrees. He chuckled. 'I'll tell you a secret. I cut them up to make patchwork quilts!'

A few days later he gave a lecture on the writing of poetry. Relaxed, wryly humorous, his white hair fluffed and wind-blown, he stood shifting from foot to foot, jigging about, bending his knees, laughing mischievously and looking quizzically at us from under his tufted eyebrows. He began to quote odd lines from those poems which had stuck to him like burrs on a country walk; lines such as Shakespeare's 'He that has power to hurt and will do none.' That, he said, had meant much to him.

Through the open windows of the Conference Centre came the zuzzing sound of crickets, swift and repetitive like a bicycle tyre being pumped impatiently. Some of the student waiters who had been clearing up after lunch now slipped in at the back to listen. Most of them were budding writers who got free tuition in return for waiting on tables. Frost continued:

> In writing prose or verse, the main thing is you have to give me something to change my voice on, sentence by sentence, so that I won't be bored by reading it. You have to plunge in from the start. Avoid intoning. If necessary, just plonk down a matter-of-fact statement. But finally it is a matter of tones. You can often tell by the tone of voice what people are really saying. If a passage of writing is good then the tone is conveyed by the context as in Shakespeare. Not like my naive friend Vachel Lindsay who thought you should convey the tone by directions in the margin such as: read this in a golden tone, a blue tone, and so on!
>
> Sometimes you think you know a poem by heart and then you hear an actor speak it, using a particular tone of voice on a word or a phrase, and suddenly it opens up a whole new dimension for you. An actor can cut your heart with these niceties.

Later that evening, after listening to the campaign results – with Adlai Stevenson winning an unanimous vote as the Democratic representative – in the lounge of the Wraybury Inn, I gave a reading of poems by Frost and Thomas. As a result I was asked to give another reading the following night in the Conference Centre. At the back of the auditorium I could see Jay Smith, one of the student waiters, seated alone and slightly apart. He had been at the Wraybury Inn the previous evening. After the recital he and I sat cross-legged on the floor in the crowded bar.

'Are you happy?' he asked. I nodded but he looked piercingly at me and repeated, 'Are you?'

'No,' I replied. 'Not if you want the truth.'

'What would you rather do?'

'I'd rather be alone with you and talk.' He nodded.

'One doesn't get very far in company with others. One presents only a superficial self. But, you can get by for now?' He then asked me to read Edward Thomas's poem *Will You Come?* As we sat facing each other, our foreheads close together, I read the poem and the whole room went quiet as everyone stopped to listen.

'Do you know,' said Jay, 'you never read that so beautifully as you did in the Conference Centre this evening when I was sitting at the back. You moved me very much and you did something new with it. You'd never read it like that before. It was the way you whispered the final word "Come!" It just caught everybody's breath. You had them.'

The moon was high, the stars brilliant, and the silence heightened by the tingling of crickets. Somewhere a church clock struck the hour. There was a smell of wood smoke lingering on the air. On a hilltop, by a silver birch, we rested: the grass spiky, cold to the touch. I lay on a rug, gazing up at the geometry of stars. Above me was his pale face with its high domed forehead, the eyes dark with shadow, the face grave and tender, the mouth curving in a smile.

'This is an hour outside time,' he murmured. 'An hour that will always be. You are beautiful, beautiful!' There was a reverence in the unveiling, his skin white and vulnerable. His body stretched upwards, the head thrown back in ecstasy, eyes searching eyes gravely. The night air stirred softly. Then came one long held look before the eyes closed, his face in a tremor of pain, and now our faces came closer together until at last the arrows sped from their bows in a shiver of cold like frost. It was ended: unexpected, happening without question, in simple acceptance. And I thought of Edward Thomas's poem:

> *Will you come?*
> *Will you come?*
> *Will you ride*
> *So late*
> *at my side?*
> *O, will you come?*

Will you come?
Will you come
If the night
Has a moon
Full and bright?
O,will you come?

Would you come?
Would you come
If the noon
Gave light,
not the moon?
Beautiful, would you come?

Would you have come?
Would you have come
Without scorning,
Had it been
still morning?
Beloved, would you have come?

If you come
Haste and come.
Owls have cried;
It grows dark
to ride.
Beloved, beautiful, come!

The 28th of August was the final day of the Conference at which John Ciardi, Leonie Adams and others had spoken, given master classes and individual tutorials. After the formal banquet and the speeches a small group of us ended up in a log cabin by the ski-run. The moon, past its zenith, an elliptical-shaped egg with grey markings, was poised in the sky in a circle of misted light tinged at the edges like a swollen bruise.

Inside the cabin candles were lit and a log fire burned. Leila Treese, Jay Smith and I sat in one corner, apart from the others, talking quietly about the solitariness of the artist, the poet. Lee told us how her husband, whom she married two months ago, did not understand her poetry. 'I don't know where he is now. He's a travelling salesman. He leaves the day I return.'

We were seated on wooden crates with a single candle on the ground in the centre. Jay collected two more crates and placed them over the candle so that the light was now concentrated, shining up through the criss-crossing bars. Our box had become a stove and we placed our hands on the top, warming them. We ceased talking, drawn together by this small fragile moment of intimacy. Then Lee read us one of her poems, one that Leonie Adams had praised, about the difficulty of communication and the inadequacy even of similes.

Almost a year later Lee was to write to me, 'Bread Loaf was so short a time and I am thankful for that last night when the three of us, who knew little or nothing about each other's lives, came to know so much about each other and ourselves in a space beyond words.'

The mists drifted slowly across the hills. The grass was heavy with dew and a single crimson leaf fell from a maple tree. It was the moment before departure. After breakfast I brushed Lee's cheek with my lips.

'I hope we meet again!' she said in a quiet nervous voice. To Jay I said, 'God bless you!' and he replied, 'And you, too!' I thought of Bernard in Virginia Woolf's *The Waves*:

> We long to embrace the whole world with arms of
> understanding. Now we must go. The moment is upon
> us, the urgency of it all is fearful. Yet we have known one
> moment of enormous peace. Now we must go.

Suddenly I was intensely lonely and homesick for England, with that sense of 'hiraeth' of which the Welsh speak, that longing for one's own roots and landscape. I realised that, rich and fruitful as the year had been, I did not truly belong here. And so I began to say goodbye to friends, booked my passage home, packed my bags, and set sail.

ACT THREE

THE RETURN JOURNEY

On my return to England I went up to Hampstead to tell Eleanor Farjeon about my meetings with Robert Frost. She spoke of the very deep relationship which Edward and Robert had enjoyed, 'such as I think only two men can have. It was love. Full of silence and reticence and dry humour, sly humour!'

We were seated in her hammock in the walled garden at the back of her cottage in Perrins Walk, among the laden apple and pear trees, the late roses and clambering creepers, while over the wall we could glimpse other gardens, chimneys, and the spire of Hampstead parish church. 'Edward inspired love in men. Ten years after his death my brother Bertie said to me, "I wake in the night sometimes and weep for Edward."' It is, I said, like the image of Perceval in *The Waves*: 'What can we do to keep him? How signal to all time that we who stand here loved Perceval, now Perceval is gone?'

On 21 May 1957 Eleanor, Robert Frost, Helen Thomas and Edward's daughter Myfanwy and I were driven to the Senate House at London University where Frost, who had arrived in England to receive an Honorary Degree from Oxford University, had been invited to speak at a reception hosted by T.S. Eliot. The lecture hall was packed and the speeches relayed to those outside but we, as guests of honour, were seated in the front row.

'This is a great occasion,' announced Professor Isaacs in his introduction. 'The greatest living American poet has, in a sense, come home. For it was in England that he received his first recognition as a poet.' Frost then rose and after cracking his usual jokes began to talk a little about Edward Thomas before reading some of his own poems.

'You know,' he paused to say, 'it is very nice coming back like this. To think how these first poems of mine have been published, read and spread about, things that I had left behind like a cuckoo's egg!' Two days later he went up to Hampstead to spend the afternoon alone with Eleanor. That evening, after he had gone, she invited me to visit her and said, 'Oh, Jimmie! Even though Robert and I may never see each other again, these few hours with him have meant more to me than anything else and will last me. When you exist on such a deep level with another human being then time is unimportant. This time with Robert just had to be!' Seated in the hammock, her head on my chest, she seemed more serene than she had been for a long time. It grew dark and I went inside to switch on the lights so that we could see them from where we sat. It began to rain and we lay back on the cushions, covered with rugs, sheltering under the canvas canopy, listening on her portable radio to Walton's *Fantasia for Harp* and two other instruments, with Benignus sprawled on our laps. We munched bread and cheese and sipped strong tea from large cups as the rain spattered down, the light from the windows filtering through the twisting branches and wet leaves of the apple trees.

We lay there, not needing to speak, while my mind went back to that moment in the log cabin at Bread Loaf, and on the hilltop under the heraldry of the stars.

'These are the only moments that matter,' said Eleanor. And I thought how those who we have loved, as Eleanor had loved Edward, do not die but live on in us. When one life touches another at such depth beyond that of lust it leaves an indelible mark. Love does not die, although it may go underground for many years. It remains waiting to be rediscovered, for each of us is the sum of all our loves.

TEACHING

On my return from America I was invited by John Fernald, Principal of the Royal Academy of Dramatic Art, to teach and also to direct productions for the Vanbrugh Theatre. Among my students were Sarah Miles, John Thaw, Geoffrey Whitehead, Dyson Lovell, Caroline Blakiston and Mike Leigh. In my teaching I used many of the exercises I had evolved in New York and word soon got around that something unusual was going on. A national newspaper wanted to interview me and photograph a session in progress but John Fernald, becoming anxious, sent for me, saying, 'You're not teaching the Method, are you?' From this distance of time it is difficult to realise how both Stanislavsky and the Method were regarded with suspicion. To this day, however, Mike Leigh as a film director still uses some of my exercises.

John Fernald became my champion and gave me a number of wonderful challenges for a young director, from Henri de Montherlant's *Port-Royal*, André Obey's *Frost at Midnight*, my own adaptation of Milton's *Paradise Lost*, to Max Beerbohm's hitherto unperformed piece, *Savanarola Brown*, which I directed at the Festival Hall, with a cast of eighty, in the presence of Lady Beerbohm. The one production, however, that stands out is Dylan Thomas' *Under Milk Wood*, which was such a success that Fernald kept asking me to revive it each term with new casts, and each time there were queues all the way down Malet Street. The production also went on tour and played before HM The Queen Mother at the Kings Lynn Festival, who spoke afterwards of 'this shining torrent of words'. Michael Codron, the West End producer, came to one of these performances and invited me to form a cast of those students who had been in my previous productions but who were now launched as professional actors. That 'Vanbrugh Theatre' production was then mounted at the Lyric Theatre, Hammersmith, with Philip Madoc as Captain Cat.

When I first saw *Under Milk Wood* at the New Theatre in London I found myself distracted by the visual detail of the set: the many small trucks that were shunted on and off. Nothing had been left to the imagination. If an actor said, 'Miles away a dog barks' then sure enough one heard a dog barking. By the time Lord Cut-Glass's roomful of ticking clocks had been trucked onto the stage we had missed half of the Narrator's description. It was as though the directors had been afraid to trust the text and felt that they must elaborate lest the audience be bored. About halfway through the performance I closed my eyes and listened to the play.

Originally commissioned for radio by the BBC, Dylan has provided his own clue to the work in its sub-title, 'A Play for Voices'. So when I came to stage the play there was no scenery and the actors were grouped in a tight phalanx on a rising plane of chairs, with a narrator on either side. No one left the stage. The actors rose or stood on chairs, leaned forward, mimed, rang their own bells, blew their own soap bubbles, provided their own cock-crows, played their own mouth organs, made their own sound effects. All was contained within the company so that the hill of chairs became the village of Llaregyb; and because each actor played many parts, with the exceptions of Captain Cat and Polly Garter, one had the feeling of generations of families, all the shared memories of a community, and that total lack of privacy that one finds in any village. All participated in the dramas and comedies of the rest; the songs that they sang were the songs that had been handed down from one generation to another. When the entire cast, rocking from side to side, sang 'Johnny Crack and Flossie Snail' they were both the children of the village at that particular moment and, at the same time, their parents and grandparents recalling these songs of their childhood.

The entire play is a canticle of praise by a religious poet, and its theme is contained in the words of the Revd Eli Jenkins' evening prayer:

> *We are not wholly bad or good*
> *Who live our lives under Milk Wood,*
> *And Thou I know wilt be the first*
> *To see our best side not our worst.*

Without passing moral judgment Dylan Thomas observes humanity with humour and compassion:

> *And all your deeds and words,*
> *Each truth, each lie,*
> *Die in unjudging love.*

In rehearsal I used a great deal of improvisation in order to open up the individual characterisations. The entire cast was always present at these sessions, sharing, as it were, in the community's collective memories – many of the improvisations showed various characters at different stages of their lives. Once this had been achieved, however, the actors sat in their rows of chairs and were literally conducted, passage by passage, line by line, sound by sound, going back and over the phrasing of a particular line, the length of a pause, or the pitch of different voices, the exact balance of a sound, a word or an inflection. The lighting or extinguishing of a cigarette, the picking up or putting down of knitting – all was carefully blocked so that nothing would distract from this mosaic of sound. All was 'plotted and pieced'; yet within this austere form the greatest freedom was achieved. Often, when I was contemplating that hill of empty chairs which, at the curtain call, always seemed so vibrantly alive, I pondered what would happen if the chairs could move, could become more intimately a part of the action, themselves playing many roles like the actors. Thus it was that some years later, in staging Laurie Lee's *Cider with Rosie*, the chairs did indeed become members of the cast!

With the opening of the Belgrade Theatre in Coventry I was invited by its artistic director, Bryan Bailey, to direct a number of productions there and then, after his untimely death, I was appointed resident director under his successor Anthony Richardson. It was at this time also that I became the presenter of *Sunday Break*, a weekly television programme aimed at young people, and dealing with moral issues.

THE YOUNGER BROTHER

One afternoon shortly before I left for America, David March observed quietly, 'You are beginning to find your wings. Soon you will not need me.' I was shocked since I could not imagine such a thing. He was my anchor. Yet he foresaw quite clearly that a year away in a new culture would be the making and the maturing of me, and that I would return a changed person. He was to prove correct. When I did return each of us had changed. One evening, boxed up in the one-roomed flat with its gas ring and shared bathroom downstairs, which we had lived in ever since I came down from Oxford, David suddenly cried out, like an animal in pain, 'Don't you love me any more?!' It wasn't that I was having dalliances elsewhere but I had matured and was now more focused on my own work and was less dependent on him.

Faced with the intensity of his emotion I did not know how to respond and so I went up to see Eleanor Farjeon in Hampstead who, disturbed by what I told her at once offered us, at a peppercorn rent, a tiny three-roomed cottage she owned in Perrins Court which had once been the village sweetshop and before that the cobbler's. It had a toilet but no bathroom: for baths we would take our towels and go across to Eleanor's in Perrins Walk. Small though it was it at least gave us a room each. Although we lived there for about three years David began to seek liaisons with others, so that living under the same roof, and in such close proximity, became increasingly painful, especially when his lovers stayed there. Later, he formed a close relationship with someone with whom he lived for forty years until he died of Parkinson's Disease. David and I remained friends and I remember, after the death of his beloved partner, sitting across the table from him in the flat that he and his partner Derek Lewis had shared, holding his hands, tears cascading down his face, as he said, 'Where is he now?'

So it was that one night, driven by loneliness, I paid my first visit to the William the Fourth, a gay pub in Hampstead. Standing ill at ease among the crush of bodies I heard a camp voice behind me saying, 'This is my first time here. I've come up from Brighton. Do you come here often?' I made no answer and did not turn round.

'You are very difficult, young man! Here am I doing my best to talk to you and you don't even answer!' Suddenly I began to laugh and it was at this moment that I saw across the room a young man who had been watching this encounter with amusement.

'Why are you laughing?' said the Brighton belle. 'I think you are very rude!' At that moment the young man who had been observing us passed me, saying, 'Would you like a cup of coffee?' His name was Hywel Jones.

If marriages are supposedly made in Heaven they are also, it seems, made in gay pubs. Because of my father I had always been ill at ease in pubs and even more so in gay ones because of the hustling atmosphere and yet, had I not gone there that particular evening, Hywel and I might never have met. It was also his first visit there. Is there a destiny at work here? Who can tell why some find the perfect partner and some never do? There remains a mystery. Where does the attraction between two people come from? How do they manage to be in the same place at that particular moment and had they missed the moment would they have remained strangers? As John O'Donoghue writes in his book, *Eternal Echoes*: 'There is a whole area of secret preparation and gathering here that we cannot penetrate with our analytical or conscious minds.'

Short, his shoulders slightly rounded as though from carrying a yoke, with shaggy black hair, glowing brown eyes, a gypsy face with the bone structure of a Nureyev, Hywel was, I learned, a farmer's son from Mid Wales, who was now working in the library at the Institute of Advanced Legal Studies in Bedford Square. He also had a very bad stammer which caused his lips to become distorted when he got excited.

Three weeks later I set off to make a solitary pilgrimage to his birthplace in Llangynog, among the Berwyn Mountains. En route I stopped at Dolgellau where he had worked in the library after leaving school and before going into the Army. At the library, a temporary wooden building with cell-like compartments of books, and windows that looked down on the grey town with its towered church, I met Elwyn Griffiths and his assistant Jeannie. His face lit up on my mentioning Hywel's name.

'He came here direct from school. He was a bright boy, very quick at learning. He soon picked it up. Now he's a man he must take the final examinations and qualify. When he went into the Army we said he could come back here, but he wrote saying he was going to stay in London. Then he wrote to me for a reference at the Institute of Advanced Legal Studies.' He smiled wryly. 'And we never even heard if he got the job! He's never been back. We wondered if it was a girl interested him there. What's he like with the girls?' At this Jeannie laughed.

'We thought perhaps he had met someone,' continued Mr Griffiths. 'He's a cheerful person, full of fun, a good chap, Hywel. How did you meet him? Oh, I thought by the way you speak that perhaps you were a speech therapist and had met him that way. How's his stammer? It used to be very bad. He'd go red in the face with it. Then when he was in the Army they sent him to a psychiatrist or something and it was much better.'

He departed to deal with someone's query and now Jeannie began to talk, shyly at first, on the defensive, with a quiet bitterness so it seemed, as of old wounds opening, as she stood sticking labels onto a pile of books.

'I wrote to him but he never answered. I got a Christmas card once but no address. I'd like to write to him. Tell him I've got a lot of news. Oh, but we used to fight and have terrible rows! Terrible! And he'd not speak for an hour. Sometimes I'd call him for his tea and he wouldn't come. Things like that. And then suddenly it would be all over. He used to cheek me something. But he could do no wrong for Mr Griffiths. He was Mr Griffiths' pet! I'd tell Hywel off about something, perhaps to put away some books, and then Mr Griffiths would come along and say, "What are you doing, Hywel? Oh, leave those!" In the end I said to Mr Griffiths, "I'm never going to tell Hywel to do anything!" Finally it got so bad that I had it out with Mr Griffiths in that room, a terrible row it was!

'When Hywel went off to the Army we teased him and had him in the end room with his shirt off and we stamped him with every stamp in the library!'

Through the windows I gazed at the town and tried to imagine Hywel looking out on such a rainy day, sorting books, drinking tea, laughing, and wondering what lay ahead of him. Then I heard Jeannie speaking in Welsh to someone and I thought of her remark, 'He never came back'. How warmly, with a spark of asperity, yet sadly too, they had spoken of him. He was indeed gone from their valley.

I hitched a lift over the Berwyn Mountains to Llangynog where Hywel, his two brothers and two sisters, had been brought up. On the edge of moorland, painted on a large cheek of rock, were the words: 'While we were yet sinners Christ died for us. Be saved' and a little further on, a similar sign but this time in Welsh. I was entering the region of the Primitive Methodists.

The mountains rose steeply on either side, the grass cropped close by sheep, with rashes of pale green bracken and rocks jutting out like the bones of the mountains. At one end of the valley was a waterfall spilling threads of creamy yellow water before flowing along the bed of the valley between banks of ash, sycamore and hazel. At this end of the valley was a stone farm, Blaenrhiwarth, nestling under a copse of fir trees, encircled by a stone wall, where Hywel's grandfather and his eleven sons lived.

At Eithen, the first house in the village, I looked down at a mud-splashed farm where hens ran squawking and a man sat removing his boots before entering the house in his stockinged feet. Next to it was Nant where lived Hywel's Uncle Tom who, as he told me, had 'lost his wife, his son, and then his arm.' Finally I entered the tiny village with its one church, three chapels, two inns and a general store.

I booked a room at the Tanat Inn where I chatted with Lyn Thomas who had been discharged from the Navy because of deafness and who now worked for the Forestry Commission. The next day he took me for a walk in the rain to Pennant Melangell with its seventh-century church tucked away at the end of the valley where the lane fizzles out. The church was not much used although the previous year, Lyn told me, there had been a service every Sunday. 'Five of us used to come. One took the service, one played the organ, one read the lesson, and one took the collection!'

Seated in the porch, looking out at the tombstones among the tall grass with the mountains to one side, and the rain drenching down, he continued, 'I don't know why this place affects me so much more than any cathedral I have visited. I suppose it's because it's been here so long, has endured, and will probably go on. But I like to come here.'

As the rain soaked into the earth I thought of St Melangell who, as a young Irish princess, had escaped to Wales to avoid an arranged marriage, and founded an order of contemplative nuns here. Then one day in AD 64, so the story goes, Prince Brockwell came hunting a hare, pursuing it down this valley. The hare ran straight towards Melangell who lifted the skirts of her habit to hide it. The Prince, amazed at her courage, took her, the nuns, and the hares, under his protection from then onwards. When she died her shrine became a focal point for pilgrims. The church and the shrine have since been restored, with daily services for pilgrims who come from all over the world to pray at the shrine, or visit the Cancer Counselling Centre that has been built alongside.

1 Aged three

2 In an early role as Hamlet at Crypt Grammar School, Gloucester. *(Gloucestershire Newspapers)*

3 Monty, the elder brother

4 As my mother wished I'd remained!

5 Jungian analyst
Franz Elkisch

6 Pick at the
Granary

7 In America, leading
an experimental
theatre workshop

8 With Martha
Graham at the
American Embassy

9 The 'Barefoot Contessa' – relaxing on the set of *Sunday Break*

10 Eleanor Farjeon with Hywel Jones at the launch of the Hampstead Theatre Club, in her Garden Room in Hampstead. *(Ham and Highgate Express)*

11 Founding the Hampstead Theatre Club. *(Helen Craig)*

12 Noel Coward
arriving for the
special matinée
performance of
*Private Lives. (Ham
and Highgate Express)*

13 David March: the
'elder brother'

14 Introducing the cast to HM Queen Mother at the world premiere of my production of *Cider With Rosie. (Eastern Daily Press)*

15 Barbara Wilkes, stage designer at the Maddermarket Theatre, who taught me so much about the relationship of designer and director, which led to a rich collaboration

16 On a visit to the 'Sage of Robertsbridge'

17 With John Hencher

18 David Hemmings in Dylan Thomas' *Adventures in the Skin Trade*, adapted by Andrew Sinclair and directed by James Roose-Evans. *(John Haynes)*

19 Mary Ure in Tennessee Williams' *The Two Character Play. (Helen Craig)*

20 An image from Deaths and Entrances, the main work created by Stage Two, as Job cries out, 'Why dost Thou hide Thy face from me? Show me my iniquity!'

21 My mother

22 Hywel with my mother

23 Bleddfa church displaying batik banners by Thetis Blacker

24 Archbishop of Wales, Rowan Williams, unveils a statue of Tobias and the Angel at the Bleddfa Centre for the Creative Spirit

25 At the Bleddfa Centre, outside the Charlesworth Chapel

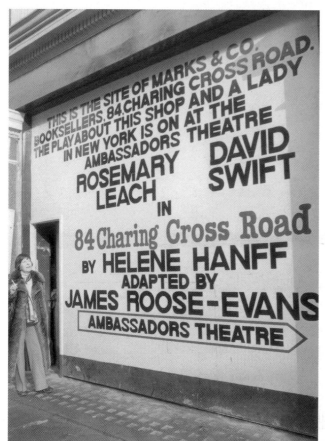

26 Preaching at the wedding of the Reverend Richard McLaren and Diana Lazenby

27 Helene Hanff at 84 Charing Cross Road

28 Helene in rehearsal with Rosemary Leach, who created the role of Helene in the stage version of *84 Charing Cross Road*

29 Backstage with Sir John Gielgud during *The Best of Friends*. *(John Haynes)*

30 With Hywel inside one of the great yew hedges at Powis Castle

On the Sunday evening I attended the chapel which Hywel and his family frequented. For my benefit one hymn was sung in English and the second lesson read in English: word having got round that there was an English visitor staying in the village. The text of the sermon was also given out in English but the sermon itself was delivered in Welsh by young Mr Mervyn Jones from Birmingham who that autumn was to study at Bala Theological College. His was the best Welsh I had yet heard, a slow sad singing voice, like a quiet pleading, as he reiterated the name of Moses: now high, now soft, now deep and thunderous, so that I began to understand the meaning of the word 'hwyl' which means, literally 'a sail', but is also used for a preacher who takes off in a flight of oratory. After the sermon Mr Edward Evans-the-Post gave out the notices in Welsh and then, speaking in English, welcomed me, saying, 'I don't know his name (Hywel had given me strict instructions that I was to remain anonymous and not mention any connection with him!) but I met him in the village yesterday, asking where to stay, and then this morning he asked me what time chapel was this evening. I hope he enjoys his stay among us.'

On my last day in Llangynog a letter arrived from Hywel announcing he was due to arrive just as I left. Already I found myself longing for a fuller relationship with him and for that completeness which comes from an intimate sharing of the daily minutiae and vicissitudes and yet which leaves room for separateness.

'We have plenty of time,' said Hywel. 'Let us tread delicately. One lives from day to day. One day at a time, because otherwise one starts building up expectations and then gets disappointed.'

And so slowly I began to learn the need for patience and for a long vision, relinquishing all holds on him so that he might be free to choose, realising he had never before been in love with anyone, and was also nine years younger. And even if this were all, I thought, it was most richly so.

Sometimes we would meet for a picnic in Russell Square near his place of work; sometimes in Eleanor Farjeon's Garden Room; go for a walk over Hampstead Heath, or to a concert at the Festival Hall. It was there that we heard Rosalyn Tureck play the *Goldberg Variations* which she had transposed for the piano and of which she had once said that as she laid her hands on the keys to play the opening bars she already heard in her head the closing bars of the work. The work is like a great river, like the Ganges, journeying towards the sea, gathering momentum, being joined by other tributaries, recalling the excitement of Emily Dickinson's 'O Sea, my River runs to Thee!'

It was at the age of seventeen that Tureck's whole approach to Bach was changed. 'I know it is unfashionable,' she said, 'to talk of revelations, but that is what I call it now. One day when I was playing a very complex fugue, the A Minor from Book 1, it came to me that I would have to change all my ideas, throw away everything I had learned and start again. And I had to form a new technique to match this concept. From then on there was no one to tell me what to do. My conviction sprang from within myself. I had to chop down every tree.' Those words of hers reminded me of Martha Graham who, too, had to scrape back to 'the original design'.

Hywel and I also went to the Festival Hall to hear Dame Edith Sitwell give a recital of her poetry. Dressed in black satin with a long black cloak held in place by a large brooch, she was already seated on stage on a throne as the audience arrived. Her face was a white mask, just the tip of her nose pink, and with two half moons for eyebrows painted above her eyes. Her skull was like a mask surmounted by a gold headdress in the design of a crown without thorns. Her eyes narrowed to a slit as, her head swinging from side to side, like a winter eagle, she watched the audience. On each claw-like hand, the nails painted red, were large chunks of aquamarine set in gold. During the interval she remained on stage, like some ancient sybil, as elderly women mounted the stage to kneel before her in homage. At the end, waving her jewelled hands at the audience, she rose and walked slowly away, the cloak trailing behind her, and I had the feeling that with her went a whole age. I thought of the opening lines of her poem *Invocation*:

> *I who was once a golden woman, like those who walk*
> *In the dark heavens – but am now grown old*
> *And sit by the fire, and see the fire grow cold,*
> *Watch the dark fields for a rebirth of faith and wonder.*

Making our way home after this recital Hywel said gently, 'Do you realise it's almost a year since we met?' And then he told me of a dream he had had.

'In it I had a telegram saying you had died and I cried as I have never cried. Then I heard you were not dead at all. Later I went into a large building – I think it was a church – and a man was preaching, saying "You must think beautiful thoughts, do good things, then you will grow. This is important." and I felt elated.'

On another evening we went to hear the Welsh poet, R.S. Thomas, reading his own poems for the first time in public at the Montgomeryshire Society in London. He spoke quietly and nervously about the background to the poems which, he said, were written to be read rather than spoken. His large hands, white and awkward, kept plucking at his thick knitted grey socks, while at other times he sat awkwardly, an elbow in one hand,

and the other supporting his chin, the bone of hand, chin and forehead seeming one, as he withdrew deep into himself, 'gnawing the white bone of a problem'.

Somewhere around this time Hywel spoke of wanting to be something, above all, an actor. 'If I don't act, I shan't do anything else. I don't doubt my talent as an actor. I know I can act but it is my stammer that worries me.' That Christmas I spent at the Granary, with Pick lying in her four-poster, the gaslight purring, her hair newly washed, falling to her shoulders like fine pale gold. She laughed with happiness that I was there. 'I've always dreamed it could be like this with you here, but never thought it possible, and this probably my last Christmas.'

Hywel had gone home to Wales for Christmas and the morning he returned he said was, 'wild with wind and the clouds flying low, then the dawn and sun rising. It made me think of Dylan Thomas' line: "By mountains where King Arthur dreams", the mountains seemed so timeless. We must spend one Christmas together in Llangynog.'

Eleanor Farjeon invited Hywel and me and Denys Blakelock to a post-Christmas party at her house in Hampstead. Suddenly Hywel began to recite the Eli Jenkins' prayer from *Under Milk Wood* which he had learnt by heart. He spoke it quietly, intelligently, without hesitation and not a single stammer. At one point he was so caught up in the speech that his head lifted as though to a strong wind, his face shining, on the words 'where the gulls come to be lonely'. Just for one moment he hesitated, a word lost, and turned towards me instinctively, trustingly, his eyes dark and glowing, knowing I would prompt him. It was the first time he had ever done anything like this in public. 'It's been a good day,' said Hywel afterwards.

'*Mai wedi body yn fore dda!*'

And so it was that in 1960 when I went to direct all six productions at the Pitlochry Festival in Perthshire, Hywel joined the company as an assistant stage manager, playing small parts. His very first role was in the opening scene of a new play by R.F. Delderfield, *Napoleon in Love* in which, as a spy, he was asked his name by Napoleon and had to reply, 'Staps!' Being able to master the 's' sound without hesitation proved a great leap forward for him. Later in the season he travelled to London to audition for the London Academy of Dramatic Art, winning a place there, as well as a grant from the London County Council. There was during this year such a sense of his speeding like an arrow to its goal, knowing the direction in which he wanted to go, following his own path to fulfilment. And it was in this summer that our relationship moved onto a deeper level of commitment on both sides.

It was in February 1961 that I wrote in my journal:

> Hywel and I have our second fierce argument in five days
> and these arguments seem a pattern of our life together.
> What terrible forces we seem to unleash in each other.
> They commence usually over some simple statement I may
> have made which he then challenges, his challenge taking
> the form of sweeping generalisations until he appears to
> be verbally attacking me and I am fighting for my identity.
> We seem to be locked in a terrible embrace. It is as though
> the whole fabric of my life, what I am, what I have grown
> to be, is being challenged and discarded. I try to follow these
> intense arguments as rationally as possible, endeavouring
> to maintain an overview, trying to pull him back from
> shooting off at emotional tangents. At such times he is like
> a puppy who, having got his teeth into something, won't
> let go! He says he used to have these fierce arguments with
> Brian, his former flatmate before he met me, and that their
> arguments invariably ended in a fight and were the undoing
> of their friendship which was simply that of two mates
> sharing a pad. I recalled how he had once told me how he
> and another boy from his village, coming home along the
> valley after school, would start to fight. And always it would
> get out of hand. Until suddenly one day he stopped and
> thought: 'What are we fighting about?

Slowly, and helped by the practice of meditation, I learned to anticipate these moments and step aside. Ten years later, however, we suddenly had an argument and I failed to step aside in time. Hywel was lying on his bed by the side of which, on a small chest of drawers, was a plaster replica of the bust of Hermes, an object which meant much to him. In my rage and frustration I picked it up and smashed its head violently against the wall. Hywel cowered back, saying, 'I'll never forgive you for that!' As the broken pieces of the head of Hermes, the messenger of the gods, fell around us I was shaken by the realisation of how easily murder can happen. I was also all too aware of my father's rages which still lay dormant within me. And what shook me further was the immediate recollection of how, only four years earlier, Kenneth Halliwell had murdered his partner Joe Orton, the playwright, in such a rage by smashing open his skull so violently with a hammer that Joe's brains were splattered over the walls and ceiling. Years later I found a bust of the young Augustus Caesar, carved in white marble, which I bought and gave to Hywel. But after that episode there were no more such incidents.

The challenge of all committed relationships is to allow the freedom of individual growth within the container of the relationship. One has to work constantly at a relationship and sometimes it can be painful as bits of the ego are chipped away in the process. As Joseph Campbell once observed:

> Marriage is not a love affair. A love affair has to do with immediate personal satisfaction. But marriage is an ordeal, it means yielding time and again. You give up your personal simplicity to participate in a relationship and when you are giving, you are not giving to the other person, you are giving to the relationship. A marriage is a commitment to that which you are. That person is literally your other half. And you and the other are one. A love affair isn't like that. That is a relationship for pleasure, but marriage is a life commitment.

As Shakespeare observes in his sonnet:

> *Love is not love which alters when it alteration finds.*
> *Oh, no! it is an ever fixed mark that looks on tempest*
> *And is never shaken.*

Throughout the fifty years of our long and loving relationship Hywel and I have confronted difficulties and misunderstandings, never seeking to evade them, enduring a variety of emotional weathers, learning as we journeyed that love has many layers, and deepens with the years. One has only to hang on when the going gets tough in order to discover the deepest layer of all, that of complete and utter trust. Now we are like an old tree that has endured many storms but whose roots go so deep nothing can shake it. And while at the beginning of our relationship I was then in the role of an elder brother, over the years it is Hywel who has taught me so much, so that now we stand shoulder to shoulder. Above all, such love, all true love, should be outflowing, and not self-enclosed, as I had learned from David March.

Which is why Mario Conti, when Catholic Bishop of Aberdeen, now a Cardinal, was so profoundly wrong when he wrote in *The Tablet* that 'there is an endemic instability in homosexual relationships.' Hywel and I are not alone in an enduring same-sex relationship. There are many that have lasted, like ours, for forty or fifty years. Although such enduring relationships may be in the minority, it has to be remembered that homosexual relationships have been made legal only within one lifetime, so that it is only now that same-sex couples are beginning to learn how to create true and fulfilling relationships in the same way that heterosexuals do. Of course there will be those who persist in regarding homosexuality as a sin, a perversion. Yet I recall how, after writing to *The Tablet* in response to Bishop Conti's remark, I received a letter from the Catholic writer Neville Braybrooke, congratulating me on what I had written and quoting what a wise priest had once said to him, 'When it comes to the Day of Judgment God will not ask how many good works you did, but: How well did you love?'

Dom Sebastian Moore, monk of Downside, describes how the official teaching of the Catholic Church is focused on faithful procreative marriage as the perfection of loving sexual relationship and that it needs to re-orient its approach and to explore, not what is or is not 'permitted' but how we should subject our sexual urges to the demands of love and fidelity in relationship. Especially, he adds, for that significant minority of humanity whose sexual orientation is towards the same rather than the opposite sex. Under the guidance of the Spirit, however, he looks forward 'one day to a deeper Catholic understanding of all sexuality. This would point towards sexual desire being fulfilled through faithful, loving relationships, whether hetero- or homosexual.' And, as Father Timothy Radcliffe, reviewing Sebastian Moore's most recent book, *The Contagion of Jesus: doing theology as if it mattered*, in *The Tablet*, writes:

> Desire, and especially sexual desire, is fundamental to our humanity and our search for God; but often the Church has been afraid of desire and has sought to control it and suppress it, fearful of its power, instead of liberating it for its ultimate aspiration, God. The Church works in terms of a narrow understanding of sex as about producing babies, which is why homosexuality is simply seen as a deviance, and is not recognised as offering a love in which God may also be found.

When a friend once asked Hywel how we had first met, he replied quietly, 'It was meant.'

My true love hath my heart and I have his
By just exchange, one for the other given
I hold his dear, and mine he cannot miss.
There never was a better bargain driven.
My heart in him his thoughts and senses guides;
He loves my heart for once it was his own,
I cherish his because in me it bides.
(Sir Philip Sidney)

A THEATRE ON A SHOESTRING

'Why don't we start a theatre here in Hampstead?'

'But where?'

'What about the Morland Hall next to the Everyman Cinema?'

It was as a result of this conversation in April 1959 with the actor and writer William Ingram that the next day, without stopping to consider the consequences, I went off to see the Vicar of the Hampstead parish church and booked the Morland Hall, which was part of the church school, for a series of dates commencing on 24 September 1959 until the following summer.

The tiny cottage in Perrins Court became the powerhouse of this new venture. Because it had once been a shop, the front door opened straight into the front room with its bow-shaped shop window before which was a table where I would sit folding circulars or eating my lunch. Passers-by would peer in and on one summer's day, with the window open, an elderly woman stood looking in.

'This is private!' I said. Without hesitation she snapped back, 'Well, you should draw your curtains then!' and strode away.

Eleanor Farjeon, who was our first patron, gave a launch party in her garden room to which were invited the director Margaret Webster, the actor Walter Hudd, the writer Pamela Frankau, John Fernald, Denys Blakelock and others. I made an impassioned appeal for help, as a result of which some gave donations, some secretarial help and some postage stamps, while others ran up and down the streets of Hampstead handing out leaflets. Ian Norrie, the dynamic and innovative owner of the High Hill Bookshop provided his premises as a box office. During the months of preparation when shillings ran short for printing or props I would spend an evening busking to the queues outside the Everyman Cinema, reciting Dylan Thomas and Shakespeare. I still marvel how it all happened, but it did. The opening production was Saunders Lewis' play *Siwan*, translated from the Welsh by the novelist Emyr Humphrys, with Sian Phillips and Robert Marsden in the leading roles.

It was indeed a venture of faith, a theatre on a shoestring and, as I announced to the local press, 'a thing of passion and vitality; a neighbourhood playhouse for the community of Hampstead.' Little were any of us to know that by the late 1970s it would be a theatre with a national and even international reputation.

The director Norman Marshall in his book *The Other Theatre* describes how as a young man in 1925 he was able to see in the space of one year thirteen plays, including Shakespeare, Elizabethan and Restoration classics, all five of Chekhov's full length plays, as well as works by Molière, Ibsen, Gogol, Calderon, Andreyev, Dostoevsky, Turgenev, Hauptmann and Benevente, while contemporary dramatists included Pirandello, Cocteau, O'Neill, Kaiser, James Joyce, O'Casey and Bernard Shaw – whose *Man and Superman* was given in its entirety that season. Of these plays hardly any was staged in the West End; rather they were staged in a theatre that was struggling for its existence in strange and out-of-the way places such as a drill hall in Hampstead (later to be christened the Everyman Theatre), and the Lyric in Hammersmith which for years had been forgotten and used as a furniture store. Then there was a small cramped cinema at Barnes where the renowned Russian director, Komisarjevsky, performed miracles with Chekhov on a tiny stage with Peggy Ashcroft and John Gielgud, to a backstreet attic in Floral Street, Covent Garden, in which the Gate Theatre, (founded by Peter Godfrey and later to be run by Norman Marshall) had just opened. And, of course, there was the Old Vic, run by Lilian Bayliss, as well as various Sunday night societies which presented one performance only, usually of new plays.

The next flowering of small theatres came in the late 1940s with the Boltons, the New Lindsay, the Embassy at Swiss Cottage, and the Q Theatre at Kew Bridge which presented a new play virtually every Monday. And then nothing until the opening of the Hampstead Theatre Club in 1959, which not only brought theatre back to Hampstead but was the first of what are now known as fringe theatres.

It was because the Morland Hall was used daily for serving school lunches, as well as for Cubs and Brownies, that we could only rent it for Friday evenings and the weekends. We rehearsed across the road in an upper room of The Three Horseshoes pub where our designer Michael Young also built the sets, which then had to be carried across the street on a Friday evening, through traffic and sometimes against howling wind and rain, for our one and only technical and dress rehearsal.

The high spot of that first season of the Hampstead Theatre Club was undoubtedly a double-bill by the virtually unknown Harold Pinter whose first play *The Birthday Party* had been panned by the critics and taken off at the end of the first week only to receive a rave review the next day in *The Sunday Times* from the powerful critic Harold Hobson. It was Hobson who now came to the tiny Morland Hall to review *The Room* which Harold himself directed and *The Dumb Waiter* which I directed.

Harold Hobson wrote:

> What worries me about Mr Pinter is why his plays do not come to the West End. It is a matter of astonishment to me how both the English Stage Company and the Arts Theatre, which can recognise a molehill at five hundred yards' distance, have overlooked this mountain. If you want to see *The Room*, or *The Dumb Waiter*, you have to go to the Hampstead Theatre Club and not the West End. The performances are crowded. Gone is the hostility which, in a moment of collective madness, greeted *The Birthday Party*. Not a jutty, frieze, buttress, nor coign of vantage but has its spectator. If the Hampstead Theatre Club keeps to this standard it not only deserves success, it will command it.

The two plays subsequently transferred to the Royal Court Theatre on 8 March 1960.

I have directed *The Dumb Waiter* several times, both here and abroad. The key to the play lies in a remark that Harold Pinter made on the first occasion we met in a pub off Charlotte Street. Removing his glasses, he leaned intently towards me, saying, 'You see, what I am interested in is: suppose you and I were locked together in a cell, what would happen to us?' And so, in the play, Gus and Ben are locked in a room, the only other character being a dumb waiter which descends with mysterious messages. The suede-shoed sophisticates who packed in to see the play at the Morland Hall would argue intensely over its meaning. To the delight of Harold and myself it was the obstreperous caretaker of the Hall, who begrudged our presence and had constantly to be taken care of with tips, who understood the play intuitively. Of all the productions that season this was the only one he watched during its entire dress rehearsal. Here were two Cockney characters who spoke his language and to whom he could relate. At the end he turned to me, saying, 'Hey, the reason that little fellow gets bumped off is because he asks too many questions, ain't it?' In that one sentence he had grasped the core of the play: if, like Gus, like Socrates, you ask too many questions you are likely to be destroyed.

That first season of the Hampstead Theatre Club, successful though it proved, was very nearly the last. The church authorities felt that we were beginning to get in the way of the Cubs, the Brownies and the school lunches and so we were asked to vacate the premises. It was at this juncture that the brewers Truman Hanbury and Buxton, who owned The Three Horseshoes pub in Hampstead offered to lease us the first-floor room as a small theatre at a peppercorn rent of one guinea a year. A leaflet was printed announcing 'London's first theatre-in-a-pub' with a quote from the theatre critic Kenneth Tynan urging support of the Hampstead Theatre Club as 'a guerilla encampment of experimental theatre.'

An appeal was launched to raise £2500 to equip the space as a small theatre seating eighty-five, and which could be adapted for either open or proscenium-arch staging, drawn up by local architect, Anthony Gough. 'It will be London's first theatre-in-a-pub' wrote J.C. Trewin in *The Illustrated London News*, 'and will continue the aim of providing a community theatre in miniature for the people of Hampstead: another achievement for a young enterprise that is already old in judgment.'

Then, unexpectedly, the Greater London Council insisted on a metal fire escape which would have cost several thousand pounds and as a result the scheme was still-born; although many years later that same room was to become the home of another theatre group, Pentameter Productions.

Finally, after many deliberations, the Hampstead Borough Council voted to give £7000 for the shell of a prefabricated building, seating 157, designed by Anthony Gough, on a site at Swiss Cottage owned by the Council, while I was left to raise £10,000 for the seating, lighting, sound equipment and other furnishings. Although I argued for a larger auditorium as being more realistic in terms of revenue, the Council refused to budge: a short-sightedness which was to create ongoing problems over the next decades until finally, in 1999, the Lottery helped finance the building of a new theatre at a cost of over £13 million. Thus, after some forty years, the temporary, prefabricated theatre was replaced by a larger, and more permanent, building.

On 3 November 1962 Dame Peggy Ashcroft unveiled a plaque marking the site of the new theatre while Dame Barbara Brooke, wife of Hampstead's then MP, Henry Brooke, agreed to chair an Appeals Committee to raise the £10,000. I spent many hours addressing and stuffing envelopes, afterwards tramping around Hampstead and St John's Wood, pushing them through letterboxes, thus learning a lot about the psychology of letterboxes. There were, for example, those that opened with such alacrity that your arm shot through only to be trapped by the metal flap as you attempted to withdraw it. Some were so stiff and unwelcoming that you had to push hard only to have your fingers nipped as you withdrew them. Others exposed your hand to the slobbering tongue and eager teeth of a waiting Cerberus. The worst, however, were those placed at the bottom of the door, which necessitated grovelling on hands and knees in total obeisance. Were these letterboxes, I wondered perhaps telling one something about their owners?

At long last, while the country still waited for its National Theatre, 'London's first civic theatre', as the press chose to describe it, opened on 16 December 1962 on a site that later was to include a swimming pool and library designed by Sir Basil Spence. The new theatre had taken only six weeks to erect but the builders were working on it until the last day. The distinguished audience, which included Lord Cottesloe and other dignitaries, arrived for a performance of Chekhov's *The Seagull* to the sounds of sawing, hammering, and the curtain accidentally opening to reveal me, unshaven, sweeping the stage!

The theatre opened in one of the worst winters, with blizzards. Each day we had to shovel our way through deep snow. There was no money to advertise and few knew where the new theatre was, tucked away, as it was then, behind derelict, bombed buildings that were being cleared for the new library. By 13 January newspapers were carrying reports that 'The Hampstead Theatre Club has been hit by bad weather and is £6500 in the red.'

Weeks of snow, without subsidy, lacking funds for adequate publicity, and the failure of the Appeals Committee to raise the required £10,000, it looked as though the theatre would have to close. I was summoned before the Hampstead Borough Council to explain our failure. It was at this point that, out of the blue, Max Rayne (later Lord Rayne and a subsequent Chairman of the National Theatre) came to our rescue and cleared all the debts. He gave a party at his home to which he invited all his friends, calling upon them to help this new theatre in every way they could.

The Hampstead Theatre Club was the very first full-time fringe theatre with its own premises but unlike the fringe theatre of the 1970s onwards it received no Arts Council subsidy. We had to survive by our wits and talent and a great deal of risk taking. From the start the programme was ambitious. Sets had to be improvised from rubbish dumps and bombed houses; actors were not paid for rehearsals and in performance received £10 a week. We mounted ten productions a year plus late night shows, Sunday entertainments, exhibitions in the foyer, and always a special Children's show at Christmas. And so for seven years, without any aid from the Arts Council, we continued to lurch from one financial crisis to another – but we survived! For those seven years we were a minimal staff on minimal wages, owing much to the support of local volunteers who acted as programme sellers and ushers, operated the coffee bar in the intervals, tended the garden on the patio outside, and regularly met to stuff envelopes with the monthly mailings to members. Everyone wanted to help and felt a sense of pride in making this theatre for Hampstead work. Operating on a shoestring it was solely this sense of passion and belief that made it at all possible. Ironically, today, with increased subsidy from the Arts Council, while office staff proliferate – in some small theatres there are as many as eight people employed full time on marketing – the actors who create the final product continue to be paid a minimum wage!

Our chief frustration in those early years lay in trying to get the critics to cover our openings for, without the means to advertise, we were entirely dependent upon their reviews for publicity. At that time there was no fringe theatre – now an established part of the London scene – and the Society of West End Theatre Managers refused to release dates of forthcoming West End openings, as a result of which our first nights often clashed with those in the West End.

It was at our lowest moment, with audiences often little larger than the size of the casts, that I decided to mount a revival of Noel Coward's *Private Lives*. Coward's reputation at that point was at its lowest ebb but I was convinced it was a work of depth as well as a masterpiece of wit and style. Our production at Hampstead was to result in a major Coward revival which Coward himself subsequently referred to as 'Dad's renaissance'.

While we were in rehearsal I wrote to Harold Hobson at *The Sunday Times*, and who had not yet visited the new theatre at Swiss Cottage, begging him to come and urging London's need for such a small theatre. I then added, in block capitals:

WE NEED YOUR SPACE!

As a result he came to the first night and wrote the review of a lifetime. The other critics followed suit and suddenly the Hampstead Theatre Club was the talk of the town. Importantly Harold Hobson went on to write:

> This is the first time I have been in the Hampstead Theatre. I have seen several new theatres, both in England and abroad, and this one, with the exception of the new National Theatre in Helsinki, excites me more than any. What makes it difficult financially is that it seats less than 160 people. But artistically this is its strength. The best work in modern drama is being done in the genre of intimate plays for small theatres.

Paris has plenty of playhouses for them – the Lutèce, the Poche, the Théâtre du Tertre; but in London there are none. But here, in Hampstead, is just what we need. This tiny, attractive, simple theatre is accurately in the spirit of Obaldia, Arrabel, Genet, Duras. In Mr Roose-Evans it has a director of unusual sensibility and knowledge. It is, of course, early days yet; but in my opinion the conditions are such that this Hampstead Theatre could conceivably do in England work of the value and fame of the Vieux Colombier in France. The trumpets are blowing for other causes than that of Mr Roose-Evans but I hope that amidst the din his clear pure call will be heard. His venture interests me more than anything I have encountered in the theatre of this nature since I first heard of Marguerite Duras' *The Square*.

Clive Barnes wrote, 'This wildly inventive production bursts across the stage like clusters of fireworks,' while Bernard Levin went wonderfully over the top with his 'This revival of one of the most famous plays of the '30s comes from the Hampstead Theatre Club, and if they give us many more like this may their names be blessed for evermore, and may a thousand flowers bloom at every step they take, and may they be heaped with gold and silver and precious jewels and pelted day and night with caviar and roses and bottles of champagne, uncomfortable though such a rain might make them.'!

As a result of all the ecstatic reviews a telegram arrived from Noel Coward in Switzerland announcing that he was flying to England for two days to dine with the Queen Mother and to see the production. However, the only time he could attend a performance was the following Tuesday afternoon and so a special matinée was hastily arranged with an invited audience which was seated by 2.15pm, with the performance due to start at 2.30pm. At exactly 2.20pm a limousine drew to a halt at the entrance to the theatre and out stepped the Master followed by the actress Joyce Carey, Graham Payne, his companion, and Lesley Cole, his secretary. Photographers began clicking their cameras while the Master paused to say a few words to the waiting journalists before proceeding to the auditorium. It was exactly 2.25pm and the curtain rose promptly five minutes later. Even a royal visit to the production (which was to follow in the person of HRH Princess Margaret) could not have been more precisely timed and as one reporter the next day observed, 'The Master's first chuckle came at 2.49.'

In the first interval Coward insisted on being photographed with the two leading actors Rosemary Martin and Edward de Souza. In the second interval he turned to the West End producer Peter Bridge, saying, 'Peter, I want you to bring this into town.' Since he had previously refused to allow a production of the play that had been on tour with Margaret Lockwood to come into the West End, this was praise indeed! At the end of the performance there was loud and deeply affectionate applause followed by cries of 'Author!' Coward stepped onto the stage, joining hands with the five actors.

'Ladies and gentlemen! This has been a lovely afternoon in the theatre BUT!' and here he shot up the famous finger of admonition, 'it wouldn't have been were it not for this delightful cast and this finely judged and beautifully paced production.' He then drove off to dine with the Queen Mother.

The following day Peter Bridge telephoned me to say, 'If I get you Coral Browne, David Niven, Ian Carmichael and David Tomlinson, will you direct it for the West End?' I declined, saying that I owed it to the actors to stand by them – after all, they had received rapturous notices – but also that I had always intended that Elyot and Amanda should be played younger than was the custom. The run was extended, and it was now that Max Rayne organised a Gala Evening to which were invited stars of stage and screen including celebrities such as Lady Diana Cooper, in order to gain us the maximum publicity. Then to the very last performance came the brilliant and innovative West End producer Michael Codron who transferred the production to the Duke of York's Theatre. A few months later my adaptation and production of Laurie Lee's *Cider with Rosie*, transferred from Hampstead to the Garrick Theatre, with Daphne Anderson as the mother, William Squire as the adult Laurie Lee, and Hywel Jones as the young Laurie Lee – for which performance he was nominated by Bernard Levin in *Variety* as 'the most promising newcomer to the West End'. The Duke of York's and the Garrick being back to back, the two casts, on matinée days, would lean out of their dressing room windows and gossip.

'See this if you really care for theatre!' proclaimed Bernard Levin of *Cider with Rosie*, 'to hold the Garrick, if the town has any sense, indefinitely. It is one of the most beautiful, touching, poetic, and imaginative offerings we have seen for some considerable time', while Clive Barnes wrote, 'Once in a while something unexpected happens in the theatre. For me it happened last night.'

For *Cider with Rosie*, Barbara Wilkes, who had designed all my productions at the Maddermarket, created an oval-shaped rostrum tilted towards the audience like an enormous mill stone, suggestive of the steep hills of Stroud and the steep bank on which the Lee cottage stood while, at the same time, suggestive of the womb of the village and family life from which the poet, Laurie Lee emerged. Some dozen chairs and a few props were the only other additions. In order to show the young Laurie in bed with his mother, it was a simple matter of arranging six chairs, three at the head, three at the foot, with a green cloth spread over the two actors like a counterpane. The same chairs quickly became the rows of desks at the village school or when placed in pairs down the slope of the rostrum, with the entire cast waving handkerchiefs and singing 'One man went to mow a meadow,' they became the charabanc taking the village on its annual outing to Weston-super-Mare. When the chairs were placed around the perimeter of the disc, the actors sitting astride, alternately rising and falling to the accompaniment of hurdy-gurdy music, and flashing coloured lights, the whole stage became the roundabout at the fair. Placed end to end with low lighting through the backs of the chairs, casting tiger stripes of shadow across the stage, they became a winter hedge at sunset. Finally, as the cast entered singing, 'We plow the fields and scatter', and placed the chairs upside down, slanting diagonally across the stage, they became the sheaves of corn in the field where Loll drinks cider with Rosie and has his first experience of sex.

Laurie Lee had only given permission for the play to be done at Hampstead and was reluctant for it to go any further, in spite of the rave reviews. He did not come to the first night but sent friends to report. Later he came, unannounced, to watch a performance. In part he found it difficult to accept the idea of young adults playing not only himself, his brothers and sisters, but doubling as other characters. Also, it was reported to me, Laurie was not at all happy at my adaptation being likened to Dylan Thomas's *Under Milk Wood*. Because Michael Codron was so keen to bring the production into the West End he and I drove down to Stroud to have dinner with Laurie in an attempt to persuade him to change his mind. It was after midnight in his cottage at Slad, surrounded by jars of homemade wine bubbling in the background, that Laurie turned to Michael and asked, 'How much do you really want to bring this in?'

'Whole-heartedly!' replied Michael.

Laurie paused and then said, 'For the sake of the light in the eyes of those young actors I will allow it to go into the West End but no further.' After its West End run Laurie refused to allow my adaptation of his book to be published or staged for many years. Even though another, more naturalistic adaptation by Nick Darke, was doing the rounds, he continued to veto my version for twenty-one years.

For Sunday evenings I began to pioneer a series of events under the title of 'An Evening with...' featuring such celebrities as Harold Pinter, Lord David Cecil, Huw Wheldon, John Mortimer, Fenella Fielding, Dame Sybil Thorndike, Malcolm Muggeridge.

MALCOLM MUGGERIDGE

The most successful of these evenings was undoubtedly that with the latter. Having grown up on the Herbert Farjeon–Hermione Gingold type revue I was interested to see if a new form could be created, dealing with contemporary issues. I wanted to turn the genre on its head and produce a darker kind of entertainment with a Swiftian bite to it. Malcolm Muggeridge, then at the height of his television fame, seemed the perfect maverick for such a project and so I wrote to him. He replied by return, inviting me to lunch at his home in Robertsbridge in Sussex.

As we drove through the country lanes I told him that I was hoping to direct Christopher Fry's play *The Boy with a Cart* and I was wondering how to portray the Chorus, described as 'The People of Sussex today'.

'My dear boy,' replied Malcolm, 'they are all tycoons with whorishly painted wives.' This would indeed, I thought, be a novel way of opening the Fry play!

Over lunch we began to explore his ideas for a new type of revue but it soon became apparent that he could not write dialogue. It was then that I suggested he adapt his book *The Thirties* for the stage, opening with a carousel on which would be seated the key figures of the period: Chamberlain, Hitler, Baldwin, Churchill, etc, all going round, up and down, on the whirligig of time. Again, however, dialogue was his stumbling block. Concepts and style were his forte, not to mention punctuation: 'Use punctuation marks as plentifully as you would the pepper pot!'

Finally I suggested we create *An Evening with Malcolm Muggeridge* to which he responded, saying that he would like to talk about those books and people by whom he had been most influenced, with Eleanor Bron, Leo McKern and myself reading excerpts from the books.

The evening at Hampstead was packed, with people sitting on the gangway steps, and so we then mounted it for a four-week run, as part of a season of documentary plays which included the production by Patrick Garland of John Aubrey's *Brief Lives*, with Roy Dotrice giving a now legendary performance as an Elizabethan Muggeridge. The Evening with Malcolm was sold out in advance and Donald Albery then invited us to do a season at the Albery Theatre. Suddenly, at the last moment, Malcolm withdrew, saying, 'I really can't bear having to listen to myself saying the same thing night after night!'

I often wondered whether this was due to an incident one night during the run at Hampstead when Eleanor had said to me, 'I can't bear to sit there night after night listening to Malcolm saying such idiotic things about education!'

'Well, why don't you say so this evening?' I replied. That evening, just as Malcolm began to pontificate about education, Eleanor made her protest. From that moment on Malcolm never repeated his views on education at that point in the programme. He was like a man who had been winded. He adored Eleanor and once confided to me, 'Had I been twenty years younger I would have been ringing her up constantly, sending her flowers, and creating all sorts of complications. Is this age, do you think, this retraction?'

It was his wife Kitty who more than anyone really understood him, and I found it deeply moving to observe how in old age they had grown together again. My lasting memory is of the two of them, seated at their kitchen table, their wrinkled hands clasped together.

It was through Malcolm that I met Leonard Woolf. Believing in the commitment of two people to one another, and knowing of the way Leonard had supported Virginia during her periods of depression, I wrote at Malcolm's suggestion to Leonard Woolf asking if I might go down to Rodmell in Sussex to visit him. He replied by return, inviting me to tea.

LEONARD WOOLF

In a room smelling of cats, wood smoke, geraniums and old books, seated in a high chair, his long head seemed carved out of the trunk of a cherry tree, while a drop of moisture hung like a miniature stalactite from the end of his nose. 'We used to play all Beethoven's quartets on that machine there, record by record,' he said, pointing to an old-fashioned wind up gramophone with a large lily-shaped trumpet. 'You had to rewind it after each record so that it took a long time to listen to each quartet, but it also gave you time to really absorb them.'

As he spoke he lifted one arm and, high above his head, his trembling fingers twisted and untwisted his thick boyish silver hair. He began to talk about the various gardeners he had had. 'I've had one for twenty-four years, one for twelve, and one for five. My first gardener was called Bartholomew.

He was a farm labourer and his wife had been a lady's maid. They met in Brighton. She was the daughter of a Colchester miller and so a cut above him. She kept the house and he learned how to garden and became very good at it. My wife used to tease Mrs Bartholomew and say to her, "One day you'll come into a fortune!" Well, one day Virginia and I came in from our walk and Mrs Bartholomew was standing at the sink, washing dishes, and she said, "I've come into that fortune, Mrs Woolf!" An aunt who lived in Italy had died and left her two thirds of her fortune. Mrs B asked me to manage her affairs, and I arranged to give £2000 to the aunt's companion who hadn't been left anything. It still left Mrs B with £10,000 which was a lot in those days. Finally Mr B had a cataract and was persuaded to go into hospital but he wouldn't stay there. He got up and came home and refused to be operated on. So he went blind. He used to sit in the basement, but he wouldn't go anywhere else. Mrs B was a real nagger, never stopped talking, and sometimes he'd go mad and chase her all round the house!'

Walking round the garden, the dog racing ahead, he observed how the heron had eaten fifty of the goldfish in the pool. 'I've always had animals of one sort or another all my life. We used to have spaniels.' Malcolm had told me that when Virginia decided to take her own life she first drowned her beloved spaniel, knowing she would then have to follow.

'I've never had an otter, but I used to have a marmoset and kept him for five years which is a record. They are terribly susceptible to cold and draughts. He used to perch on my shoulders but often he would snuggle inside my jacket. Do you know that stretch of road outside Orleans? It's ten miles straight to the horizon. I had an old Lancaster and was driving at seventy miles per hour with the hood down, and the marmoset in the back seat. I'd forgotten all about him until suddenly he was on my shoulder, biting my ear, and furious. He didn't like the draught!

'He used to escape up trees. In order to get him down I would put honey on an old tin lid, place this inside a butterfly net and then, climbing a ladder, try and tempt him down. Once, at dusk, he climbed the lime tree by the back door and just wouldn't come down, whatever we did. My wife and I stood there. And I kissed her. Well, that did it! Immediately he made such a noise, chattering away, and was down that tree in a flash, furious with jealousy! So after that, whenever it happened, all I had to do was to kiss my wife!'

Back in the house we sat in the kitchen, eating homemade cake, he holding his cup with trembling hands because of his Parkinson's Disease, and talking of the various actors and actresses he had known, especially Sybil Thorndike, Peggy Ashcroft and Paul Scofield:

They're not like actors; you think of them as real people. I remember Enid Bagnold, the playwright, shouting over the church wall to me about Edith Evans, 'The Dame doesn't know her lines!' Enid's hat had blown off at the Goodwood Races and she called in to see us, thinking we'd understand. Poor Enid, she never felt she was a real professional!

ENID BAGNOLD

I'm delighted that Leonard Woolf should have mentioned to you the talk over hedge. I was looking at the churchyard and saw a grey head appearing and disappearing. A weeding gardener? And then I thought, but it's Leonard Woolf! Dare I? Shall I? and did. I'm so glad I did.

Enid Bagnold had sent me a copy of her most recent play *Call Me Jacky* which everyone else had turned down, with a note saying, 'I am like a beggar with a little talent to sell, and no market.' Shortly after this came an invitation to visit her in her home in Hove.

She had first made a name for herself with her novel *National Velvet* which was subsequently made into a film starring the young Elizabeth Taylor. Of her subsequent novels *The Squire* is one that deserves republication, hailed at the time as an important mark in feminist history for she was the first to write frankly about the pains as well as the joys of giving birth. But the play by which she is best remembered is *The Chalk Garden*, which owed much to the brilliant editorial imput of the Broadway producer Irene Selznick who, over a period of two years, made Enid rewrite until it was in a form ready for the stage. By the time I met her, her husband Sir Roderick Jones had been dead a number of years, and she was an old woman frightened by death, and bitter that she was not recognised as the playwright of the century, nor had been made a Dame of the British Empire.

She was seated in a small courtyard off her garden, having tea with the actress Kathleen Nesbitt, who had been one of Rupert Brooke's lovers and who, even now, was strikingly beautiful. As birds swooped and darted, Kathleen, with fingers stretched diagonally from arthritis, splashingly poured the tea while Enid sat plump, sturdy and erect, like a small girl on a pony, holding an umbrella against the sun.

'Once in church I knelt and prayed, with my teeth on the wood of the next pew, "O God, make me famous!"'

'Well, you are!' laughed Kathleen.

'Not enough – not blazingly! I am paid out for wanting fame for such bad reasons. That damned ambition! Oh, I've been what I wanted to be – a writer. I wish I had been a better one. I would have bartered love for that. I would rather have had fame and been a virgin for seventy years!'

Slowly we walked through her kingdom of small gardens, paddocks, orchards, kitchen garden, stables: the beds all carefully weeded, the edges of the lawn neatly trimmed (the gardener even kept a daily diary of the garden). Her husband had originally bought the white clapboard cottage that had belonged to the painter Burne-Jones and then gradually acquired the other adjoining cottages until they became one dwelling with thirty rooms. 'And for his eightieth birthday,' said Enid, 'I built on a thirty-first room for him!'

Opening off her study was a small conservatory where she bedded out seeds and small plants on shelves. 'I'm not allowed to stoop or garden anymore. That's what age does to one.'

Most of the rooms smelled of neglect. Shelves from floor to ceiling were crammed with books, tables piled high with manuscripts, documents and journals; while every bit of wall space was crowded with paintings, framed photographs and letters (one from Charles Dickens). Most of the frames had pieces of paper stuck on with Sellotape and each inscribed in Enid's handwriting: 'Given to me by.... especially drawn for me by.' It was as though the house were a museum of her own ego. Why does she place these labels on the front, and not on the back? I wondered. It was like her conversation, peppered with the names of the famous and yet, how quick she was to blame for the failure of her plays those actors who had starred in them: Sybil Thorndike in *Call Me Jacky*, Edith Evans in *The Chinese Prime Minister*, and John Gielgud and Ralph Richardson in another. 'I have been writing plays for twenty years,' she said bitterly, 'and except for one, *The Chalk Garden*, they have not been a success. Now it's too late. Do you think you can persuade Celia Johnson to do my play? Is there a chance you'll do it at Hampstead?'

THE FIRST SEVEN YEARS

In those first seven years at Hampstead we presented new plays from Australia, Africa, America and Europe, alongside new plays by John McGrath, John Bowen, James Kennaway, Peter Terson, Peter Kenna, Donald Howarth, David Hare, Barry Bermange, Jack Pulman, Giles Cooper, Colin Spencer, Frank Marcus, Andrew Sinclair, Kenneth Ross, Tennessee Williams and Clive Exton.

We also mounted classics, often with large casts, ranging from the extraordinary 1500-year-old Sanskrit classic *The Little Clay Cart* which had never before been staged in England and which I directed, to Euripides' *Hippolytus*. I also commissioned from Peter Luke an adaptation of Fr. Rolfe's novel *Hadrian VII* which, unfortunately, was too ambitious for us to stage, and was given its première at Birmingham, subsequently transferring to London, with Alec McOwen receiving rave reviews for his performance as Pope Hadrian. Another innovation was the mounting of seasons with a theme, from *The International Theatre Season* (with plays by Strindberg, Feydeau, Durrematt, Duras) to *The Living Theatre Season* which was a programme of documentary plays including Michael Hastings' *The Silence of Lee Harvey Oswald*, Patrick Garland's memorable adaptation and production of John Aubrey's *Brief Lives*, to Heinz Kipphardt's *In The Matter of J. Robert Oppenheimer*.

This latter, taken from the actual trial records of the American physicist was a play that at the time no one dared risk publishing or staging, because of the threat of massive libel writs from those depicted in the play. I was determined, however, that it should be staged. Our solicitor Laurence Harbottle said that the actors would have to be warned that there might be only one performance of the play and that he himself would need to be in the audience on the opening night, ready to receive any writs that might be served. I replied with some passion that I was prepared for the theatre to be closed down but that we had to do the play. Fortunately the first performance passed without any trouble and the production transferred to the West End for a short run and was subsequently published.

By Christmas 1964, with the Boroughs of Hampstead, Holborn and St Pancras about to merge into the Greater London Borough of Camden, Max Rayne felt that it was high time this so-called 'civic theatre' should receive civic support and so he tactfully withdrew. Without Max's generosity and enthusiasm the theatre would not have survived its first two years at Swiss Cottage. Even so, it was to be seven lean years before the theatre finally received Arts Council support.

In 1965 a report was drawn up for the new Camden Council in which I pointed out that our policy was to present a vital and varied range of plays appealing, not to a single coterie, but to the many tastes and temperaments that are to be found in any community. As I saw it this was essentially a neighbourhood playhouse similar to that of the Neighbourhood Playhouse in downtown Manhattan.

John Mortimer, in his introduction to the report, wrote:

> In the pages that follow is set out, in all modesty, a record of one of the most remarkable and exciting achievements in our local life. The Hampstead Theatre has been built on nothing but devotion, enthusiasm, artistic integrity and private charity. The devotion, enthusiasm and integrity will continue; the charity cannot, nor should it. It must be time that we made ourselves responsible for a theatre that has proved itself so completely. It no longer has to be argued that the provision for live theatre is a public service which we need as much as baths, libraries, drains, schools, and dustmen. Investment in a living theatre is purely practical; we need to produce informed and enlightened citizens if our businesses are to expand; we need to provide a full local life if our towns and boroughs are to prosper.
>
> A healthy theatre must be able to afford to take risks and make discoveries. It should at least pay its actors a wage they can live on and work in dignity. Its Director is as important to the community as a local Editor, Doctor, Headmaster or Clerk to the Justices. His salary should not be that of a competent typist. The new buildings at Swiss Cottage in Sir Basil Spence's design, establish our right as citizens of Camden to read Chaucer or James Bond, learn Judo or Fencing or the crawl, in the best and most pleasing surroundings. None of these is less important than the theatre: the theatre is the living commentary on all we do. Where it is lacking it has to be built up but where it already exists it must surely be supported.

It was a masterly defence by an eminent barrister and playwright. Due in part to his championship there then began discussions with the local authority for a new, purpose-built theatre which, as I wrote, 'must serve the community, have ample foyer and restaurant space, as well as room for lectures and seminars, demonstrations and exhibitions. *It should provide a meeting place throughout the day.* A theatre is the coming together of people under one roof, sharing in a common experience, and going to the theatre must become as simple and as natural as going to the library for a book or to the pool for a swim.' Today I find it very satisfying to see the new theatre humming with activity, from young people's workshops, and various study groups, as well as locals using the foyer as a place to meet and have coffee or a snack.

In the early years I was often challenged: Why, if it is London's first civic theatre was it a club, restricted to membership? There were two answers to this. One was that the annual membership fee was our main source of income for several years. The other answer was that as a theatre club we were not subject to the Lord Chamberlain's censorship. Even so, in January 1967, we incurred the wrath of our principal champion Harold Hobson when, in a review of Colin Spencer's *The Ballad of the False Barman*, he was so disgusted by the sight of a male bottom that he wrote: 'It is hideous and disgusting and should be stopped. The licence our stage has arrogated to itself goes far beyond any limits which a decent society should permit. There is today a campaign to get the censorship abolished. What in actual fact is needed is that the Lord Chamberlain should exert over theatre clubs as well as theatres the authority which a recent legal decision has shown that he possesses.'

Within months, however, the Lord Chamberlain's powers were finally abolished, thereby enabling Colin Spencer's next play, *Spitting Image*, to transfer to the West End. The play is a satirical comedy about two young homosexuals, one of whom has a baby by the other, an event which throws the medical and political worlds into a conspiracy to hush up the whole matter lest other gays should follow their example. I was attracted to the play because it not only dealt brilliantly with homophobic attitudes in society but also for the way in which the author so movingly portrayed the two central characters who were, as the critic John Russell Taylor observed, 'an entirely believable married couple, living and growing together and apart. Few heterosexual plays have done this so well.'

But although the Lord Chamberlain's office had been abolished there remained a vociferous element of the public which continued to exercise its own censorship: the Gallery First Nighters, a coterie of theatre-goers led by 'big Sophie' who, in her youth, so it was reported, had been a groupie of Tallulah Bankhead. During the final scenes of the play on the first night at the Duke of York's Theatre I was startled by prolonged and ugly sounds coming from the gallery. Racing upstairs I found Sophie and her friends in the front row of the 'gods' booing and jeering. The actors had ground to a halt but, leaning over the balcony, I called out to them to continue. It was clear that Sophie and her gang were determined to wreck the play as, only a few months earlier, they had booed and heckled at the first night of Joe Orton's *Loot*. By delaying their protest until the closing moments of the play they had skilfully avoided being ejected.

Quite early on I had received a letter from a student who lived in St John's Wood, who was waiting to take up a place at London University to read English. He was, he said, very excited by the whole idea of a theatre for Hampstead and asked if he could help in any way. He was surprised, as he later told me, to receive by return a letter, followed by a phone call inviting him to help out in the box office at £1 a week. Little did he know how desperate we were or how much we had to rely on voluntary help. As the person in charge of the box office was leaving, this student's letter was indeed timely. His name was Nicholas de Jongh, later to become the formidable theatre critic of *The Evening Standard*.

After a while, emboldened by his success at being appointed to such a responsible position, he went to our able administrator Richard Cottrell to ask if his salary could be raised so that he might at least cover his fares. Richard, who had worked for Prospect Productions after coming down from Cambridge, and was himself a talented director, had a very bad stammer which he also knew how to use most effectively when negotiating business deals! On this occasion it was very pronounced.

'Well d-d-dear! You sh-sh-shall have… ' and here followed an interminable pause as his lips vibrated until finally, he stammered out, 'th-th-thirty shillings a week!'

Those early years owed almost everything to the shared commitment of those involved, in creating, often literally, something out of nothing. We were never able to afford understudies but there was one occasion when this nearly caused us a very real problem during Andrew Sinclair's adaptation of Dylan Thomas' *Adventures in the Skin Trade*. This was the production that Antonioni came to see twice and, as a result, cast David Hemmings, who was playing the young Dylan, in his first leading role in the film *Blow Up*.

Barbara Keogh who was playing Robert Eddison's wife suddenly announced that for one performance she would not be able to arrive until the interval as she was filming. There was consternation until Bridget Turner, who was playing opposite David Hemmings, said, 'Well, Jimmie must go on for her!' And so, for the first and only time in my life, I became a transvestite. I quickly learned the lines, got into the costume – the high-heeled shoes were not easy – and played my scenes with Robert Eddison. In the interval Barbara arrived and took over for the second half. The strangest thing is that nobody in the audience appeared to notice any difference! Certainly no one made any comment afterwards.

TENNESSEE WILLIAMS

Tennessee Williams came twice to see this production and wrote me a fan letter, saying how much he wanted me to direct one of his plays. 'God knows,' he wrote, 'I have waited a long time to have you direct a play of mine, especially since I saw what you did so marvellously with *Adventures in the Skin Trade*: your wildness, your sense of fun, your way of making a difficult thing work.'

We had met originally as a result of my having been sent a copy of his play *The Milk Train Doesn't Stop Here Anymore* which had just opened to disastrous notices on Broadway with Tallulah Bankhead in the lead. In spite of the reviews I was riveted by the play and sent Tennessee a ten-page analysis of it, together with a copy of *The Epic of Gilgamesh* as a gift.

> Dear Jimmie,
>
> I went home to Mother at Easter and when I got back last night I found your package containing Gilgamesh, your letter, and your marvellous synopsis explication of my play. I took the published version home with me and started to tackle again its many problems, the principal one being its lack of concentration, excess superfluity.
>
> You see the design of the play as it should be, the tent-posts of it. That's why I feel it would be wonderful if we could spend some time together somewhere, sometime soon, perhaps in Ischia? To 'smooth down the matted hair', to borrow a phrase from Gilgamesh, and to anoint it with the oil of a sure direction. I think if we can get *Milk Train* finally right, I will be happy to confine myself, henceforth, to simpler undertakings. The meaning of the play is like a sentence on a blackboard which is scribbled over with irrelevancies so that the true sentence can hardly be noticed.
>
> I read Gilgamesh till I fell asleep last night. It is enchanting. I read it every night and the poetry moves me deeply and it puts me in the mood for work the next morning. I am going out now to a showing of Orson Welles' great film, *Citizen Kane*. In theme it is very close to *Milk Train*. It is one of those spring days that remind you New York is a seaport, so I will say *au revoir* and go out wandering.   Fondly, Tennessee.

Whenever Tennessee was in London, Hywel and I would go out for a meal with him. Often we would meet in Gerald Street at the home of his great friend Maria St Just. Sometimes he would sit drinking brandy, abstracted, swivelling his eyes, cracking his jaw and lolling his tongue.

'Ten, stop cracking your jaw and rolling your eyes!' Maria would say. Often he would appear completely withdrawn. Once he surfaced to say, 'I am gonna read you a poem of mine. It's guaranteed to make you laugh!' The poem was about two guys meeting in a hotel and having sex. Afterwards, each lights a cigarette and they fall asleep with the cigarettes in their mouths. 'And that's how big hotels come to be burned to the ground!' is the last line of the poem. I thought of this some years later when I was on a lecture tour of America and staying in a small hotel in Charlottesville in Virginia. On the table beside the bed was a printed notice asking one not to smoke in bed, and adding, 'if, however, you insist, please inform the management where you would like your ashes sent.'

Sometimes with Tennessee I would wonder, where was the real man? Perhaps the work was the man and everything else a drifting mass of sensibilities? Would he ever find a true friend again? It was his restlessness, plus an increasing addiction to drugs, that had destroyed the one true friendship of his life, with Frank Merlo, affectionately known as the Horse. Tennessee was incapable of being monandrous. They parted. When Frank died of cancer of the lungs (he was a heavy smoker) Tennessee never really recovered. It was at this period I met him and in his first letter to me he wrote, 'Love is a green and fertile place. Since Frank's death there has been no love in my life. There is only work.'

Sadly I failed to get a production of *The Milk Train* off the ground. Then Tennessee entrusted me with the English première of his most recent work *The Two Character Play* which I directed at Hampstead with Mary Ure and Peter Wyngarde. The play was deeply personal to Tennessee, being based upon his relationship with his sister Rose, who had spent the greater part of her life in a psychiatric institution. In the play two leading actors, brother and sister, are on tour with a two-character play and arrive in some kind of no-man's land at a theatre where there is no staff and no audience. I was moved by Tennessee's trust in me for he regarded the work as 'my most beautiful play since *Streetcar*, the very heart of my life.'

The production was sold out in advance. Harold Hobson in *The Sunday Times* wrote: 'The audience listened with absorbed attention, but it would be rash to say they were not bewildered.' In *The Observer*, however, Ronald Bryden wrote: 'It seems to me his finest work for a decade, the most successful piece of sustained theatrical writing he has achieved since the first act of *Sweet Bird of Youth*. It is good to see the poet laureate of lost grip recover his own.' Tennessee continued to rewrite the play and another draft was later performed in America under the title *Outcry!* It remains a densely written and often obscure piece but, nonetheless, a work of importance in the whole canon of Tennessee's writing as reflecting his continuing obsession with his sister Rose.

Finally, after seven years, the theatre received official recognition. The producer Oscar Lewenstein, one of our Board of Directors, and I were summoned to St James's Square where we were ushered into a large room, in the corner of which was a desk. Behind this loomed the large figure of Lord Goodman, black tufts of hair springing from his ears. He listened to us attentively and then, lifting the phone, dictated in immaculate prose, without any hesitation, a letter saying why the Hampstead Theatre should be given a grant. I was subsequently, with Lord Goodman's permission, even to the illustrations by Brian Robb, to create a central character named Mr Goodman in my sequence of children's books, *The Adventures of Odd and Elsewhere*.

BEYOND THE THRESHOLD OF WORDS

From 1959 onwards, with first the responsibility of launching the theatre and then from 1962 in the new theatre, the stresses and strains of mounting ten or more productions a year, under-staffed and overworked, left little time for experimentation outside of the narrow confines of particular productions. After ten years I and everyone else were still being paid a pittance. I had no assistant, there was only one secretary, no full-time press representative and only temporary script readers. It was little wonder that I began to feel I was on a conveyor belt and yet, as we entered our second decade, it seemed to me important that rather than rest on our laurels or collapse from exhaustion, or seek greater financial gain elsewhere, we should be taking time out to search and research.

In his journal the sculptor Isamu Noguchi wrote: 'I wanted to find other means of communication – to find a way of sculpture that was humanly meaningful without being realistic, abstract and yet socially relevant. I wanted to find out what sculpture was all about. Sculpture, I felt, had become a captive, like the other arts, to coterie points of view.'

If one substitutes for the word 'sculpture' the word 'theatre' then this sums up exactly my own feelings and reflections during the latter half of the 1960s. It seemed to me that the drama in England was merely repeating itself in various styles of naturalism and that it was being saturated with words. It is not that I despise words, quite the contrary, but that I sensed the need to go beyond the threshold of words.

It was at this juncture that David Herbert of Studio Vista commissioned my next book *Experimental Theatre*. It was as a result of researching for this book, as well as experiencing the work of many of those in experimental theatre at that time, including Martha Graham, Alwin Nikolais, Peter Schumann and his Bread and Puppet Theatre, the Living Theatre, the Squat Theatre, The Polish Laboratory Theatre of Jerzy Grotowski, The Roy Hart Theatre and others, that my own thoughts became clearer about the direction I wanted to take.

Then in 1968 I was encouraged to apply for an Arts Council Bursary and on St David's Day that year I flew to Finland to work for a month with young actors at the National Theatre in Helsinki. Those four weeks were to provide the time out for reassembly that I needed. It was as a result of the work done with those young actors that I decided the time had come for me to form a theatre workshop where I could pursue the exploratory work I had done in New York. This I decided would be the experimental wing to the Hampstead Theatre and for that reason I called it 'Stage Two'. From Finland I began to write letters to colleagues in England, outlining my ideas: a small core of actors to train for twelve months without any need to perform publicly during that time. They would not, during this period, work on any specific texts but explore images and create their own works. In order to achieve this they would need to do intensive work on movement and voice, acquiring a variety of skills.

On my return I laid my plan before the Board of Directors who gave it their blessing, and an appeal for £10,000 was launched. The long haul had begun again.

'THERE'S DUST EVERYWHERE!'

George, Barbara Hepworth's assistant, was chipping at a dome of stone, his blue beret, overalls and face covered in fine white powder. 'There's dust everywhere!' chuckled Dame Barbara as she appeared in the doorway of her studio at St Ives, leaning on a stick, her hunched shoulders giving her the appearance of an owl. 'Marble, stone, plaster — there's dust everywhere. It even leaves white footprints all the way down the street!'

It was March 1969 and I had travelled down to St Ives to try and persuade her to create a setting for Stage Two in which the audience would arrive in a Hepworth landscape and pass through before taking their seats. As the action unfolded, this landscape would be transformed by lighting as well as by the actors' use of it, elements of which would be able to pivot, glide or be elevated. At the end the audience would once again move through this landscape but seeing it now in a different light. I wanted the setting to be part of the action rather than merely a decorative background. Dame Barbara had written back, inviting me to visit her, but pointing out that she felt her designing days were over as she was severely crippled with arthritis. She had only twice before designed for the stage: once for Michel St Denis' production of *Antigone* in which Peggy Ashcroft had played the lead, and once for Michael Tippett's opera *A Midsummer Marriage*.

We sat in her large upstairs room which was crowded with furniture, statues, paintings, and cupboards full of rare glass which she had been collecting over the years, and fur coats thrown down anywhere. After tea and chocolate biscuits she produced chunky glasses into which she poured generous quantities of whisky, while she chain-smoked from a box of cigarettes at her side. 'This year I shall have lived in St Ives for thirty years. I am torn between the Aegean and this part of Cornwall. Here you have the sea on both sides so that you get the sun and the moon in the sky together and we also have the Northern Lights. Nature has to be the inspiration. Life and art are affirmation. We must go on creating else the world and the Philistines will close in. Sadly I see too many young sculptors who have lost their roots as well as all sense of tradition.' Hearing about the intensive movement training planned for the actors of Stage Two, she spoke of how when she was younger she used regularly to attend a ballet class and later loved to watch the Diaghilev Ballet in rehearsal. Returning home from a day's work in her studio she would always put on some music and dance to it, finding this relaxing.

'In sculpture there's a need to walk around and through it, sensing also with one's feet. It is my feet, as much as my eyes, that know this place with all its ramps and steps, hills and twisting lanes.'

In responding to my ideas for a décor that would involve both the spectators and the actors she told me about her most recent work for Japan, a small maquette of which stood on the table at my side, which had three interlocking screens with a hole in each 'so that people can sit in one, lean through the second, and climb through the third'.

'Sculpture is no longer something to be admired on a pedestal. I love to see my work out of doors, at different times of the day and the year, perhaps mantled in snow or fallen leaves, gleaming in the rain, or looming out of a thick sea mist. I love, too, to watch people in a landscape, especially when they are alone, perhaps silhouetted against the sea, or hurrying along

Oxford Street, their noses way ahead of them! And I love sitting in St Mark's Square in Venice and watching people enter the challenge of that space: some clinging to the sides and others striding boldly across!'

It was dusk and someone came in to switch on the lamps. She struggled up with the aid of her stick, making her way across the room.

'I'd like to give you this,' she said, handing me an artist's proof of one of her most recent lithographs, entitled '*Ithaca*', knowing that I shared her love of Cafavy's poem of that name.

'It will remind me of journeys yet to come!' I said, as I looked at its abstract suggestion of a ship sailing towards an unknown horizon.

STAGE TWO

Over the months I auditioned actors, looking for those who were physically free, emotionally open, and imaginative in their responses, as well as willing to commit themselves for a year. The final company was composed of Hywel Jones, Kevin Costello, Paul Saunders and Di Trevis, who later went on to direct at the National Theatre and at the Royal Opera House. On 26 May 1969 we began, at first in various rented studios while I continued the search for permanent premises. Finally we negotiated to rent 109a Regents Park Road, a Victorian church hall that for forty years had been used as a wood veneer factory, Souhami and Sons, but had been standing empty and neglected for the past two years. It was filthy inside with both dry and wet rot. However, we set about the task of cleaning, stripping and renovating. Occasionally passers-by would look in, but not offer to help – appalled, I think, by the task in hand. By June, I, too, had begun to realise the enormity of what we had taken on, and that we could not attempt it all ourselves as well as continue the daily training and research. Suddenly I thought of the actor Raymond Platt, who had been at RADA, and who lived nearby and who was, I knew, extremely practical: how practical I was only later to discover. I called round to see him, to ask if he could help.

'Yeah! I could take that on.' He yelled upstairs. 'Hey, Fella!' A lanky, begrimed youth appeared, with a shaggy mongrel behind him. 'Fella, this is Jimmie. He wants some help with a building down the road. You'd like to work on that, wouldn't you?'

It transpired that Fella, also called Derek, was heaving sheets of iron in Camden Town and was bored with it. He was saving money to go to Gibralter and from there planned to go round the world, working his passage.

The three of us, followed by the dog, then walked to Regents Park Road to inspect the property. Raymond, small, urchin-like and dynamic, began to make a list of tools he would need for stripping, sanding, sealing and cementing. I agreed to pay them ten shillings an hour, and sighed with relief. But whenever I could I would spend four or five hours a day, heaving out rubbish and pulling up the rotten wood block floor in the smaller hall.

In the weeks that followed Raymond was like a Napoleon, directing operations with the authority, temperament and eccentricity of a great general. At intervals we all worked under his instructions, while the Friends of the Hampstead Theatre lent a hand painting the 60ft-high walls of the main hall which was to be our performing space. Frequently Raymond would disappear into clouds of dust like a miniature Elijah. Once, receiving an electric shock, he fell off the scaffolding tower, 40ft high, laughing all the time but totally unharmed. Outside the building Fella, swinging an iron bar to remove the large enamel signs 'Souhami – Wood Veneers', had one fly back at him, vooming like a thunder sheet. As blood gushed from his hand, he looked down at it, grinning. 'Now I've given my blood!' he said.

One night, passing the building, we noticed lights on and went in. We found Raymond, washed, shaved and jacketed, walking up and down, elegantly smoking a cigarette.

'I feel like Wagner!' he grinned.

He had that day completed the rewiring, and fixed studio lamps in the hall which were now turned up to illuminate the raftered roof.

'I've decided to paint the roof white,' he announced. 'That way it will reflect the light off the floor, especially when I've sanded and sealed it. Underneath all that dirt you can see the wood is a rich golden colour.' Raymond had a vision of the building and already with one wall smashed through, a floor ripped up, and the walls thrice washed and painted black, the identity of the building was beginning to emerge. He was already making shutters for the windows, and creating a 'green room' for the actors, and had painted the floor of the office yellow. Continually he planned, improvised, invented. Without him it would not have been possible.

After three months we began to focus on our first work, an exploration of what we felt to be the last taboo in our society today: Death; and which we entitled *Deaths and Entrances*. Slowly we began to assemble images. We imagined commencing with a procession of shrouded figures, some walking, some being trundled in wheelbarrows – 'Let the dead bury their dead'. We explored images of death as a sleep and graves as beds. We examined images of claustrophobia and the fear of being buried alive. We read about the background to All Souls' Night as well as the many versions of the Resurrection story, and Gilgamesh's search for everlasting life. We looked at recurring images of a Final Judgment and listened to a recording of Benjamin Britten's setting of the *Lyke-Wake Dirge* with its reiterated

This aye night and every night
And Christ have mercy on my soul.

This led us to consider Requiem Masses and the Book of Job with Job's cry (which we used in the final work): 'Why dost Thou hide Thy face from me? Show me my iniquity!' Slowly this first work became a dramatic meditation on death: seeing death in its many forms: from the death of a love, a relationship, to the death of an ambition, as well as physical death, for we die many times in one lifetime.

So it was that day after day, week after week, through many improvisations, a pattern began to emerge. We worked daily from ten in the morning to eight in the evening. One day Di Trevis, returning to her partner, was asked what she had been doing. She replied, 'I've been sweating all day over a hot thigh!'

10,000 MILES ACROSS AMERICA

In October of that year I went to America on a ten-week lecture tour of Women's Clubs and universities to raise money for Stage Two. The tour had been organised for me by Malcolm Muggeridge through his agent in New York, W. Colston Leigh, who was the top agent for such tours. Malcolm advised me to wear a very good pair of shoes. Why the latter? I asked.

'Because, dear boy, seated at a table on a platform, that is what the audience is going to be looking at!' The other valuable piece of advice he gave me was always to start with a joke – 'That relaxes an audience!'

I went armed with a glossy brochure bursting with quotes from Noel Coward, Tyrone Guthrie, Sybil Thorndike, Michael Redgrave, Tennessee Williams and Harold Hobson. On arrival in New York I went first to meet Mr Colston Leigh who had once been a champion heavyweight boxer. Unlike his top lecturers I was low down on his list but he still took 50 per cent. Towering above me, he boomed, 'I have only two pieces of advice to give you. One: it is no good being just good in this game; you have to be superlative!' I replied that I intended to be, and then asked him for his second piece of advice.

'You will find that the Women's Clubs are not interested in what you have to say – only in *touching*.' Although mystified by this remark I was soon to learn what he meant.

My first engagement was with the Women's Club in Houston, Texas, newly opened by Princess Alexandra, and set in parkland. I arrived to find a red carpet and canopy at the entrance, and a liveried attendant to greet me. Inside were Aubusson carpets and Impressionist paintings. In the new chandeliered dining room some five hundred ladies in flowered hats were about to sit down to a vegetarian lunch. I was sat at a table on a platform with the President of the Club. Behind us, against a large window a curtain was drawn. As I rose to speak I could see the silhouette of a mouse running up the material. At once I screamed and stood on my chair and so, faithful to Malcolm's advice, got my first laugh.

After reading a selection of poems and answering questions I descended from the platform and moved among the tables. It was then that I discovered the meaning of Colston Leigh's remark. At once the ladies began to surround me, touching my arm, caressing my silk cravat, and murmuring, 'Oh, he's so purty!' I began to feel like a relic of Olde Engand as one after another told me how their great-great-grandfather, or mother, had come from England, and so on.

At the universities I spoke about theatre and especially about what was happening experimentally. I had already had several books published, two of which were then on the reading list of campuses at that time: *Directing A Play*, and *Experimental Theatre*, while the latter was on sale at every major airport in the United States.

At Raleigh, North Carolina, I was met by Dr James Elder and a group of his students of Elon College. The following morning I was driven by one of the students to Sunday brunch at Jim Elder's house. Wearing a Union Jack apron with the words 'Sir Jim Elder' stitched on it, he was busy cooking bacon and scrambled eggs, with Earl Grey tea to drink, and Oxford Cooper's Marmalade for one's toast. Becoming aware of a continuous background of music and then of cheering crowds, horses' hooves, followed by a fanfare of trumpets, I suddenly realised that we were listening to a recording of the Queen's Coronation. Then, as the assembled congregation in the Abbey began to sing the English National Anthem, the students and Jim Elder stood to attention, joining in the anthem which they sang with increasing fervour as they reached the phrase 'God save *our* Queen!' It was like stumbling into a secret society of Anglophiles. I asked if they were doing this just because I was there. 'Oh, no!' they replied. 'We do this every Sunday morning!'

SHADOW PLAY

Before leaving for America I had suggested to the actors at Stage Two that they might experiment with shadows and shadow play. By the time I returned they had mocked up a huge screen and begun to project images onto it from behind, using torches and various props. In many ways this work, called *Dreams*, was perhaps the most accessible. Of it Nicholas de Jongh wrote in *The Guardian*: 'It is the twenty minutes long *Dreams* which marks the experience and achievement of Hampstead Theatre's experimental wing, Stage Two, as important. It is possessed of real missionary gleams, and the team of actors are in full command of their material. This could grow into something of true theatrical significance.'

By May 1970 we had completed the removal of the gallery at one end of the hall but then came a shock. The seating, which had been ordered months before, could not be installed until a day or two before the official opening on 2 June and meanwhile the cost had doubled. Tickets were already on sale, newsletters mailed, posters distributed, and still we had no staff, not even a stage manager. Most worrying of all we had no money in the bank while bills, including the next quarter's rent, were mounting. Consistently the Arts Council ignored our applications for aid, as also did the Greater London Arts Association. Then, at the last moment, we were saved by a generous loan from Eddie Kulukundis, with the result that on 25 May the scaffolding for the seating arrived. Eddie was a Greek ship owner, a millionaire, who passionately loved the theatre, and eventually became a West End producer, later marrying the actress Susan Hampshire.

In the following days we painted, sawed, and swept, sweat streaming down, and then we rehearsed. The actors had wired up lamps, built platforms, removed the hundred-year-old iron gallery, sewn the costumes, made the props, solved all design problems, and done their own stage management. In a very special way they had not only created the works they were about to perform, but they had made the building their own. And so on 1 June, after only twelve months' research, Stage Two presented its first two offerings, *Deaths and Entrances* and *Dreams*, with a programme note which stated:

> The aim is not work for its own sake nor as a kind of private
> therapy, but for an audience. It is important to stress this.
> The whole point of the Stage Two workshop is to search
> and research; to experiment, to make mistakes, to grow, and
> then share this work in performance, making no claims. In
> five years, perhaps, we may be able to say we have achieved
> this or that, but not now. This is only a beginning.

This note was added because I knew that certain individuals at the Arts Council, and others, had begun to regard what we were doing as private therapy, totally ignoring the hard discipline and professionalism of the work. By 2 July the bank manager was refusing to advance any more money and on 20 July we received the final rejection by the Arts Council of our third application for funding. In reporting the Council's decision the letter stated that 'the Drama Panel had not liked the first programme.' Apart from the question of what 'liking', a purely subjective response, has to do with Government funding of the arts, this statement was wholly false. We had kept records of every person who came to the performances and in fact only one member of the Drama Panel had been, and that was the theatre critic, Ronald Bryden, who in *The Observer*, had praised the company's achievement. 'Unlike the failed ballet that so often passes for avant-gardery' he wrote, 'this is properly trained, professional, authoritative. With this augmented armoury you can imagine the actors tackling works buried till now under the limitations of traditional theatrical skills'. Similarly, in *Dance and Dancers*, its editor, Peter Williams, had written: 'This is obviously a laboratory situation of the highest order.'

Each day the future seemed more bleak, approaching a cul-de-sac. On 3 September we performed various exercises and some new sequences for a small select audience which included Ron Vawter, then a leading member of the Wooster Street Theatre group in New York, and Anthony Strilko, my composer from the Julliard days.

'You are much too modest,' said Strilko. 'It is very exciting. There is nothing like this in New York.' After lunch that day I talked to the actors, explaining that I had failed to raise any more money. I had already given all my savings, as well as my royalties from my West End production of Jack Pulman's *The Happy Apple*, the play which made a star of Pauline Collins. And so I said we must close. We cleaned the building for the last time and I departed once more to America to raise money to clear Stage Two's debts.

At the obvious level Stage Two as an experiment was clearly a failure. Had it received Arts Council support and been able to go on to explore specific texts as Ronald Bryden had suggested, it might have been very different. In the eyes of the Board of Directors of the Hampstead Theatre Stage Two had failed and pressure was eventually brought on me to resign. I was given a cardboard handshake of £250. There was no farewell party, and I walked out into the wilderness. Had I been more streetwise I would have anticipated all this and networked to secure another appointment.

However, the following decade in the wilderness, when it seemed I had had my chance and blown it and was now without a base from which to work, was to prove productive in unexpected ways. I had founded a theatre against the odds, with little practical experience of running a theatre. I had run it for nearly ten years on a shoestring, directed four plays in the West End, written a series of children's books, as well as two books on the theatre, and done two long lecture tours of America. It was time to take stock and stand still. A character in Charles Morgan's play *The River Line* says at one point:

> *O proud, impatient man, all owe to Earth*
> *Her seasons. Growth and change require their winter*
> *As a tired child his sleep. Thou art that child;*
> *Lie down. This is the night. Day follows soon.*
> *Wake then refreshed, wiser for having slept.*

INTERVAL

The following few years were a hand-to-mouth existence familiar to the vast majority of actors, directors, designers and writers who work in theatre. I directed a number of commercial tours, including one of *Private Lives* with Joanna Lumley and Simon Cadell, several productions at the Shaw Theatre including *The Taming of the Shrew* with Susan Hampshire, a production of *A Streetcar Named Desire* in South Africa, and an experimental version of Sophocles' *Oedipus* for the Contemporary Greek Theatre in Athens. I was chosen by Harold Hobson as his successor to be the chief adjudicator of the National Student Drama Festival, and also the National Drama Festival of Zambia. I made trips to America to teach and lecture, was a regular book reviewer and, in my capacity as a children's author, I made visits to schools and libraries. On one occasion I and a number of other children's authors travelled to London from Birmingham with 400 children en route for the Children's Book Fair. Each compartment had its own author telling stories. In my carriage I spread the rumour that there were fleas on the train. When we arrived in London 400 children dismounted, frantically scratching and saying, 'There's fleas on the train!'

One of the most unexpected and creative challenges was an invitation from the National Trust to create a Victorian Extravaganza at Plas Newydd in Anglesey. Spread over three evenings, it took nine months to plan, and there were scores of events in different parts of the grounds. Each evening as Queen Victoria arrived in an open landau, ten trumpeters appeared on the roof to blow a fanfare of welcome. Then, at the end, as night fell, Queen Victoria would appear on a floodlit balcony to speak to her people in Welsh and in English. Below her, some thousand spectators stood with flaming torches and sang the National Anthems of Wales and of England. But this was not the climax! As the orchestra began to play Handel's Fireworks Music, so a display of fireworks exploded over the Menai Strait, with Snowdon in the background.

Then in 1979, the year my mother died, I was encouraged to apply for the post of Reader in Drama at the Middlesex Polytechnic (now University). I was given instant tenure – which meant I could not be sacked – the relief of a regular salary and the promise of a pension at the end. However, all my initiatives to break new ground, to create a really radical and professional programme, were met with resistance. After three months I handed in my resignation. More than anything, however, I had come to realise that, tempting as it was to have financial security, academia was not my world. It felt too much like a betrayal of the real theatre to which I belonged. My passion and my greatest joy is working with actors in the creation of a production. And so, although I had no job to go to, I once again walked out into the unknown.

In the summer of 1980 I went to teach a course in experimental theatre techniques in Grand Rapids, Michigan. My assistant and chauffeuse there, Susan Kruger, to whom I shall always be indebted, gave me as a parting gift a slim volume of the letters between Helene Hanff and 84 Charing Cross Road, the antiquarian bookshop of Marks and Co. It was in this way that I came to acquire the rights to adapt it for the stage, an event that was to prove the turning of the tide in my outer journey in the theatre.

However, it was when I was invited to direct the Chester Mystery Plays for the 1973 Chester Festival that another and quite unexpected stage in my inner journey was to unfold.

MYSTERY

Dean Addleshaw, I have a problem. What did Jesus wear at the resurrection? We read that the shroud was neatly folded in the tomb. Was Jesus naked, or had he found a local tailor to run up a suit for him? What does the actor playing Jesus wear?

At that moment all the clocks in the Dean of Chester's house began to strike and chime the hour of seven in the evening. 'Dear me!' replied the

Dean. 'No one has ever asked me that before! I shall have to consult my books. Can you come back in three days?'

In the autumn of 1972 I had been invited by Alexander Schouvaloff, Director of the North West Arts Association, to direct the Chester Mystery Plays for the 1973 Chester Festival of the Arts. The plays, presented every five years, were usually spread over two evenings: the Old Testament on one, the New on the other, and repeated over a period of two weeks. My brief was to prepare an adaptation and production that could be performed nightly. Alexander Schouvaloff also suggested I bring a fresh approach to the plays and break with the customary style of production which employed some two hundred local people, all in medieval costume, together with pupils from the local ballet school as angels.

Throughout the early stages of preparation I had in mind that our audience would not be wholly Christian, while many would be agnostic, even atheist. How was I to communicate these stories to them? Krishnamurti once remarked that if only we could read the Bible as great poetry it would yield up many more levels of meaning, and so I was determined to approach the plays on an archetypal level, seeing the stories as myth. As Joseph Campbell says: 'Myths are stories of our search through the ages for truth, for meaning, for significance. Myths are the clue to the spiritual potentialities of human life.'

Thus the story of the Garden of Eden is a metaphor for a very real human experience. The loss of innocence, and its corresponding movement towards new knowledge, is something we all experience. And so, in staging this scene, I had all the women play Eve and all the men Adam, with everyone eating apples.

It was only after auditioning several hundred local people that I finally selected a company of thirty actors, plus a group of scruffy small boys on bicycles who were to be the angels, delivering their messages, ringing their bells boisterously, singing *Glorias* hoarsely, always a little breathless with excitement, and often late!

For the following nine months I travelled up to Chester every weekend. I began with workshops for ten actors at a time. The aim was to build up an atmosphere of trust in preparation for when all three groups would come together. These sessions enabled me to observe more closely the actors I had chosen, for it was to be several months before I cast the various roles.

One weekend was spent exploring the Lord's Prayer. Curiously the Chester Cycle gives nothing of Christ's teaching and so I decided to insert into the second half both the Beatitudes and the Lord's Prayer. As Jesus spoke the prayer so the others repeated it after him, phrase by phrase, each in his, or her, own way. Thus the all too familiar words, chanted in rote and at a gabble as they usually are in churches, became a living reality for each actor.

The day that the full company assembled for the first time was a shock. Suddenly it seemed like a lot of people and yet all too few for the task ahead. I suggested we all sit in a circle, close our eyes, and out of the silence speak whatever was our strongest thought. One senior drama lecturer commented on the unique experience of the workshops, how they had all been able to relax because there was none of the customary pressure to get the show on. Another, a teacher, observed how the improvisations had given her the feeling of belonging to a group, of being totally at ease and able to reveal her deepest emotions. For myself I spoke of how inadequate I felt to the task, not in any negative sense but in the realisation of my responsibility. In *The Tempest* Prospero says, 'I have promised to deliver all', and at such a moment a director cannot but feel like Captain Cook leading his sailors on a voyage into the unknown. Over the remaining months we used these Quaker-like silences on a number of occasions.

Alexander Schouvaloff had suggested that I stage the plays inside a big top on the Cathedral green rather than in the open air as in previous years. With the help of the designer Bruno Santini I designed a large circular stage from the centre of which rose a 30ft-high pine tree, its branches lopped off to short stumps. This was the Cosmic Tree, the axis between Heaven and Earth, down which Lucifer at the start descended. Later, hung with baskets of apples, it became the Tree of Knowledge of Good and Evil in the Garden of Eden. It also served as the mast of Noah's ark and, at the end of Part One, when Mary enters the Temple for the blessing of her child, it became a giant Christmas tree, hung with evergreen garlands and storm lanterns. In the second Part it became the Cross. The auditorium, which seated eight hundred, was arranged in a semi circle, and the actors wore their own clothes for the production.

Religion is in essence symbolic, speaking of truths beyond finite comprehension. One of the most valuable of Jung's achievements was to have re-opened the way to symbolic thinking, enabling us to appreciate and understand the religious ideas of every culture, and to rediscover them for our own generation. And so I knew that when we came to the staging of the Last Supper and of the Crucifixion we had to avoid the conventional representation of those scenes. In such instances one always goes back to the text to ask: What is really happening here? It is what in the theatre we refer to as the sub-text. One of the books we studied was *The Ceremonies of Judaism* by Abraham Z. Idelsohn from which we learned that from the oldest times the Jews have celebrated their festivals with special lights, the obligation to kindle which rested on the women. Also, before all meals at which bread is served, the devout Jew is obliged to wash his hands and while doing so pronounce a blessing. This is because he is to be purified for the table, just as a priest is for the altar on which sacrifices are to be made.

Jesus, however, took the traditional Passover meal and charged it with new meaning as an agape, a love feast in which the body of the beloved is eaten. The more I meditated on the Last Supper I saw it as a mandala with Jesus at the centre, himself the feast, ringed round by his disciples, and the whole enclosed by a circle of fire like the tongues of flame at Pentecost. And so, at the beginning of the scene, the entire company entered singing an Alleluia. The women, each with a towel over an arm, carried wooden bowls filled with water, and stood around the perimeter of the circular stage, while the men washed their hands. The actor playing Jesus remained in the centre, naked to the waist, wearing white cotton trousers. The men then lowered over his head a circular cloth that had a hole in the middle until he was standing in the centre of the cloth, tucked in at his waist, and the disciples kneeling round him, holding the material taut, so that it had the appearance of a round table. While this was happening the women re-entered with seven-branched candelabra holding lit candles which they set down in a circle around the stage. The women then remained, kneeling, for the rest of the scene.

Jesus, taking a flat circular loaf, blessed and broke it, leaning forward from the centre of the 'table' to each of his friends in turn, saying 'Eat my body.' And similarly, after passing the cup saying, 'Drink my blood.'

One Saturday I took the men for a special session relating to the Last Supper. Seating them in a close circle I asked them to focus on the young farmer who was playing Jesus and to be aware that this was the last meal they would have together. They were to memorise this moment for all time, rather like Garbo as Queen Christina in the film when she says, 'I am memorising this room. In the future, in my memory, I shall live a great deal in this room.' The hour, the place, each other's faces, the departure of Judas, everything that Jesus had said and done, even though they could not wholly understand it, they were to be conscious of, knowing it was for the last time. I wanted the intensity of this moment to communicate itself to the audience. Then at the end they were to sing a hymn, as the disciples did, before leaving for the Garden of Gethsemane. For over half an hour the actors sat in silence and then very quietly they began to sing:

Abide with me, fast falls the eventide,
The darkness deepens, Lord with me abide!

As they sang, so the words gathered an intensity of emotion peculiar to the situation, the disciples looking to Jesus on the words 'I need Thee every passing hour' and he, the actor playing Jesus, looking upwards, towards his Father, on the words 'O Thou, Who changest not, abide with me! Help of the helpless, O abide with me!'

During the singing of this hymn the actor playing John spontaneously reached forward to touch the hand of Jesus who sensing this, took hold of his hand and then with his other reached for the hand of Peter. One by one the actors began to link hands as they knelt in a circle. Slowly the actor playing Jesus lifted them to their feet, raising their hands in the air like a benediction and then, deliberately, letting go, breaking the link – for they must learn how to detach themselves from his physical presence. Gently he took John's hand and placing it in the hand of Peter, sealed up the ring once again, while he stood outside, ready to depart. It was out of many such improvisations that the whole production grew.

The scene that took the most preparation and was only possible because of the months of workshops was the staging of the Passion and the Crucifixion. In one of our group discussions we talked about the Crucifixion as an historical event, but then went on to ask: What is crucifixion? Daily we crucify one another: husbands and wives, parents and children, teachers and pupils, politicians, clergy, civil servants. We are all guilty of cutting one another down to size, castrating one another emotionally and psychologically, dragging people down into the mud. It was this sudden appearance of the word 'mud' which finally led the way into how to stage the scene.

The actor playing Jesus stood in the centre of the stage, facing Pilate, while the rest of the cast stood upstage, holding long poles with which they began to taunt Jesus, elongating the sounds of the word 'Ba–ra–abbas!' into a frenzy of hatred and rejection. At the climax of sound, one of the actors began to throw mud at Jesus, and the entire cast began to drag him around the arena until he was blackened from head to foot, finally thrusting him up onto the tree where he hung suspended from two of the stumps. There, in long elongated sounds, he cried out repeatedly, '*Eloi! Eloi! Lama Sabachthani!*' ('My God, my God, why have you forsaken me!') Slowly, as they realised what he was saying, the rest of the cast began to climb the tree until they all hung from it like a swarm of bees, taking up the cry of '*Eloi! Eloi! Lama Sabachthani!*' over and over.

For what we had realised is that Calvary is both the experience of one person in history as well as a universal experience. For has not each one of us, at some moment or other, had this feeling that God does not exist and that life is without meaning? As in the great aria of lament in Gluck's *Orphé*, when Orpheus sings, on the death of Eurydice, 'What is life, if thou art gone, Eurydice?'

As a result of this new way of seeing the Crucifixion, avoiding the conventional image of the Cross, many non-believers and agnostics who saw the play were deeply moved. There were also those Christians who were shocked, while many, especially monks, nuns and priests, wrote to say how deeply they had been affected, shaken and even changed by the experience. The intensity of hatred in the cries of 'Ba-ra-abbas!' and the voice of Jesus cutting across this with the long phrases of '*Eloi! Eloi! Lama Sabachthani!*', the actor's voice spanning several octaves, was something the actors never lost. The whole sequence of the Lamentation from the Cross lasted seven minutes, a very long time in theatre. Always, of its own volition, it would cease and then, in the ensuing silence could be heard the voice of Jesus saying, 'It is finished!'

Alexander Schouvaloff came to see a run through.

'Months ago I explained to you that I wanted this production to break away from the traditional presentation in the manner of a pageant and, instead, be done in such a way as to be meaningful for today's audience. Well, your production and your company succeed in a way which I never imagined or hoped for, by creating something really wonderful which makes sense and will make people think. It is, of course, a production which people will not expect and perhaps one which some will not like. This is what I really wanted. It is also funny. The total balance is there. Your production is a re-discovery and your company of actors make it so. I do not think that professional actors could achieve this degree of commitment.'

The production broke all previous box-office records, and the theatre critic Andrew Porter, who had just returned from reviewing Peter Brook's *Orghast in Persepolis*, wrote *in The Financial Times*:

> This is an exhilarating, exciting and moving experience, and Mr Roose-Evans has come closer to catching the spirit of a communal and contemporary dramatic presentation of matter familiar to all – closer to the spirit of these mystery plays – than one could have thought possible in the twentieth century. The actors played, declaimed, moved freely and fully, without self-consciousness. Ian Lever's strong, unaffected Christ, and David Burrows' shining Abraham and also Peter, were exceptional.

After the final performance David Burrows handed me a poem:

> *We must not weep at end*
> *For there is no end.*
> *We are not what we were.*
> *We cannot lose what we have gained.*
> *We have met, we have touched each other with smiles,*
> *Exchanged unknown emotions.*
> *We have embraced without shame.*
> *We have met for a reason,*
> *A brief interlude in time,*
> *And so we part, the purpose done.*

In *The Empty Space* Peter Brook wrote, 'The search today is for a necessary theatre, one which is an urgent presence in our lives, speaking to its audience at a depth of feeling that precedes the dissection of man into social and psychological categories, *speaking to a man in his wholeness.*'

This production of the Chester Mystery Plays was, and remains for me, one of the most fulfilling experiences of my life, drawing upon my work in New York and with Stage Two. It made me reflect more deeply on the teachings of the Gospels, on the role of the sacred in our lives and the deep hunger in people for the things of the spirit, and, above all, there came with it the gradual awareness of another door opening.

ACT FOUR

ANOTHER DOOR OPENS

As I stepped forward and knelt down it felt as though I was being buried alive in a cave of darkness as the Bishop's hands pressed down firmly on my head, while the hands of some fifty clergy also hovered over me. It was as though I were being pushed down under the waters of this new baptism. Then, as the cloud of hands withdrew, I was released and stepped back, shaken and shivering. Now the cloud was moving in again for the next candidate, followed by the same solemn and unwavering words of consecration.

For three days, those of us who were to be ordained in July 1981 in Hereford Cathedral by Bishop John Eastaugh, had been in retreat at the Bishop's Palace. Unable to find anywhere quiet in the house, I had gone across to the cathedral hoping to find somewhere there where I might spend the next two-and-a-half days. As I entered the cathedral I was greeted by a blare of music and spoken commentary from a television screen showing a film about pilgrims. I fled from this to the Lady Chapel and knelt, but even there the ceaseless coming and going of tourists made it difficult to focus. It was then that I noticed a small chantry chapel to one side, the door of which was locked. Obtaining a key from the head verger I proceeded to lock myself in.

Above the altar hung a two-dimensional portrait of Mary and the Child in carved and painted wood. The sturdiness of the baby sucking at the mother's teat, its hands reaching up to hold each side of the breast with a passionate intensity, like that of a lover, moved me deeply. As I made this the focus of my meditation so the organist began to play Bach's *Wachet Auf* – *Sleepers awake!* which he had played some months earlier for my mother's funeral in the Lady Chapel.

From time to time tourists would try the handle of the door but, finding it locked, went away. Then, on the second day, as I lay prostrate on the floor before the Mother and Child, I heard someone try the door. I took no notice. Then came a knock.

'Who is it?' I called out.

'It's Kevin! May I join you?'

It was one of the other ordinands who clearly had experienced the same difficulty in finding somewhere quiet to meditate. So then there were two of us in that chapel. Later, when Kevin had left, I curled up embryonically on the floor of that womb-like space and gazed at the Child suckling at that eternal fountain. I allowed thoughts, images, to flow freely, as I absorbed the deep eroticism and spirituality of this image, and I was filled with joy in the concentrated stillness of that small chapel, knowing that on the next day some 1500 people would be filling this cathedral and with one voice affirming their wish to see us ordained. These were now my last minutes in the chapel before Evensong after which the cathedral would be closed until the morrow. What had those last minutes to say to me? What had this chapel of the Mother and Child to say to me over and above the deep comfort it had given me? As I lay prostrate, allowing blessings to descend, I prayed for an increased awareness of what it is I have to give, or what might be given through me.

On the final evening we were all gathered for the Bishop's Final Charge:

> You are called, not to do a job, but to live a life. From tomorrow your lives will be different. You will be leaping into the void. Until you have made the leap you cannot know what sacrifices and demands will be asked of you. Before, life was easier, your own. But in the void are God's arms and you will be leaping into them. He will never ask of you anything for which He has not prepared you, and for which He will not give you the strength.

It is not surprising that that night I had the most appalling nightmares of being trapped in violent, bloody and dangerous situations with death the only way out. Two weeks later I began rehearsing my production of *84 Charing Cross Road* in Salisbury.

ONE MAKES A PATH BY WALKING

How did all this come about? Although without any religious background as a child – as a family we never went to church – nonetheless, from an early age I have always been conscious of another and deeper dimension to life, one that led me first to be confirmed as an Anglican, and then to be received into the Catholic Church, and all this was deepened by the years of Jungian analysis. Eventually I ceased practising as a Catholic and whenever I had to fill in a form requiring me to state my religion I would write the single word 'Seeker'. Then, in the late 1950s, a School of Meditation was set up in London. I enrolled and was given a mantra. The process was complicated, however, by the fact that every week the voluntary counsellors kept changing and each seemed to give contrary direction. In the end I stopped going and persevered on my own. This search for a deeper spiritual centre was happening at one of the most demanding periods of my life when I was founding the Hampstead Theatre in London.

Throughout this time my parents were unofficially separated, my father having gone to live and work in America. Then in 1970 my mother informed me that my father was returning to England and that they had decided to live together again. They were then both in their seventies. 'Is that wise?' I asked.

And so the search began for a house large enough for us all. In August of that year my mother found The Old Rectory at Bleddfa in Radnorshire, a move that was to have unexpected consequences. Bleddfa itself was a hamlet with a scattering of farmsteads and cottages and less than a hundred inhabitants. It had an inn, a school, and in those days a tiny shop which also functioned as a sub-post office.

My father returned from America and within weeks the drinking and the rows were resumed. My mother had a small heart attack and the local doctor was sent for. Taking me on one side he said bluntly, 'There is only one thing wrong with your mother: your father!' and so I had to break it to my father that he should return to America, saying that it was no one's fault: 'It's just that you and mother don't get on.' In the years of my growing up I would dream of avenging myself on him and yet when the moment came I found I had mercifully moved beyond such adolescent fantasies and was able to understand him as well as what I had inherited from both of my parents.

The house being next to the village church, I felt it my duty to join the tiny congregation of four whenever I was in residence. Then, in 1973, the Rector informed me that the church was on a provisional list for closure. For a year I pondered this. Having founded a theatre on a shoestring, the last thing I wanted to do was to get involved with a church in the least populated county in Britain (which also had no traffic lights)! Eventually I asked the Rector to come and see me, and said that if he wanted to save the building it was no good waiting until it was declared redundant, for by then it was usually too late. I suggested that, while continuing to be used as a place of worship, it could be developed as a Centre for Sacred Art, offering a programme of exhibitions, seminars, retreats, concerts and workshops. I wrote to George Pace, then the leading church architect in Great Britain, who generously gave his services in drawing up a scheme for re-ordering the church so that it could be used in a variety of ways. At the launch of our appeal in 1974 I said that we had only to reach out our hands to share, and other hands would come to join ours in an ever-growing circle of friendship. It was in this way that the Bleddfa Centre for Caring and the Arts (later to be re-named as A Centre for the Creative Spirit) was born, based on my belief that the arts should nurture and enrich people's lives. It was registered as a charity, The Bleddfa Trust, with the aim of 'providing a centre for those seeking through prayer, through the arts, and through encounter with others, a deepening of spiritual understanding.' And over the years it has, as a local doctor remarked, become a place of pilgrimage.

There is a Buddhist saying: 'Look at the ground on which your own feet stand' and another, 'A journey of a thousand miles begins on your own doorstep.' One starts with what is at hand; and so the long hard slog for funding began, especially as it was discovered that the roof was held together simply by inertia: the wooden pegs holding each stone tile having long rotted. In the end, aided by grants from the Historic Buildings Council for Wales, and the Welsh Churches Act, the entire roof had to be re-battened, re-felted, and re-tiled, one major beam replaced, two new sets of trusses installed, the pews taken up and replaced with chairs, the choir stall pit filled in, and much of the floor re-laid with stone slabs, while the whole building had to be rewired.

There began a programme of concerts by Leon Goossens, the York Winds of Toronto, the Claydon Ensemble, and others, together with workshops on the environment, retreats, special days for children, and exhibitions of work by artists such as Thetis Blacker, and Peter Eugene Ball.

I wrote hundreds of letters and the money came in, but there was opposition from a number of local inhabitants. One woman tackled me in the churchyard saying, 'It's evil what you're doing!' And because we had workshops on meditation another inhabitant spread the rumour that we were smoking pot in the church! Interestingly most of the opposition came from those who never came anywhere near the church.

What changed this situation came about on one Christmas Eve. On Christmas Day the usual congregation of four people increased to seven and

I suggested to the Rector that if there were to be a simple service of carols and readings on Christmas Eve he would find the church packed because, I argued, this is very much a threshold time when people feel utterly lonely: their children having grown up and left home, or partners having died. He resisted this but I persisted until he said, 'Oh, all right then, provided you organise it and all I have to do is give the blessing at the end!'

Instead of the usual rows facing the altar, all the chairs were placed in a circle, several rows deep, around a manger filled with straw. The church was packed with church and chapel people as well as visitors. The raftered roof was softly illuminated but otherwise there was darkness: a warm hushed atmosphere as everyone sat pondering the words, 'The people that sat in darkness have seen a great light.' Then, at a given signal, from outside, the village children, wrapped and muffled against the cold, could be heard singing a Gloria, as they advanced up the path with a boisterous ringing of handbells, gourds, tambourines and drums. Inside, everyone waited. In the porch there was a hushed consultation and whispers of 'Go on, Robert!' Robert gave three loud bangs on the doors of the church.

'Who is it?' I called out.

'It is the Christ Child!' he answered, to which I then replied, 'Let the Christ Child enter!'

The doors opened and the children appeared, two-by-two, carrying tall candles, farm lanterns, baskets of mince pies, and finally a brother and sister bearing a life-size figure of a naked new-born male child which they placed in the manger. Candles were distributed and lit and then, very softly, all joined in singing 'Away in the manger'. The faces of young and old, church and chapel, believers and non-believers, friends and visitors, were reflected in the light from the flickering candles. Melodion, cello, flute, made music, as carols were sung, a poem read, then a short meditation and prayers, then more carols. The mince pies were blessed and then people began to move about quietly, eating mince pies, drinking coffee, talking, not wanting to leave, staying for over an hour, content to be there in the candlelight, in the warmth and security of that ancient house of prayer, with the winter dark and cold outside.

In 1983 came the opportunity to acquire the village school which had closed because of lack of numbers. With its closure the village seemed to go dead; parents no longer gathered to deliver or collect their children, or gossip in the little shop. I was determined therefore that it should remain a public building, drawing people to the community, and not be converted into a bungalow. Once again I sat down to write hundreds of letters. Aided by grants but also, once again, by the contributions of many hundreds of people, the school was converted into a gallery, tea rooms and shop, with a landscaped garden (made possible by a grant from the Prince of Wales' Trust) and the whole formally opened by the Marchioness of Anglesey.

A few years later some adjoining land, plus two tumbledown barns, came on the market. Thanks to three individuals who gave generously, as well as a grant from the Foundation for Sport and the Arts, Bleddfa now has a handsome Shaker-like Barn Centre, which comprises a large studio, reception area, and small meditation chapel, built around a central courtyard with a fountain. To one side is an orchard, and below is a large meadow used for parking.

In AD 2000, to mark the Millenium, a statue of Tobias and the Angel was commissioned from the Irish sculptor Ken Thompson and unveiled by Dr Rowan Williams, then Archbishop of Wales who, subsequently, as Archbishop of Canterbury, has become the Centre's chief patron. A Bleddfa Annual Lecture was also set up with its first speakers including Neil McGregor, Director of the British Museum, the Right Revd Dr Rowan Williams, Archbishop of Canterbury, Sir Peter Maxwell Davies, Master of the Queen's Music, and Jonathon Porritt, CBE.

In all the ebb and flow of fortunes that the Bleddfa Centre for the Creative Spirit (as it is now named) has experienced since 1974 it has continued to explore the relationship between art and life, between the creative and the spiritual, for I believe that the majority of people possess, no matter how unused, real creative and imaginative faculties, so that the question is less one of educating people to appreciate the fine arts than of providing facilities and environments in which they can be and are actively encouraged to use their own creative faculties. In her novel *The Rector's Wife* Joanna Trollope observes how 'so many people lack the capacity to live life richly at any level.'

In the Barn Centre at Bleddfa, in the reception area, are some words by Lorca, painted on wood by the calligrapher John Hencher:

> *The poem, the song, the picture*
> *Is only water*
> *Drawn from the well of the people*
> *And it should be given back to them in a cup of beauty*
> *So that they may drink*
> *And in drinking*
> *Understand themselves.*

Those words sum up for me what the Centre for the Creative Spirit represents. True creativity is closely linked with the inner spiritual life of each person. Yet strangely this is an area in which the Church, in general, still shows little interest, despite Rowan Williams' observation that we 'need to encourage creative expression in everyone, as this is a way of helping us to be fully human.' Or as the writer, Jeanette Winterson remarked in a radio interview with Bel Mooney: 'One of the reasons I am passionate about art is because it is so large and because it opens cathedrals in the mind where you can go and be and you can pray and you are not small. We have to be able to put meaning back into the lives of ordinary people.'

I believe that every aspect of one's life, from washing the dishes, preparing a meal, digging in the garden, collecting a child from school, or helping a neighbour, can be an opportunity for being creative, for creativity expresses itself in many ways: from the creation of a garden, a home, to a relationship, while the greatest of all arts is life itself.

In *News from Nowhere* William Morris wrote: 'It is the child-like part of us that produces the works of the Imagination.' Morris was indeed someone who kept the child alive in himself and never lost his eagerness or joy in things, and his desire to experiment. In an early letter he wrote, 'My work is the embodiment of dreams', and I feel that is also true of everything I do, whether it is writing children's books, founding a theatre, directing a play, creating a garden, nurturing friendships, or simply cooking a meal for friends. If I could never direct another play – and my greatest joy is working with actors – or write another book, I would not cease to be creative. Creativity, like a stream or river, will always find its own outlets.

VOCATION AND AVOCATION

Setting up such a centre, however, took up an enormous amount of time and energy and was, of course, entirely voluntary, while I continued to struggle to earn a living by directing and writing. Then, one day in 1973, John Hencher, a close friend and priest, who was much involved with the work at Bleddfa, said to me, 'James, why don't you take Orders?' meaning, why don't you seek ordination? John and I shared much in common and, although he was four years younger than I, he was very much my elder brother in spiritual matters. He had been an actor in his youth, working for the Royal Shakespeare Company, when one day he felt the call to the priesthood. For many years he was part of the Education Team for the Hereford Diocese and then became the much valued chaplain at the Monmouth School for Boys. He also played a key role in the work of the Bleddfa Centre, while his partner John Cupper brilliantly developed the potential of the Old School Gallery.

While I understood in part what he was saying I was also quite clear that I was not meant to give up working as a director in the theatre, which is my prime craft. Eventually I learned about the non-stipendiary priesthood, then a new experiment in the Anglican Church, comparable to the worker-priests in France: a group that includes stockbrokers in the City, farmers, doctors, teachers, and others – I was to be the first theatre director – who continue to earn their living like other people but who, as a result, are often more able to function in a priestly way at the margins of society, though some are wholly committed to conventional parish work.

It was about this time that I had a dream which clearly signalled the approach of a major change and I was fortunate that I was able to share this with Franz Elkisch. In the dream I was giving a lecture to young people about the creative process, explaining how always out of *nothing*, whether it is a blank canvas or sheet of paper, a block of stone or wood, *something* is created. As I spoke I was also projecting images onto a blank screen with the aid of a projector. Then the screen dissolved and became a glass window through which I could see the sky and from far away, from out of space travelling towards me, I could see a shape that I recognised as being a deeper aspect of myself. The question with which I was then faced was: Do I hurl myself through the window and go to meet it, even if in the process I wound myself? Or do I sit here, quietly waiting for its arrival?

'You must wait,' counselled Franz, 'because to try and anticipate what is already in motion in order to make it happen sooner would be an act of the ego and result only in harm. Your task is to wait patiently for this aspect of the Self to reveal its purpose.' The path to ordination did indeed unfold of its own accord although I had many doubts from the start.

'What a relief!' laughed Canon Murray Irvine, the Director of Ordinands for the Hereford Diocese. 'Most people who come to me think they are God's gift to the Church!' Because Franz Elkisch had urged me not to let the authorities send me to a theological college – 'They will only try to brain-wash you' – and because I was convinced that I was called to 'a hidden ministry', I told all this to Canon Irvine and that I also had a problem with the word 'God'! He seemed totally unfazed, replying, 'Clearly you are *sui generis* and our task is to devise a special form of training for you, provided you are accepted by ACCM (Advisory Council for the Church's Ministry). Let me talk with John Eastaugh, our Bishop.'

A week later I drove through narrow twisting lanes in the hills above Brecon to meet David Shapland, an Anglican priest who with his wife Julie had created at Llanerchwen a retreat house for those monks, nuns and priests, both Catholic and Anglican, who were experiencing vocational crises. I had met him once before and recognised not only that he had a fine intellect but was also someone who saw clearly through people and, when necessary, could be blunt. After all, I thought, this idea that I might have a vocation to the priesthood could simply be a narcissistic illusion, and I was already full of doubts and uncertainty. I needed therefore to test myself by being grilled by someone like David Shapland. He listened intently to what I had to say and then, looking at me directly, said, 'If I were a Bishop I would ordain you today!' He invited me to return the following week to meet a colleague of his, Canon Laurence Reading who was a skilled counsellor and also adviser to the Bishop of Hereford.

Laurence Reading, with his grey beard and watchful eyes was a Gandalf-like figure in whom I sensed a deep wisdom; indeed, over the years I was to learn much from this elder statesman. David Shapland sat in on our meeting but said nothing while I was being probed. 'What you are seeking,' said Laurence Reading finally, 'is authority. Ordination gives one authority to carry out one's task and at the same time it acts as a brake, preventing the ego from becoming inflated. It means that by being subject to authority you will be less likely to be acting from your ego.' Laurence Reading subsequently briefed the Bishop about me and I was asked to go and see him.

It was during this period of doubt and questioning that I wrote the following in my journal:

> I know that with ordination a subtle shifting of attitudes will take place and that, increasingly, more opportunities will be revealed, and a greater burden laid upon me. I have an awareness of gifts as yet untapped within myself and which, in this second half of my life, are waiting to be harnessed. I am not moving away from the theatre or from writing but, rather, with ordination these gifts will be enhanced and woven into a richer pattern. If I am asked how precisely I see my 'ministry' I have to reply: I do not know. I cannot give a simple answer or say that it is to do this or that. In so far as I can discern an emerging pattern it will be to act as a bridge between opposites, and to be within myself such a bridge. But, I know that it has primarily to be 'a hidden ministry'.

In due course I drove to the Bishop's Palace in Hereford to meet the Bishop, John Eastaugh. I was ushered into the library where a large marmalade cat sprawled luxuriously before the fire while through a tall window I could glimpse a magnolia tree in flower. The Bishop entered, wearing a rose-pink cassock with a silver cross on a chain. Inserting a cigarette into a holder, he then poured two large gins and proceeded to gossip with me about the theatre. It was like being with Noel Coward, and I began to wonder when we were going to get down to business. Then, with a flick of his ash, he changed mode, and revealed his essential gravitas. He had been informed that I did not want to go to a theological college, but he seemed unfazed by this. He suggested that I visit Brother Alban, the Guardian of Glasshampton Monastery at Shrawley in Worcestershire, which is the contemplative centre for the Society of St Francis of which the Bishop was then the titular head. 'If Brother Alban can devise a form of training for you then I will accept that. But you will have to go before ACCM, the selection board first. There's no other way. But don't mention my plan to them! I am happy to be your sponsor and to ordain you.'

On 7 July 1978 I received a letter inviting me to the Bishops' Selection Conference at Ecton House in Northampton:

> Sheets and pillow-cases are provided, but please bring your own soap and towel. The cost of the Conference to candidates will be £7, payable at the Conference. If you are not in a position to pay this, please let us know. You will be able to claim for travelling expenses in excess of £5 for coming to the Conference and going home again by public transport; except for travel from overseas.

Immediately on arrival I was plunged into a deep depression, wanting to drive straight back to London. There were eighteen of us being considered for ordination and on the first evening we sat in a circle and were each given two minutes in which to say something about ourselves. A bell was rung at the end of each two minutes. The session was chaired by a jolly, be-spectacled, pipe-smoking avuncular Bishop much given to telling funny stories and talking to us as though we were all children. Over the three days we were subjected to various tests and interviewed by members of the Selection Panel. When the Revd Huw Thomas questioned me about training and I told him about Glasshampton he tut-tutted, murmuring, 'All highly irregular! But it seems from the correspondence I have been shown that everyone seems eager that you should be ordained but are waiting for someone else to give the green light!'

Convinced that I would be rejected on the grounds of being too much of a maverick, too individualistic to fit in, I returned home to read Martin Buber:

> I am in favour of every religion in its beginning. Then it is fresh and spontaneous, filled with joy and love. If only

it would stay that way! But then it becomes codified and organised. It becomes a mechanical repetition of a formula which has lost its original meaning. Look what happened to the Hasidim! And nothing can hide the face of God from young people as organised religion does.

Is becoming a priest an essential part of my life's development? I wondered. I shared all this with John Hencher, my priest friend who had first suggested ordination. He told me that in his letter of recommendation to ACCM he said that whatever form my ministry took it would be unorthodox and not like anyone else's. 'My advice to you is to take one step at a time,' he now said. 'Don't try to see to the end of the journey. It's very tempting, especially as one gets older when there is a greater urgency and sense of the brevity of time. You will be led each step, and with each step there will be a chance to say no.'

After being accepted by ACCM. I drove to Glasshampton to meet Brother Alban. The track up to monastery is across farmland, full of ruts, winding uphill until one comes in sight of the red brick building with a clock tower in the centre: the former stables of a grand house that had been burned to the ground. I sat talking quietly with Brother Alban in his small cell with its desk piled with books and papers, and a strong smell of tobacco. I told him that what I was seeking was a Zen-like preparation of silence, prayer, study, and manual work. We then spent an hour together in the chapel in silent meditation and after supper returned to his room. 'Come and be here whenever your work permits, and we shall leave you to your own devices,' he said. 'But you will know, and I will know, when the time has come for me to say to the Bishop: He is ready to be ordained.'

And so in November of that year I entered Glasshampton, a white wall of mist surrounding the monastery and moisture dripping from the bare apple trees onto the blackened leaves that littered the wet grass. Spending long hours in the chapel I found myself wondering whether we need to approach Christianity more as a faith than a religion. Is it the Church itself, the institution, which has come to stand in the way of the teachings of Jesus? I wondered. And yet all faiths need some form of container, some structure, which is why temples, synagogues, churches, and sacred scriptures have evolved; and yet in the earliest years of Christianity there were no churches; people simply met in each other's houses and, as Wendell Berry has pointed out, in Jesus' teaching there is no mention of bricks and mortar, only of where two or three people are gathered together in his name.

At Pentecost we read how 'all believed together and they had all things in common; and they all spoke with one voice.' What has happened that this unity now appears so fractured and fragmented? Once upon a time there was the great barque of Peter sailing alone on the seas of Time. A century later there appeared another vessel, the ship of the Orthodox. Then with the Reformation there came a whole Armada of lesser ships, rowing boats, coracles, rafts. But now how many of these have sunk, or are foundering while even, some think, the great barque of Peter has sprung leaks, and the *Ecclesia Anglicana* appears often to be rudderless, with its passengers and crew often bitterly divided? So much then for Jesus' prayer 'that they may be one even as Thou and I are one'! There is much talk of re-union in the ecumenical movement but the danger is that it would be on an academic and bureaucratic level, with everyone agreeing legalistically on certain points of doctrine, theology and morals, accepting the Pope as Chief Pastor of such a Church. I keep thinking of the words of Eliot from *The Four Quartets*: 'Be in the difficulty of being.'

And so, over a period of two years, in full summer, deep snow, during the time of my mother's death, in spring, summer again, and autumn into winter, and then another spring, there at Glasshampton I experienced peace, crisis and growth, learning from many hours spent daily in silent meditation in the chapel. My usual companion there was Brother David, the oldest member of the Society of St Francis and its first Provincial Minister. Born in North Wales he had been a priest for fifty-six years. Bird-like in his movements, reminding me of a wren, he was extraordinarily youthful, taking his turn in the laundry, or washing up in the kitchen. In the chapel he would sit on a chair in front of the Blessed Sacrament, a brown wool plaid blanket wrapped round him: 'It belonged to a Scottish shepherd and it is more than a hundred years old. I have had it for fifty years.' He would read, pray, or fall asleep. We were always aware of each other's silence as we sat there, hour after hour. One learns so much just by sitting and listening to the silence beyond the silence. I had asked to come to a place where I might have a Zen-like preparation, a place of quiet prayer, study and manual work and it was in those long hours spent in the chapel with Brother David that I learned so much. It is less what a person says than what he is.

But my ordination nearly didn't take place. Because I am bi-domiciled, with a home in Wales and another in London, Bishop John had forgotten to secure for me from the then Bishop of Edmonton, the Rt. Rev, Bill Westwood, a licence for London. I was sent for by Bishop Bill who looked very worried when I spoke about a 'hidden ministry'. When I commented on this he replied, 'Yes, I am very worried!'

He asked nothing about my spiritual practice, nor how I saw my work in theatre relating to my ministry but became like an Army Captain. 'If you were to be licensed by me you would have to get down to the nitty-gritty.

I would want you to put in so many hours hospital visiting, so many hours doing Nativity plays in schools, taking so many services each Sunday, and I would need you to report to someone tougher than Prebendary Chitty who knows you too well. And I would want to be the one who advises Bishop John when I think you are ready to be ordained.' I found myself wondering what made him so aggressive.

'I am not impressed by distinguished, powerful, famous people,' he continued. 'I've buried too many. Nobody asked you to join the Church. You aren't doing us a favour. It's your soul I am worried about. Father, why haven't you got a spiritual director?'

I told him that he had the wrong idea about me. He then looked at me and said, 'Father, is there anything else that, as your future Bishop, you ought to tell me?' I replied that he was welcome to ask me anything.

'Are you a bachelor? Have you ever thought of marriage?' Having told Bishop John as well as those at ACCM about my long relationship with Hywel I refused to tell this man. He had asked all the wrong questions in this aggressive manner and found answers of his own making. He was a committee man, an institutional animal, and all my horrors of the Church as an institution returned. It was clear that Bishop Bill regarded me as unreliable, with a bad track record, too favoured by the Hereford Diocese (I suspected also that he did not approve of Bishop John) and thought that I needed toughening up, put in my place. There was nothing wrong with that but it was his manner that was so deeply off-putting. When I told all this to Graham Dowell, the Vicar of Hampstead, he replied, 'I have never felt that Bishop Bill has ever listened to a single thing I have ever said!'

It was clear that Bishop Bill thoroughly disapproved of the unconventional way I had been allowed by Bishop John to prepare for ordination and, as a result, it looked as though I might never be ordained. This was both a painful and a fruitful time. I rang Johanna Brieger, who was not only my doctor but a Jungian analyst, asking if I might have an hour of her time professionally. She listened to me and then said, 'I have only one question to put to you: Have you ordained yourself?'

It was a very Jungian response but I understood what she meant about an interior commitment and so I replied immediately, 'Yes'. For I did not have any doubts that I was meant to exercise a priestly role, even if it meant as a layman. 'Then that's all that matters,' she answered.

The interview with the Bishop of Edmonton and his accusation that my life was 'tacky' (his word), plus his superficial judgements and his refusal to give me a licence were, nonetheless, wounding. I drove to Hereford to discuss matters with Bishop John and his close adviser Canon Laurence Reading. The problem, declared Bishop John, was that 'the Bishop of

Edmonton is very ambitious and can block things. He is likely by now to have spoken to Gerald Ellison, the Bishop of London. But I'll try to get to him first and explain things. I don't want to put too much in a letter. These things are best done on the spot. But it may mean my putting off your being ordained deacon. I need time to sort all this out. It is my fault. I ought to have cleared London first. Did Bishop Bill question you about your sexuality? He himself is very anti-gay. I wouldn't be surprised if he hasn't already sent for your ACCM papers. I think there was some phrase in them such as "perhaps his sexuality needs clarifying". I think I told you that you were the first person I know of, as an acknowledged homosexual, passed through ACCM. But we have to handle this carefully. I look upon you not as an experiment but as an exploration. The Bishop of Edmonton will see himself as acting in all sincerity in the best interests of the Church. After all, he might think: he could end up marrying gays in church or even setting up the James Roose-Evans church!'

In the end Bishop John decided to go ahead and ordain me initially just for the Diocese of Hereford and so on the morning of St David's Day 1981 he came early to Glasshampton to ordain me a deacon in the presence of the community. I rose at 3am to spend a vigil in the chapel, until at six o'clock I went to bathe, shave and change. I then went outside to watch the dawn and reflect on those words from *The Four Quartets*: 'Through the unknown, remembered gate…between two waves of the sea… quick, here, now, always, a condition of complete simplicity costing not less than everything.'

As the sky lightened with delicate saffron and primrose yellows I could see the lights of a car slowly ascending the farm track as a chauffeur driven white car came into view bearing Bishop John and Canon Laurence Reading. After robing, we entered the chapel, where we sang 'Guide me, O Thou great Redeemer,' to the tune of *Cwm Rhondda*, as it was St David's Day, and my favourite hymn, 'We love the place, O God, wherein Thine honour dwells.' After the giving of the Peace I went in turn to each of the community to give them the Peace, as well as to Hywel who was present, and then we all gathered round the altar for the Communion. A week later Bishop John wrote to me:

> My dear James, last Sunday seemed to me absolutely right: a hidden ministry, dedicated to God, in the presence of those who have helped you on your way and one or two friends. This must be the way for your immediate future, and my only worry is that you may be tempted to advertise this hidden ministry in lights! By lights I mean

dog collars, cassocks, and other ecclesiastical wear to proclaim your identity. I have deliberately ordained you to a hidden ministry and after Peter-tide I want those in your profession and others whose lives you touch to discover for themselves that they have a priest living and working with them who is there to serve them and meet their needs as one who works and lives alongside them and is not set over and against them as a priest of God. This will require considerable humility on your part, the kind of humility not generally associated with the theatrical profession, if I may be so bold! You will need patience as, under the hand of God, your ministry gradually unfolds itself, but you will need a great deal of patience and waiting upon the Holy Spirit to point the way in which you should go.

A few months later I was priested in Hereford Cathedral with a licence only for the Diocese of Hereford at that time (although afterwards I was licensed for London, and since then also for the Church in Wales). 'I am ordaining you to be a presence,' wrote Bishop John, 'to exercise a ministry that is hidden but not secret. Not to play a role.'

Only a handful of friends knew what was happening so that it was startling when I was telephoned by *The Guardian* wanting to make a story about my being the first British theatre director to be ordained yet continuing to work in the theatre. I explained that I did not want any publicity, that I needed time in order to learn how to manage these two roles. The last thing I wanted was for colleagues and others to say, 'What on earth is he up to now!'

Seven years later I did 'come out' when Richard Barber, the Editor of *Woman* magazine, offered me a weekly column, as a kind of spiritual agony aunt, which I called *Something Extra* because I believed, and believe still, that while people are often put off by conventional religious practices nonetheless many are searching for 'something extra' in their lives. I wrote this column for two years and at one point I asked my good friend Dom Jerome Hodkinson, OSB, then Abbot of Belmont, whether he read my column. He replied, 'Jim, I can hardly go to our local newsagent and ask "Have you got my weekly *Woman*?"!'

BUILDING BRIDGES

Slowly, quietly, over the years, while continuing my work in the theatre, I have grown more sure of my particular ministry: to build bridges between opposites, to be on hand in unlikely places and situations, and to be more aware of 'other' patterns at work.

How is it, some have asked, that I am now back in the Anglican fold and an ordained minister of it, while still practising my craft as a director in the theatre? How, some have challenged, can you be a member of a Church that represents barely one per cent of the population and continues to dwindle? A Church that is controlled by Parliament, a secular body, and without any authority, unlike that of Rome, and that seems fated to disintegrate. What kind of Church is that?

The answer lies in the fact that deep down I believe there is a Church beyond all Churches. As the Duchess of Malfi says in Webster's play, 'I trow, sir, in the Eternal Church it will not be so.' As human beings we need tangible signs; we need structures, institutions and disciplines. The institutions act as containers for the teachings and the wisdom that each has inherited. But these truths are no more than signposts, especially because they have to be expressed in some sort of limiting formula. They point towards a reality but they do not contain the reality. As Father Daniel O'Leary has written:

> To be sure we need Churches. But the warnings of Jesus must burn in our hearts. The moment the Churches begin to believe in themselves more than in the Spirit entrusted to them, believing that they are chosen where others are not, then they are confusing institutional elitism with working for the Kingdom.

What people are giving up on is going to Church. It is in the institution, not God, that they are losing faith. I cannot believe in the division of faiths, let alone of the one Faith. I do not believe that Jesus came to found an institution. When Jesus prays 'that they may all be one' I do not believe he was praying for ecumenical unity, all under the one leadership of the Pontiff of Rome. I believe that there is a deeper unity that lies beyond institutional differences, the kind of unity that Thomas Merton found when Christian and Buddhist monks joined together in meditation. On that occasion Merton asked everyone to form a circle and join hands, saying: 'We are going to have to create a new language of prayer, and this new language of prayer has to come out of something which transcends all our traditions and comes out of the immediacy of love.'

There can be but one God under all. Each of us approaches the Eternal Reality, however we define it, along a particular path: cultural, geographical, biographical. The primary goal of such an inter-religious movement must surely be the unity of all mankind, for the most negative aspect of religion today is its role in dividing humanity into rival blocs and groups. So much of the conflict among human beings today has an ethnic or religious label. And yet the power of true religion is always to transcend, in an all-comprehending love of the whole of humanity, whereas today, instead of transcending, religions tend to reinforce the barriers that divide and separate.

Unity does not mean conformity, however, nor does it mean the elimination of differences. Some differences are valuable and have to be celebrated, while others have to be eradicated or resolved. Each religion must be humble enough to recognise the good aspects of other religions, and to foster these in their own communities. What is needed today is a global ethic, such as that proposed by the Baha'i movement as expressed in its paper, *Valuing Spirituality in Development* for the World Faiths and Development Dialogue at Lambeth Palace in February 1998: The concept of unity in diversity is a way of expressing the principle of the oneness of humanity. It stands in contrast to uniformity. Each of us depends upon the wellbeing of the whole. We need to respect one another, as well as the Earth itself.

Above all, the focus of today's spirituality is in the recognition of God's presence within ourselves. We are rediscovering what our ancestors were so aware of: the presence of the sacred in all creation; in contrast to an other-worldly spirituality reaching out to a God beyond this sinful world.

Most Christian prayers end with the words: through Jesus Christ, our Lord. These words suggest to me the image of Jesus as a window through which we see God more clearly. Jesus, the man, revealed God-ness more fully than it had ever been revealed before, and I believe that we are all called, whatever our religion, or none, to be filled with God-ness. All truly good people, of whatever faith or none, are like windows, revealing a deeper dimension to life.

And so I have found that it is, above all, in the practice of silent meditation that true unity can be found, when people of all faiths, or of none, can enter into a silence beyond words and concepts, sharing at a very deep level. Ultimately all we can do is to prostrate ourselves at the threshold of Mystery, of the Unknown, of Silence, sensing that from beyond comes the answer to our deepest needs. Silence is at the core of Buddhism and nowhere is this more obvious than in the story of the Buddha's great wordless sermon. How can there be a sermon without words? it might be asked. The Buddha simply holds up a flower. Only one of his disciples understands. That disciple smiles and the Buddha smiles back at him, and in that silence between them the silence was passed on from the Buddha to his first successor, the monk with the understanding smile. Ever since the tradition of Buddhism is passed on in silence. This is at the heart of all religions: the need for inner silence, inner emptiness, and inner transformation.

But what, someone will ask, do you actually do, James, in your capacity as a priest? My main work has been that of helping people, as individuals or as groups, to create rituals for various occasions. All major rituals are rites of passage, marking a transition from one mode of being to another, working a transformation within the individual or community at a deep psychological, physical and spiritual level. Today, however, we lack rituals which can mark and celebrate essential rites of passage. Today we have no rituals for a boy coming to puberty, for a young woman's first menstruation. 'No wonder,' wrote Harvey Cox, 'we undergo identity crises until we die.' There are no rituals for pregnancy, none for a broken marriage, a broken relationship or a broken home. We have no rituals for a woman who has been raped, beaten or battered; no rituals for parents who have had to experience an abortion, a miscarriage, or a still-born baby. What rituals do we have for a child moving to a new school or a new neighbourhood, or a young person going off to her first job. As Rosemary Manning has a character observe in her novel *The Open Door*, 'Oh, God, why is there no satisfactory ritual for parting? The pain is raw at the edges: no healing balm of sherry.'

What rituals exist for the elders of our society, be they the wise women and men in our midst, or those fragile victims of senility or Alzheimer's whom we must support? Why do we so often wait until someone is dead before we say how much we valued them? We have need also of rituals for ageing, as each of us grows into old age and moves towards our eventual departure. And while each of the major religions has precise rituals for the dying and the dead, what rituals do we have to offer to those of no specific faith or tradition? As May Sarton writes in her novel *As We Are Now*, 'What rite of passage is there for the dying, especially where there is no faith in God?' and even among existing religious institutions which have their own ancient liturgies there is often felt the need for alternative forms. A nun, having read my book *Passages of the Soul: Ritual Today* wrote, 'I'm especially interested in and inspired by your exploration of drama spilling over into liturgy, creating our own liturgies that are relevant to us today – *and all this rooted and fed from our deepest centre.*'

On one occasion I was approached by someone who worked for the London Symphony Orchestra who asked if I would baptise his two year old daughter. The mother, a Thai, was a devout Buddhist, and when the child was born she was given a Buddhist ceremony of welcome. Now, however, the mother was dying of cancer and wished the child to be baptised. As a

Buddhist she had refused all medical treatment and, in fact, died ten days after her daughter's baptism. It was clear that something special was called for over and above the traditional Christian baptism, especially as I knew there would be a number of Thai people present.

Instead of using the font which was tucked in the far corner of the church I assembled chairs in a four-sided formation. On one side of me sat the parents with their daughter. The mother, although yellow from the cancer, was beautifully dressed and totally 'present' throughout the ceremony. On the other side sat the Guardians, as I prefer to call them rather than god parents.

The previous day, it being autumn, I had gathered a basket of fallen leaves, and at the start I held up one of these, explaining to those present that we were about to honour two great spiritual traditions: the Christian and the Buddhist. I told the story of how the Buddha, during one of the last days of his life, was out walking with his disciples when he stooped and picked up a fallen leaf. 'This,' he said, 'represents what I have been able to teach you. But look at all the other leaves on the ground!'

I then linked this story to the end of St John's Gospel where the author says that there are not enough books in all the world to contain the things that Jesus said. In case some of those present might think what we were about to do unorthodox, I described how at Stanbrook Abbey in Worcestershire, an enclosed order of Benedictine nuns, there had recently been staying two Buddhist monks sent by the Dalai Lama. They had lived, eaten, and worshipped alongside the community. When I asked Dame Felicitas Corrigan, one of the most senior members of the community, how this could be, since normally no men are allowed inside the Enclosure, she replied, 'The Holy Father has asked that there be greater dialogue between Catholics and Buddhists.'

I now asked a small boy – whom I had baptised in that same church – to hand out to everyone present a leaf from the basket which they could keep as a memento of this day. As he did this I noticed that many of those present were weeping. Most of them knew that the mother was dying so that at that moment the distribution of autumn leaves became also a leave-taking. Such moments I would describe as Holy Theatre.

At the moment of baptism it became clear that the little girl was too shy to come forward and so, quite spontaneously, I sank down on my knees, squatting on the floor. Immediately the parents and the little girl and the Guardians all followed suit and we carried out the baptism in this informal manner. When it was all over, another spontaneous thing happened. The Thais had all brought food and, suddenly, there were little groups picnicking all over the church: a simple yet sacramental sharing of food.

What is important to realise is the need to meet people where they are, and be prepared to respond imaginatively, even if it means departing somewhat from the book of rules. Imagination is surely the key to a living liturgy. Rituals must be made meaningful for those taking part otherwise they become merely esoteric, remote, and therefore alienating.

Ritual is one of the neglected forms of theatre. Although certain rituals are timeless, perfected and handed down across the centuries in the form of the great liturgies of the major faiths, and are capable always of rediscovery, other rituals need to be created for a specific time, place and need. A true testing of a ritual is, as the British theatre director Peter Brook had observed, when a strong presence of performers and a strong presence of witnesses 'can produce a circle of unique intensity in which barriers can be broken and the invisible becomes real'. It is when these two worlds meet that 'there is a burning and fleeting sense of another world, in which our present world is integrated and transformed.' It is when a community of individuals bring to the creation and enactment of a ritual such a total dedication that then the invisible becomes real.

'It is puzzling and frustrating', wrote Dom Laurence Freeman OSB, in an article in *The Tablet*,

> to try to understand how the mainline Churches, despite all their determination and resources, still seem unable to connect with the profound spiritual needs of our time. For so many young people, ready for idealistic and sacrificial commitment, hungry for inspiration, the Church could give the sense of belonging that they seek as citizens of the global village. But instead of discovering an inclusive vision, a comprehensive philosophy of life, a spirituality, they dismiss what they find as narrowness of mind, intolerant dogmatism, internal feuding, inter-denominational sectarianism, medieval sexism, and so on. It seems disloyal to re-iterate it all. Perhaps the best way of dealing with it is to ask why – the unkindest cut of all – the most damning criticism is that Christianity lacks depth. It is all very well for practising Christians, who have the grace to see the Church in a mystical as well as an institutional light to say that this assessment is extreme. Of course it is. It is, nevertheless, what an increasing number of people believe. A more deeply contemplative Christianity seems the only possible future for a Church which will be smaller, less grand perhaps, when stripped of its secular pomp

and prestige, freed from obsessive single-issue theological politics, self destructive divisions and excessive clericalism.

Society can only be renewed by renewing individuals. And in order to do this we have to give individuals an opportunity to contact their own inner resources. As Ira Progoff has written, we gradually discover that our life has been going somewhere, however blind we have been to its direction, and however unhelpful to it we ourselves have been:

> We find that a connective thread has been forming beneath the surface of our lives, carrying the meaning that has been trying to establish itself in our existence. It is the inner continuity of our lives. As we recognise and identify with it, we see an inner myth that has been guiding our lives unknown to ourselves.

Crossing Hampstead Heath with the actress Stephanie Cole once, she stopped suddenly.

'What is it?'

'It's something you've just said,' she replied. 'It hit me hard. You said, "I no longer have a career. I have a life. And anything that comes to me in the way of work in the theatre is a bonus."'

Life is indeed so much richer than any talent one may have, and in one's senior years one can no longer talk in terms of a career. That is something that is built in the first four or five decades of one's life. At the end of one's life what will count is not necessarily how many plays one has directed, books written, or roles played, but what kind of person one has been.

84 CHARING CROSS ROAD

Japanese girls in tight skirts, carrying parasols, were walking elegantly down Fifth Avenue, followed by brass bands, groups of senior citizens, and representatives of many different trades and ethnic groups. It was Labour Day and so once a year the citizens of New York have the centre of the stage as they walk the length of one of the most fashionable streets in the world, waving to their friends and supporters.

It was September 1982 and on a smaller stage nearby I was auditioning actors for the Broadway production of Helene Hanff's *84 Charing Cross Road*, which I had also adapted for the stage, and which was to open at the

Nederlander Theatre, designed by the eminent Oliver Smith, with Ellen Burstyn as Helene Hanff, and Joe Maher as Frank Doel.

At the age of thirty-eight Ellen, feeling she had failed as an actress, had given up acting and gone to live in Europe for four years. Then, out of the blue, she was sent the movie script of *Alice Doesn't Live Here Any More* which was to make her a Hollywood star. When we first met she said,

> It seems as though it is only when you have let go and given up that life changes. I'd like to be able to use that experience in playing Helene: how for years she wrote plays that never got anywhere and she felt a failure. And then, suddenly, she writes this small book which makes her a household name. The loneliness of the long-distance writer, that's what I'm after! To find the real chinks in her armour, the places where I can show the loneliness behind her barrage of verbal fireworks.
>
> What happened to her when she was twelve? Did she compete with her brothers for their father's attention, being the only girl? Did she dress up in men's clothes and earn a reputation as a whiz-kid on the block? What gave her the drive to be so independent? Do you remember what she said on the Dick Cavett Show? That one doesn't really change as one gets older. 'You remain a twelve year old still,' she said, 'with all the same feelings like: I'm still scared of making a fool of myself!'
>
> Oh, I'm so excited! There's so much to this role and I'm only just beginning to tap it. Watching Rosemary in London it seemed very easy. But now I know it isn't.

The play, like the book – which is based on the original correspondence between Helene and the staff of Marks and Co, the antiquarian booksellers – begins with the image of an impoverished and unsuccessful writer in New York who, dreaming of the England of Chaucer and Donne, begins ordering books she cannot really afford simply in order to have a link with the England of English Literature. Her brash, abrasive Jewish humour begins to thaw the very English reserve of Frank Doel who deals with her requests, signing himself F.D. until they are eventually addressing each other as 'Dear Helene' and 'Dear Frank'. Slowly she begins to acquire a surrogate family in England as one by one the other members of the staff start writing to her and exchanging gifts. The first act builds to a climax when Helene announces that she is coming to England for the coronation of Queen Elizabeth II.

The second act opens on this note of expectation. Then comes the big disappointment when she announces that she has to cancel her trip because of having to move to a new apartment. From this point onwards the mood of the play changes. Frank begins visibly to age, becoming absent-minded. He, his wife and children had all been so looking forward to meeting Helene, and now it seems it will never happen. And, as in the famous Agatha Christie story, the other members of the staff begin to depart until only Frank is left and then he dies.

Helene is shattered. As she herself said: 'I was a failed playwright; a TV playwright whose experience in live TV was useless in the age of film. I was nowhere. I was nothing.' It was into this void that the news came of Frank Doel's death, as well as that of Mr Marks, the owner, and the closure of the shop. 'Coming when it did, the news was devastating. It seemed to me that the last anchor in my life – my bookshop – was being taken from me. I began to cry and I couldn't stop.' It was then that she realised she had to write the story of her relationship with Marks and Co.

The question always, however, was how to end the play. I puzzled over this until by chance I was given a copy of Helene's sequel *The Duchess of Bloomsbury* in which she describes how she finally comes to England for the publication of her book, even though the shop had been closed down. And so, in the play, as Helene hears the news of Frank's death and the closure of the shop, the lights lower, and over the sound of a jet plane, we hear a pilot's voice announcing that shortly the plane will be arriving at Heathrow. When the lights come up all the books have vanished and the shelves are empty. The shop is empty and bare. Then, through the windows we see Helene coming down the street. She pauses to check the address and then, as she enters the shop and looks around at the empty shelves, she says, 'How about this, Frankie? I finally made it!'

The production was launched at the Salisbury Playhouse and just two of the national critics were invited by way of testing the waters. On 13 August 1981 Helene wrote:

Dear J-R-E,

Just got the mail from friends in London. Two marvellous reviews (*The Times* and *The Telegraph*) of your production of *84 Charing Cross Road*, from which I gather you bring off a miracle. God (and I) bless you for it! Please let me know if it ever gets to London – well in advance, so that I can save up the fare. Helene Hanff.

Seven West End producers came to see the production and as many Broadway producers expressed interest. One producer, Michael Redington, came several times to Salisbury to see it and it was he who acquired the rights for the West End, but we nearly did not make it. We were offered the Ambassadors Theatre but Redington was unable to raise all the capital required and so another play opened there instead. I remember being invited to the first night by the theatre critic Nicholas de Jongh who, observing that I was dressed entirely in black, remarked, 'Such funereal elegance must mean you are trying to put a death wish on the play!' Whatever the reason, the play closed within three weeks and once again the Ambassadors, the ideal theatre for our play, became vacant. Yet still Michael Redington had difficulty in raising enough backers, given that we had no major star. It was at this point that I decided to pre-empt matters. I sent a telegram to Tinker Jay, the owner of the Ambassadors (it had been built by his father) which read:

YOU HAVE A JEWEL OF A THEATRE

WE HAVE A JEWEL OF A SHOW

LET THERE BE A MARRIAGE

I followed this up with a second, and a third telegram, each sent on the same day, but differently worded. Tinker Jay then telephoned Michael Redington saying, 'Look, I am getting all these telegrams from James Roose-Evans! Perhaps we should meet.' Forty-eight hours later a deal was struck and I then sent my final telegram:

TINKER JAY, HIP-HIP-HOORAY!

One afternoon during the previews at the Ambassadors Theatre we all crowded into Rosemary Leach's dressing room to listen to Helene giving her *Letter from New York* for the BBC's *Woman's Hour*. It was to be her last broadcast before flying to England for the West End opening. In it she described how all her life she had had two ambitions: one was to come to England which she finally achieved when the book was published over here by André Deutsch; the other was to be a playwright. She had written scores of plays none of which had ever been performed. 'and now someone I have never met, James Roose-Evans, has turned the book into a play, and they are presenting it in the West End, and I have been asked to the First Night, and when do you think they have fixed it for? Thanksgiving Day! I nearly refused to go!'

Little did Helene Hanff know when she sat down to write the story of her relationship with the bookshop that the resulting slim volume would become, not only an instant success, but a cult book, celebrating the friendship between the two countries. Letters poured in by the hundreds, invitations and gifts arriving by each mail: cheeses from Wisconsin, pecan nuts from Georgia, even a proposal of marriage from a fifteen-year-old boy with terminal acne. 'I was totally unprepared for this,' said Helene, 'and I didn't know how to handle it.'

However, it was the book's adaptation for the stage and, subsequently, as a Hollywood movie starring Anthony Hopkins and Ann Bancroft, which was given a Royal Command Performance in the presence of HRH The Queen Mother, which finally changed Helene's life for it was the first time she had made any money. Ironically the sales of the book never did, for a reason she explained on the Dick Cavett Show. 'For every fan letter I received, and they were countless, I would write a reply – but only the one! – and the cost of the aerogram equalled the amount of the royalty on each copy of the book!'

On her arrival in London I entertained Helene, Michael Redington, Rosemary Leach and David Swift to lunch at the Garrick Club. Helene, in her dark trouser suit, with a red, white and blue silk scarf at her neck, stood with legs astride, one hand on hip, a cigarette angled from her mouth. Even during lunch she had a cigarette lit the whole time, taking a puff between each mouthful. When the head waiter quietly whispered in my ear that smoking was not allowed I replied, 'Try telling that to Miss Hanff!' Crouched in her chair behind a cloud of smoke, she shot off zany sharp cracks like a small boy showing off. Fiercely independent, I quickly sensed that there was no way one could direct her from point A to point B because she was always darting off at tangents and would not be diverted. After lunch she insisted on looking at every portrait and was indignant that she could not find one of Bernard Shaw!

Then suddenly it was Thanksgiving Day 1981 and the First Night in the West End of *84 Charing Cross Road*. Just before the curtain rose John Barber, theatre critic of *The Daily Telegraph*, beckoned to me, saying, 'The boys – (meaning the other critics) – and I would like to see Miss Hanff take a curtain call.' There was only ten minutes to go before curtain up so I dashed backstage to explain to Rosemary and David how it could be done, then raced back to my seat in the dress circle before the curtain rose. I could see Helene seated in a box with her publisher André Deutsch, holding a large glass of gin and smoking throughout the first act!

In the interval I got her to sit next to me in the dress circle, still clutching her glass, but minus her cigarette. At the end, as the applause began, I hurried her down the stairs and pushed her through the pass door, before slipping into the stalls to watch the curtain calls. All the actors came on followed by David Swift and then Rosemary Leach, but still no sign of Helene. Apparently she was saying, 'Where is James? I'm not going on without him!' until our company manager Brian Kirk pushed her through the door of the shop. As Helene and Rosemary embraced, the whole audience rose to its feet, applauding loudly, with reiterated cries of 'Bravo!'

Later Helene was to write of that moment:

> One of the critics described my walk to the bookshop door to join the cast on stage at the curtain call in these words: 'and the audience rose to her.' I hadn't seen that in the darkness beyond the footlights. I stared at that line till I couldn't see it for tears. Somehow, with that image, the dream week I had lived through in London was suddenly, overwhelmingly, real. The suite in the hotel, the flowers and the messages were real, the Opening Night was real, even the wildly improbable plaque I had to unveil.

Although the original bookshop had been razed to the ground, Michael Redington had got permission to have a brass plaque erected, marking the site and this was unveiled by Helene herself. It is there to this day and reads:

> 84 CHARING CROSS ROAD
> THE BOOKSELLERS, MARKS AND CO
> WERE ON THIS SITE WHICH BECAME
> WORLD RENOWNED THROUGH THE BOOK
>
> BY HELENE HANFF

The reviews were ecstatic. In *The Daily Telegraph* John Barber wrote: 'I found my throat lumpy and my eyes in tears. It does not often happen.' Similarly in *The Times* Irving Wardle, not easily given to being moved, wrote:

> The sight of Helene Hanff on the set of the bookshop she made famous, and blinking under the applause of the town she could never afford to visit, made last night's opening into the end of a fairy tale, obscure affection finally crowned with public acclaim.

The play received four nominations from the Society of West End Managers for: Best Actress, Best Actor, Best Play, and Best Director, and won for Rosemary Leach the award for Best Actress of the Year. A year later it was to win awards for Best Actor, Best Actress, Best Director, Best Play for the Broadway production.

Two Broadway producers, Liz McCann and Nell Nugent, who had transferred various productions from the Royal Shakespeare Company to Broadway, including the much acclaimed *Nicholas Nickleby*, had drawn up a contract with Michael Redington to present our production in New York, but were waiting to see it before signing their half of the contract. In due course, but with no haste, Liz McCann came over to see the production and then asked to meet me.

'What we have to do,' she said, in her tough, abrasive manner, stubbing out her cigarette as though on a raw wound, 'is to cast two sexy young people in those parts. The audience has to believe they would have got into bed had they met.' I politely tried to explain that this was not what the play was about, nor what Helene intended, but she cut me off abruptly, saying, 'I have to tell you that I don't like people who wear two hats. I don't like having the author to direct. I would want someone else to direct it on Broadway.'

'Then you would be making a grave mistake,' I replied. 'My adaptation is a director's *mise-en-scene* and the success of the piece, as theatre, lies less in the adaptation than in its staging.'

While waiting for her partner to see the production the contract remained unsigned except by Michael Redington. A few days later I received a call from Alexander Cohen, one of the most senior and distinguished Broadway producers, and for whom some years earlier I had directed in the West End Jack Pulman's comedy *The Happy Apple*.

'Jimmie, I have just seen your production of *84 Charing Cross Road*. I love it, and what you have done with it. And I want it for Broadway.'

'Oh, Alex!' I replied. 'I wish you could but there is this contract with Liz McCann and Nell Nugent… '

'Have they signed it?'

'No, only our producer, Michael Redington, but… '

'Jimmie, let's meet. How about breakfast tomorrow at the Savoy?'

At once I telephoned Michael Redington who said, 'But you can't! There's this contract!' while my agent said the same. I over-rode them both, replying that we should all meet at nine o'clock the next morning.

'Alex understands the play,' I said. 'And those two women don't. They would kill it. Besides, they have had plenty of time to see the show and sign the contract and all they have done is drag their feet!'

Within twenty-four hours a new contract was drawn up and a deposit paid, and I was flown to New York for preliminary discussions with the eminent stage designer Oliver Smith. The play opened on Broadway in November 1982 and ran for three months, receiving further awards for Best Actress, Best Actor, Best Director, and Best Play. Helene never ceased to express her gratitude:

> What fortune teller would ever have had the nerve to predict that the best years of my life would turn out to be my old age? As long as I live – and however many times I say it – I will never be able to tell you what you have done for me, but not the least of it is the financial security that keeps rolling in – this time from the production in Australia – to give me, for the third year, a worry-free old age I never expected to have. It's just indescribable. God bless you a thousand times, as the Irish say, for dramatising it.

There was a curious consequence arising out of the success of this production. In February 1983, by way of celebrating the 500th performance of the London production I took our producer Michael Redington to dinner at the Garrick Club and in the bar I was greeted by Laurie Lee, whom I had not seen since that evening in Stroud. Pink and cherubic and now white-haired, he greeted me effusively, saying some five or six times, 'You're a genius! What you did with that unlikely book *84*, you put magic in it as you did with my book.' After all the vicissitudes we had been through I was taken aback. 'I have to admit,' he continued, 'that I was jealous. I thought it would come off after four weeks but now you are famous and wealthy and not interested in me!'

Michael and I then urged him to reconsider *Cider with Rosie* for the West End. 'No, there's a slump in the middle of the book. It is nothing to do with you. It's in my original material. My book is episodic. Perhaps if we could work together on it?'

The following year I was asked by Alan Strachan to direct a new production of *Cider with Rosie* for the Greenwich Theatre and this time Laurie agreed to let me do a fresh adaptation, and in addition permitted Samuel French at long last to publish it. Since then, not a year goes by but amateur companies up and down the country are performing it.

THE BEST OF FRIENDS

Out of the hundred or more plays I have directed one other stands out in these later years as a special bonus: the opportunity of working with the idol of my youth on a play that resonated deeply with my own life.

Although I had known John Gielgud for more than forty years, having first been introduced to him by Esmé Percy, we had never worked together. Then Michael Redington commissioned from Hugh Whitemore (whose plays *Pack of Lies* and *Breaking the Code* he had produced in the West End) a play entitled *The Best of Friends*, based upon the correspondence between George Bernard Shaw, Sir Sydney Cockerell, Director of the Fitzwilliam Museum in Cambridge, and Dame Laurentia McLachlan OSB, a famous Abbess of Stanbrook Abbey, an enclosed order of Benedictine nuns outside Worcester. Redington, who had also produced *84 Charing Cross Road*, wanted me to direct it.

What he did not know was that Stanbrook Abbey had been an important influence in my life. I first went there in my early twenties, at the suggestion of Dr Elkisch, and over the years I have formed key friendships with individual members of the community. And so, on my way to the first production meeting, I went in to Westminster Cathedral to visit the Chapel of the Blessed Sacrament to light some candles and say a prayer for the production. As I lit the candles I heard a whoosh! and smelled burning. Simultaneously a large black woman moved swiftly towards me and ran her hand through my hair – which was on fire. I was entirely unaware of this. So, when I arrived at the production meeting I announced that I had nearly gone up in flames like Elijah in his chariot!

At that first meeting we were all agreed that Gielgud would be the ideal casting for Sir Sydney Cockerell but we also realised there would be no point in sending him the script. Then aged eighty-three, it had been a decade since he had last acted on stage, appearing only in films. So we sent the script to Alec Guiness, Paul Scofield, and other leading actors but each turned it down, saying they did not see how the play could work on the stage. After three months we appeared to have reached an impasse. 'Let's send it to Sir John,' said Michael Redington. 'After all, we have nothing to lose!'

Thirty-six hours later Gielgud telephoned to say he would do the play. Hugh Whitemore and Michael Redington drove from London to Wootton House in Buckinghamshire where Gielgud lived in stately splendour, while Hywel and I, driving from Wales, got lost and were half an hour late in arriving. On arrival Hugh whispered to me, 'He's changed his mind. He isn't going to do it!'

As Gielgud entered the great hall with its gilded ceiling, its marble busts on pillars, and a raised gallery at one end, he remarked, 'I've been telling them, Jimmie, that I'll do it on the radio, but I don't really see how it will work in the theatre. It's too static!'

He had a point there. The opening stage directions read:

> The downstairs room of a house at Kew. A neatly bearded old man, Sydney Cockerell, sits propped up in bed. On the left is a writing desk. Here sits the familiar figure of George Bernard Shaw. On the right French windows open onto a conservatory where a Benedictine nun is seated, Dame Laurentia McLachlan, Abbess of Stanbrook Abbey in Worcestershire.

Throughout the rest of the text there were only three other stage directions. And there was no plot. Just as with *84 Charing Cross Road*, I knew that it was not sufficient to have characters seated at desks reading letters, even though Hugh Whitemore had artfully broken up the letters into conversations, creating a series of movements as in a piece of chamber music. Somehow I, as director, had to find a way to physicalise the play. It was only when I grasped that all the dialogue was taking place in the memory of Cockerell that I began to see the play as a box of memories. In real life, except on one occasion, Cockerell and Shaw would only have met the Abbess in one of the parlours at the Abbey, separated from her by a large metal grille. In memory, however, people can come and go, engage in various activities, which in actual life could not have happened. Memory transcends space and time.

'I'll do it as a radio play,' repeated Gielgud, 'but I don't see how it can work on stage.' It was at this point that Michael Redington, knowing that I had done a lot of preparatory work on the production, said, 'Jimmie, tell Sir John how you see the play working.' As I described how I saw each scene being staged Sir John began to get more and more excited so that when his companion Martin Hensler came in with a tray of tea, followed by their dogs, he said, 'Jimmie, tell Martin how you see the play being staged.'

Three hours later, and after a walk around the gardens, followed by a curious peacock, John finally agreed to do the play, provided, he added to Hugh, 'You make my part larger and put in a few more jokes!' Hugh and I then went off to Stanbrook for several days where we sat at a long table in one of the larger parlours, with a tape recorder in the middle. A nun brought in twenty or more bound volumes of the original correspondence between Dame Laurentia and Sir Sydney. Hugh would take one volume,

I another, and if either of us found something we thought either dramatic or funny, we switched on the machine and recorded it.

Once the new draft had been completed and sent to Gielgud he began to learn his part well in advance of the rehearsals. With the role of Cockerell cast we then offered that of the Abbess to Rosemary Harris, and that of Bernard Shaw to the Irish actor Ray McAnally, who had recently played the Cardinal in the film *The Mission*.

Once we had cast I began to ponder the difficulty of playing the role of an enclosed nun, something so entirely outside the experience of most actresses. I wrote to the then Abbess, Dame Joanna Jamieson, asking permission for Rosemary to spend at least one day inside 'the enclosure', beyond which no outsider may normally go. The Abbess replied saying that while she understood the need for an actress, especially one of the calibre of Rosemary Harris, to get under the skin of her character, nevertheless my unusual request would require the consent first of the Council, then of the whole Community, and finally the approval of the Abbot President. As a start, she said, she had consulted the Council of nuns at Stanbrook and they were unanimous in the opinion that the Community would not approve.

I had also written separately to the formidable Dame Felicitas Corrigan who had been a nun under Dame Laurentia and who had written the book *In A Great Tradition* which had first suggested to Michael Redington the idea for the play. Dame Felicitas was then in retreat at the sister Abbey of St Cecilia on the Isle of Wight and as the writer Rumer Godden was also staying there, Dame Felicitas had sought her opinion. It had so happened that when Rumer Godden was writing her novel *In the House of Brede*, largely based on Stanbrook, she, too, had applied for permission to spend a day inside and had been similarly refused. Rumer Godden then wrote to me to explain why she concurred with the decision taken by the Abbess and the Council. She considered that Rosemary would quickly feel too bewildered, benumbed and tired to assimilate much, and that Dame Joanna's refusal was as much for Rosemary's sake as the community's.

I at once wrote back to Dame Joanna, pointing out that this was no fictional Abbess that Rosemary was being asked to play, as in Rumer Godden's novel, but their former, and most famous, Abbess. It was, I stressed, essential for the actress to have some experience of the life and routine inside the enclosure. Finally on 2 November 1987 the Abbess wrote back to say that she had now presented the matter to the whole Community and she was happy to report that they were willing for Rosemary to spend one day inside the enclosure.

And so on her arrival from America I drove Rosemary to Stanbrook where, on the second day, she entered the enclosure at 5am, the start of the monastic day. Later that afternoon I was with Dame Philippa Edwards, one of the younger nuns, when there was a knock at the inner door of the parlour in which we were sitting. Dame Felicitas entered, leaning on her stick, accompanied by Dame Hildelith, Stanbrook's distinguished printer, who had also known both Cockerell and Shaw. Behind them was a third nun whom I did not recognise.

'James, I don't think you have met a new member of our Community,' said Dame Felicitas. 'This is Sister Laurentia.' It was Rosemary, dressed in full habit, and looking as though she had been a Benedictine nun all her life! The Community had given her a cell with a sign outside announcing: Dame Laurentia. She had been attending all the sung Offices in the Abbey church, eaten her meals in the Refectory, following the daily routine of the community in every detail.

More than twenty years later when I directed a new production of the play, with Patricia Routledge as Dame Laurentia, Michael Pennington as Cockerell and Roy Dotrice as Shaw, Patricia was allowed to spend *three* days inside the enclosure, being given a place in the choir next to the Abbess. By then a precedent had been created and there were no problems! Indeed, at the end of our tour of that production we gave a special performance of the play for the community in their recreation hall, the first time in the history of Stanbrook that actors had performed a play inside the enclosure!

How a director works on a production varies with individual directors; some have a set way of approach which the actors are expected to subscribe to. I am more pragmatic in that my approach varies according to the requirements of the play and the actors. Usually I like to creep up on a text, like an archaeologist digging down to various layers, leaving what is called the blocking of the moves until the actors feel ready. Once an actor knows the character she or he is called upon to play, moves and business will flow almost spontaneously. Blocking moves at the very first rehearsal is indeed very old-fashioned. However, given Gielgud's age and his apprehension about returning to the stage after such a long gap, I felt it important to have all the furniture and properties present from the first day of rehearsal. We began with the opening scene in which Sir Sydney Cockerell has a long soliloquy. Having roughly blocked it I suggested we might go back over it. 'No, no,' he replied, 'Go on!'

And so we proceeded, scene by scene, until at the end of the first day we had blocked the first act. The next day he insisted on going on with the second act, saying 'I want to see how it will end.' When we got to the end of the play there was a wonderful smile on his face as he realised that Hugh's play would work as a piece of theatre. For privately, before rehearsals began, he had written to his old friend, the publisher John Murray, describing the play as 'a recital of letters' and expressing his anxiety as to whether, after all, he should have done it on the radio. Clearly what he needed therefore was the reassurance of a physical framework to the play with the speeches anchored in various activities. That this was important became increasingly clearer as the days went by for, although he had learned his part beforehand, he suffered from periodic blackouts and each time he dried he would stamp his foot in frustration. Indeed there were days when rehearsals limped along as, again and again, he had these blackouts. On other days, however, he would have marvellous bursts of energy and creativity.

But he could be critical of his fellow actors! In one lunch break when he and I were alone he said of Rosemary Harris, 'Of course Edith Evans ought to be playing the Abbess!' In those early days Rosemary was inclined to be too emotional, something she subsequently controlled. 'You see, Edith had a small iron door in front of her heart and only once or twice during a performance would she let it open and we would see inside. Then she would slam it shut again! That's how the Abbess should be!'

On another occasion, listening to Ray McAnally tackling Bernard Shaw's long speech about *The Black Girl in Search of God* he said to me, 'Why does Ray speak it like that? If I were playing Shaw I'd do it quite differently.' I replied, 'But, of course, John. You are a different actor. You and Ray and Rosemary each work in a different way.' Where Gielgud would always go for the musical cadence of a speech, Ray McAnally would break down each sentence into smaller units, finding the meaning in each. Only when he felt really inside a speech would he then fuse together all the units. Some actors work from the outside in, while others work from the inside outwards, and it is the task of a director to be sensitive to each actor's way of working.

He never interfered with the production although one day he complained that once Shaw and the Abbess had 'died', he didn't like being left alone on the stage for the final scene. 'Couldn't they just stay on stage, seated on their chairs?' he suggested. I thought this a daft idea but I said, 'Well, let's try it.' We did and at the end he grinned, saying, 'No, no, you are quite right. It's like sitting in Pharaoh's tomb!' Deep down I suspected that he was nervous at being left alone on the stage in case he might not be able to hold the audience for the final ten minutes which, ultimately, he did most movingly.

Before the first preview Gielgud was very nervous, perhaps recalling what he had said to the publisher John Murray in a note about 'being very apprehensive at the responsibility of acting in the theatre again after so many years.' But as the curtain rose and the audience applauded loudly he rose to the challenge, seizing hold of the opening soliloquy in a way he had been unable to do in rehearsal, and suddenly delivering it with enormous pace and energy. However, because he kept having minor lapses of memory, we provided him with two prompters, one on either side of the stage. It was at one of the final previews that he achieved his most spectacular dry. The audience that night was packed with celebrities: Steven Spielberg, Paul Newman and Joanne Woodward, Tom Stoppard, Lady St Just, Edward Fox, and others. In one of his speeches Cockerell describes how he built up the collection at the Fitzwilliam Museum.

'I would find a man with a lot of money and no children and get myself invited to dinner. Then, over the wine, I would say to him, "What are you going to do with your collection when you die?"' At this particular performance John suddenly said, 'I would find a man with a lot of children and no money...' He paused, immediately correcting himself, 'I mean a man with a lot of money and *no* children!' and then fell back in his chair laughing, and the whole audience laughed with him. Afterwards I said to him, 'There, you've broken it! So long as you don't worry, the audience isn't going to worry either.' That night he finally overcame his fear of drying.

During the previews I made it my job, as I always do, to watch the play from every part of the house in order both to check the sight lines and the audibility of the actors. One evening, up in the gallery, I observed people straining to hear John and so I had to tell him, he of all people, one of the great voices of the British theatre, that he couldn't be heard! 'Right!' he said. 'I'll speak up!' was his immediate and realistic answer.

In his first night note to me, thanking me for everything, he wrote, 'I hope you will continue to correct my faults and be on the look-out for any small improvements I hope to make.' At each performance he continued to hone his role and often, at supper afterwards, he might say, 'Did you notice tonight how, by telescoping that line about the man with no children and a lot of money, I got a bigger laugh?'

Like Henry Irving, Gielgud never ceased working on his part. And always, after each performance, as he stood on stage at the curtain call he would look like a boy in love, laughing, seeming years younger, knowing he had done it once again! He was also conscious that one of the reasons the limited run was sold out was that everyone sensed this would probably be his last performance on stage. That he returned to the stage when he was thought to have retired took everyone by surprise. He gained an especial amusement from the closing line of the play: 'The Angel of Death seems to have quite forgotten me.' At the age of eighty-three – during the run he celebrated his eighty-fourth birthday – audiences were as aware as he of the irony of this line. Then with a twinkle he would add, 'On the other hand, I might pop off tomorrow. Who knows!'

After the last matinée, and before the final performance, as he came off stage he said to Ray McAnally, 'Tonight is the last night' meaning that he would not return to the stage; not for him the smaller and smaller cameo roles, except on film. He had returned in triumph and that was enough. The audience that night surely sensed all this for, at the final curtain call as Rosemary and Ray deliberately stepped to one side, as they had planned, leaving John alone in the centre of the stage, the entire audience rose to its feet, from the stalls to the circle, from the upper circle to the gallery, cheering, drumming the floor with their feet, pouring out their gratitude for this 'most parfait and gentil knight', for his lifetime of work in the theatre. And it was not only the actor they were saluting but the man himself. Acting, as David Hare once observed, is a judgment of character in that we respond to the actor's inner qualities rather than to the trappings of technique. Michael Billington, referring to this in his review, added,

> We were moved, not simply by the sight of a great actor returning to the stage at the age of 83. Gielgud's own qualities of grace, charity, humour and pathos, touch us to the heart. When, at the end, as Cockerell, he declares friendship to be the most precious thing in life, we go beyond the artifice of impersonation to touch something real and true. I believe this happens with all truly great actors in their last years; an essential nobility of spirit shines through the mask of characterisation.

We who worked with him on that production, from Michael Redington who conceived the idea of the play and commissioned it from Hugh Whitemore, to everyone involved, we knew that we should not look upon his like again.

A year or more before this I had been asked to direct Maureen Lipman in a one act play by Anthony Horowitz for a Jewish charity in aid of refusniks in Russia. It was as a result of this that I received a letter from Maureen saying, 'Now we have met I am not going to let go of you!' In one of our meetings she told me that she had been approached to make a television programme about Joyce Grenfell and suggested I should write it. I replied by saying why not do it first for theatre? As a result my agent negotiated with Reginald Grenfell, Joyce's husband, for me to write such an entertainment, eventually titled *Re:Joyce!* And so, in the autumn of 1987, I began researching into the background of Joyce Grenfell, sitting in Joyce's attic study where I discovered all her notes for broadcast talks and newspaper articles, sketches, songs, as well as albums of newspaper cuttings and photographs, many of them including her own water-colour caricatures of friends; as well as her paintings (she was a talented amateur painter). Then one afternoon, opening a drawer, I came across a series of folders containing thousands of handwritten letters, each of which bore the opening inscription, Darling Ma.

Although Joyce was very much the archetypal Englishwoman she was more American than English, being the daughter of an American mother, Nora Langhorne, who was born and brought up in Virginia, and an English architect, Paul Phipps. Her mother was a born story-teller and loved making up characters and from a very early age Joyce also played at being other people. She would have long made-up dialogues with her mother who would feed her as a stooge feeds a comic. 'My mother was two hundred times more talented than I was,' Joyce once wrote. 'The only difference was that I grew up to turn it into a job.'

When Joyce's parents broke up Nora married Maurice Flynn, an Irish American known as 'Lefty' for his ability to kick with his left foot in Yale football games. Hence these weekly letters to her mother in North Carolina. Joyce's way of writing these letters was in journal form, often a day-by-day account of her doings. How Joyce entered the theatre, never having before performed on a professional stage, in a Herbert Farjeon revue, and acting with Hermione Gingold, is told in these letters with all the breathlessness of a cliff-hanger. After her London debut in 1939 the *Daily Mail* carried the headline. 'LONDON HAS A RUTH DRAPER!'

After I had edited a selection of the letters, Gerald Isaaman, the Editor of the *Hampstead and Highgate Express*, showed them to Ion Trewin at Hodder and Stoughton and they were published in 1989 under the title *Darling Ma*.

While working in Joyce's study I also came across all her journals and especially those she kept when, in the last two years of the Second World War, she travelled thousands of miles in the Middle East and Asia entertaining troops. *Darling Ma* ends with Joyce and her pianist Viola Tunnard about to sail to Italy and the Middle East to entertain the troops under the auspices of ENSA (Entertainments National Service Association). In both these journals and in the letters to her mother, there is an urgency to record things exactly as they were at that moment just because there might never be another. And so Ion Trewin suggested I also edit the wartime journals which were published under the title *The Time of My Life*.

When I had written the script of *Re:Joyce!* Michael Codron undertook to produce the show and arranged for it to be tried out first at Farnham. It was unfortunate that the dates coincided with rehearsals for *The Best of Friends*. These, at Gielgud's request, always ended at four o'clock. I would then lie down for an hour, and at five o'clock go down to a smaller studio to rehearse with Maureen until nine o'clock. It is the first and only time, thank goodness, that I have had to rehearse two shows back to back! And so, in due course, at the same time that *The Best of Friends* was playing in the West End, *Re:Joyce!* also opened in the West End, simultaneously with the publication of *Darling Ma*. For Maureen Lipman it was a personal triumph, while reminding many of the enduring quality of Joyce Grenfell.

WITH EDWIGE IN PARIS

'Jim, did you ever in your wildest dreams imagine that you would be in Paris directing the legendary Edwige Feuillère?' Hugh Whitemore and I were walking from our hotel to the Théâtre des Champs Elysées for a reading of *The Best of Friends* which had been translated into French by Pol Quentin, under the title *Les Meilleurs Amis*, and was to star Edwige as the Abbess. Starring opposite her as Cockerell was Guy Tréjan, a member of the Légion d'Honneur, and who had made the welcoming speech when Edwige, the first woman to be elected, was made a member of the Légion. The role of Shaw was to be played by another fine actor, Henri Virlogeux.

Edwige was the grande dame of the Paris theatre. As *Le Monde* wrote after her death in 1998, 'Edwige Feuillère was our Marlene Dietrich, our Irene Dunne and our Greta Garbo, all in one.' When she first appeared in London in 1968 in *La Dame aux Camélias* and *Phèdre* Harold Hobson in *The Times* described her as the greatest actress he had ever seen. I remember seeing those performances and walking the streets for an hour or more afterwards, unable to speak to anyone, such was the impact she made on so many of us at the time. And now here I was working with her. She had been to London to see the production, realised it was something she wanted to do, and had especially insisted that I direct her. Although she was eighty-two, in rehearsals she was indefatigable. Some days she was like a girl in love, full of laughter and the excitement of discovery. On other days she was clearly tired, and suffered a lot from pain in her neck and back.

'It's not surprising,' she smiled. 'I am paying the price. You see, in Jean Cocteau's *L'Aigle à Deux Têtes*, every night I had a sensational fall backwards down a great staircase, ending always with the back of my neck on a particular step. And I did this for over 200 performances. Then, in *La Dame aux Camélias* I had another incredible fall backwards.'

All this had damaged her spine so that she was in pain a lot of the time, as well as having arthritis. But being a perfectionist she refused to allow this to get in the way of the work. On one particular day when she suddenly felt dizzy, Guy Tréjan urged her to go and lie down. At this Edwige banged the table very hard with her fist and replied, '*Si je cesse maintenant, je cesse toujours!* If I give up now I give up for always!' and went on rehearsing.

Before rehearsals began she had gone to stay at the Benedictine Abbey of Saint-Louis du Temple at Vauhallan on the Ile de France, about 20km outside Paris. She had a strong conviction that this would probably be the last play she would do, as indeed it proved.

As rehearsals progressed she insisted on wearing her costume. At one point I had to tell her that she was being much too flirtatious for an enclosed nun, let alone the Abbess. 'Darling James!' she laughed. 'You forget I have a reputation for being the great courtesan of the French cinema!' and then, as always, she immediately applied the note. On another day I had to remark that she was being much too sad as the Abbess.

'You are quite right,' she said. 'You are absolutely right to pick me up on that. Deep down I am a very sad person. It is the blows of life.' Always, as with Gielgud, I shall hear that famous voice, like a cello playing unaccompanied Bach.

I love theatre because it is a live animal. Dame Edith Evans used to compare acting in the theatre to riding a horse. She would stand in the wings each night and listen to the audience. Some nights, she would say, 'the audience is so unruly that, as you come on, you have to pull on the reins and dig in the stirrups and get it under control before you can canter away. Other nights you gallop away from the start!'

A play is a living, breathing thing, constantly shifting and changing, however subtly, from performance to performance. The text alone is not theatre: it only becomes theatre through the actor's use of it. Unlike the cinema the theatre is an ongoing and organic process and each performance is different because the audience is different. One of my great delights as a director is watching an actor try various possibilities for a scene. Although often, to an outsider, the director may seem to be doing nothing he is like a naturalist, watching the actors closely, observing the processes at work. A director does not have to justify his presence at rehearsal. The simple fact that he is there, alertly watching, is often all the stimulus an actor needs. On the other hand there are days when the director is in full spate and the actors having to race to keep up with him! The director has to veer between being a pilot and also a pioneer who challenges his actors, daring them to make discoveries, and above all, to experiment.

In a good production the overall concept of the play, its basic style, even much of the detail, will stem from the director who, like Prospero, has 'promised to deliver all'. And yet in the final design it should prove impossible to separate the various threads contributed by the director, the author, the designer, the actors, and the technical staff. A good production is like a seamless robe. It has often seemed to me that all a good director has to do is to blow gently on the embers until they begin to glow, and then to go on blowing until they suddenly burst into flame. It is at that moment that the actors begin to inhabit their roles, and all a director has to do thereafter is to keep a gentle eye on the production during its run.

DOORS OPENING AND CLOSING

A week before my mother died in 1981, the year I was ordained, she was staying with me at the Old Rectory for Christmas and clearly not at all well. Late one night I sat on her bed, cradling her in my arms, when she said, 'Before you were born, we wanted a girl. Well, you haven't done too badly!' I laughed and replied, 'What a thing to say to a man of fifty-one!'

'I don't know what I would have done without you,' she said, holding me more tightly. Then, as I went to leave her room after saying goodnight she sat up swiftly in bed, sprightly as a young girl, laughing, with arms outstretched. 'Goodnight, my darling, and thank you for everything!' Those were the last words she spoke to me.

A few weeks after my mother's death I was walking across Oxford Circus when suddenly I looked up and there, in the sky, I saw her. It was as though the sky was tilted, as though another dimension of reality was breaking through, rather like one slide being placed across another. There she was, but much younger, vibrant with laughter, and in that moment I knew that she understood me as she perhaps had not before, and that she would continue to watch over me. Such experiences are, of course, far from uncommon. They are not emotional fantasies. Such experiences, as is known from research, remain a constant and do not fade. As Edwin Muir expresses it:

> *That was the real world: I have touched it once,*
> *And now shall know it always.*

Many months later, on my fifty-second birthday, I was staying with Hywel and two other friends, Joyce Grant and Dr Johanna Brieger, at the Old Rectory in Bleddfa. Over breakfast we talked quietly and then at eleven o'clock Albert Thomas from the village post office arrived, accompanied by his two daughters, Beth and Leah, who were carrying an enormous birthday card made by the children of the village school. When they had gone, Hywel put on the *Bach Double Violin Concerto* which Joyce had given me. Listening to it with closed eyes there came a point in the music when my mother 'arrived' and was present with all her warmth, vitality, humour and love. Blessings seemed to be descending on my head. Mother 'recognised' Joyce, 'welcomed' Johanna, and Hywel. The kitchen was full of presences. Then I discerned Franz Elkisch, my old analyst, and he was laughing. Tears poured down my face. I felt so abundantly blessed, surrounded and supported by love. I realised in that instant that Franz and my Mother were protecting me, that they were my true parents. Then I heard whispers. It was Hywel talking quietly to Joyce about getting in the rest of the apples. Slowly I was returned to the present moment. Even if science cannot explain such moments it is enough to accept them.

One December morning in Wales I took a long walk. In the thick mist the nests of rooks appeared like dark smudges on the ghosts of trees; every bush, thorn, twig and branch had its replica in ice while the topmost twigs of a line of hawthorns glittered and sparkled in the sun like fine spun glass, and from the pine trees thick scales of ice tinkled like Japanese wind chimes. As I climbed the old track with the long shaggy grass stiffly frozen, so the mist grew thicker. Telegraph wires, thickened with frost, spun the lane below like a spider's web. In the thickest part of the mist, down in the valley, although I could see nothing, I could hear the sounds of a farm beginning its day: the sudden chuckling of ducks being released, a cockerel crowing, children's voices, and cattle lowing in a barn, waiting to be milked. Next came the clip-clop of a horse travelling along a lane, then over grass, then over cobbles, and a boy's voice shouting, 'Hey up!'

Climbing higher still, the wind was blowing the mist along until suddenly a huge wall of cloud advanced towards me, surrounding me, so that I lost all sense of direction and could go no further. I stood still, wrapped in a white blanket of mist, listening to sheep nearby munching. It is often when all sense of direction is lost and there are no answers that all one can do is wait until the mists rise. It is by waiting in this cloud of unknowing, enveloped and surrounded by mystery, that the truth is often to be found, and not in argumentative debate.

Jonathan Miller, theatre director and doctor, once observed in a lecture that there are some people who are 'neither fish, flesh, fowl nor good red herring;' those who have a quality of not being either this or that, neither here nor elsewhere. They are people on whom we cannot easily affix a label. Such he termed an 'interstitial' person, one who stands at the cross-roads of society, at a frontier, at a place not easily classifiable. The shaman, the priest, the healer, he maintained, are such people. Their task is to stand at the inter-section of paths and hold the tension of the opposites within themselves. And it is there, at the crossroads, that I know I belong.

The pattern of our lives is different for each of us and our task, as we grow older, is to watch the pattern unfold and to assist it in reaching its completion.

The task is continuous. It is like gardening. A garden has to be toiled over, weeded, dug, forked, fertilised. One may clear a whole patch in an afternoon and yet, within a week, the weeds will have returned. A garden left to itself quickly reverts to wilderness. So with ourselves. We have to work at life, at love, at art. And only then will life and love and art be seen to be One.

I was fortunate that in my early seventies I had cancer of the thyroid and had to deal with fear. I learned, as Holderlin expresses it, 'Where danger is, grows also the rescuing power'. I was on my own when I realised I had cancer, as Hywel was away in India. The fear was almost suffocating and yet I was glad to be alone to deal with it. As Virginia Woolf wrote:

> We do not know our own souls, let alone the souls of others. Human beings do not go hand in hand the whole stretch of the way. There is a virgin forest in each; a snowfield where even the print of birds' feet is unknown. Here we go alone.

One night, at the peak of the fear, I awoke to hear an interior voice saying, 'You are not alone. You have an angel working alongside you.' And from that moment the fear began to subside so that when I went in for the four-hour operation, not knowing whether I would be able to speak when I came out of it, for the vocal organs are perilously close to the thyroid, I was totally unafraid.

Who is to explain the origin of that 'voice?' It is possible that it came from the unconscious, that repository of wisdom that lies beyond the intellect; but I do not discount, any more than does the biologist Rupert Sheldrake, that there may be angelic powers. In the Celtic tradition there is a strong sense that each of us has an invisible companion who walks the road of life with us, and one of the poverties of modern life is the loss of belief in such presences. The late John O'Donohue, in *Eternal Echoes*, observed how the Christian tradition says that when we are sent here on earth a special angel is chosen to accompany our every step, breath, thought and feeling.

> This is your guardian angel, who is right beside you, as near as your skin. In your angel you have as much shelter as you need. You are not on your own. If you could see your path with the eyes of your soul, you would find that it is a luminous path and that there are two of you walking together. You are not alone. When loneliness or helplessness overcomes you, it is time to call on your angel for help and courage.

Schopenhauer points out that when one is at a certain age you look back on your life and it seems to be almost as orderly as a composed novel – although it may well not be the novel one had imagined one was going to write! And just as in Dickens' novels little accidental meetings turn out to be the main features in the plot so, in our lives, what seem to have been mistakes at the time, turn out to be critical turning points. And so one asks: Who wrote this novel? Jung was convinced that each of us comes into the world with our own blueprint and that our task in life is to realise this design. It is this which leads Schopenhauer also to ask the question: 'Can anything happen to you for which you are not ready?'

Looking back over the course of my life I can see how going to live with the Pollards, having a breakdown, going to Ampleforth, meeting David March, being encouraged by Kenneth Williams to direct, being offered my first theatre, meeting Martha Graham and going to America – each person and event has been like beads in a necklace; Proustian beads because, as I touch them, each holds vivid memories, each acting as a key, opening doors and windows of opportunity.

Each of us has to learn how to wait for our own door to open. Although a few people seem to know from the start where they are going, most of us have to learn to wait for our door to reveal itself. And once we go through it we are no longer outside but inside, no longer elsewhere but here.

Epilogue

In my former home, the Old Rectory at Bleddfa in Powys, the study looked onto a terrace, a tree enclosed garden and the hills beyond. People who visited were often startled when they looked through the windows of the study from the outside and saw the garden, the trees, the sky, and the hills, inside the room, reflected in a large Victorian mirror at the far end. Eight feet high and six feet across it was the exact dimension of the French windows.

I used to love sitting in the garden after twilight, seeing the house lit up like a lantern. Often I would approach my study windows and peer in: observing the desk with its empty chair, the white painted bookshelves, the green carpet like a stretch of lawn, the prints of birds and animals on the walls, the large pedestal lamp with its silk shade patterned with autumn leaves, and the rocking horse of waxed unpainted wood. Then I would see my own face palely reflected in the mirror, peering in from outside, as the moths around me thumped against the glass. I would gaze quietly, sensing the silence within the empty room where so much life was lived, and I was content to be both outside and inside. It was as though I were a revenant, come back after my death to look at my old home.

For so many years I felt I never belonged, that I was always on the outside wanting to be on the inside. Now I am content to be both on the inside and the outside, but it has taken a lifetime to arrive at this stage. I think back to my early twenties, when I was at Oxford and broke down at a party, crying with all the intensity of youth, because I did not know whether I was meant to be a monk, an actor, a writer, a teacher. I did not then know about the role and work of a director. It has taken a series of life crises to realise and accept that I am all of these things, and the challenge has been to weave these seemingly disparate strands into one pattern. It is like the task faced on the first day of rehearsal by a director in the theatre: how to weld a group of individual actors into an ensemble so that each complements the other. As so often, Emily Dickinson sums it up in one of her graphs of the human heart:

> *The props assist the house*
> *Until the house is built,*
> *And then the props withdraw –*
> *And adequate, erect,*
> *The house supports itself;*
> *Ceasing to recollect*
> *The auger and the carpenter.*
> *Just such a retrospect*
> *Hath the perfected life,*
> *A past of plank and nail,*
> *And slowness – then the scaffolds drop*
> *Affirming it a soul.*

Acknowledgements

I want especially to thank those friends who have read various drafts and given me invaluable feedback, from Faith Evans, Jenny Pearson, Michael Ford, Barry Turner, Celia Read to Antony Wood of Angel Books who read the ninth draft twice and offered invaluable editorial help, as well as to Carl Miller who provided the final stimulus that I needed. Throughout I owe so much to the encouragement and support of Tony Morris whose friendship and expertise has guided this book towards publication, and I also want to thank Laura Perehinec at The History Press who has patiently overseen this book and also *Finding Silence: 52 Meditations For Daily Living*. And lastly I want to thank the Rayne Trust for its generous support.

By the Same Author

BOOKS ON THE THEATRE

Directing a Play
Experimental Theatre
One Foot on the Stage: the Biography of Richard Wilson
London Theatre: from the Globe to the National

CHILDREN'S BOOKS

The Adventures of Odd and Elsewhere
The Secret of the Seven Bright Shiners
Odd and the Great Bear
Elsewhere and the Gathering of the Clowns
The Return of the Great Bear
The Secret of Tippity-Witchet
The Lost Treasure of Wales

The Magic Magic Man (unpublished)
The Christ Mouse

OTHER

Inner Journey: Outer Journey
Passages of the Soul: Ritual Today
Darling Ma: the letters of Joyce Grenfell to her mother (ed.)
The Time of my Life: the Wartime Journals of Joyce Grenfell (ed.)
The Cook-a-Story Book
Finding Silence: 52 Meditations for Daily Living
In Preparation: *Holy Theatre: Rediscovering the Sacred in Worship*

STAGE ADAPTATIONS

Helene Hanff's *84 Charing Cross Road*
Laurie Lee's *Cider with Rosie*
Re:Joyce! an entertainment about Joyce Grenfell, written for
  Maureen Lipman
Augustus, or *Eminently a Victorian*, based on *The Story of My Life*, by
  Augustus Hare

STAGE ANTHOLOGIES

A Celebration of Gardens, toured, and then broadcast for BBC 3
A Pride of Players, actors of the nineteenth century
Oh, Mr Porter, What Shall I do! Travel by rail and sea
The Journey Thus Far, a celebration of age

BBC RADIO DOCUMENTARIES

The Female Messiah
A Well-Governed Stage
Topsy and Ted

AVAILABLE NOW

A fresh, original and inspiring collection

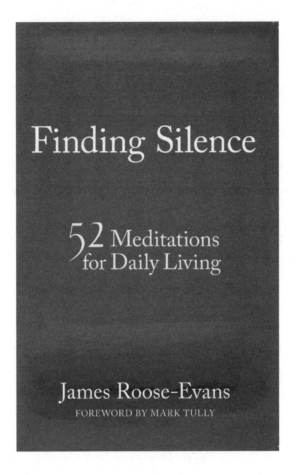

ISBN 978 0 7524 5405 4
Price £8.99

Growing out of a meditation group led
by James Roose-Evans, *Finding Silence* is a
collection of practical and inspiring thoughts
about meditation, creativity and spirituality.

See www.thehistorypress.co.uk for details

Visit our website and discover thousands of other History Press books.

www.thehistorypress.co.uk